The

Significance

of Sibling

Relationships

in Literature

The Significance of Sibling Relationships in Literature

Edited by

JoAnna Stephens Mink

and

Janet Doubler Ward

Bowling Green State University Popular Press
Bowling Green, Oh 43403

Library of Congress Catalogue Card No.: 92-75707

ISBN: 0-87972-612-1 clothbound
       0-87972-613-X paperback

Cover design by Laura Darnell-Dumm

For our siblings—

Bonnie, Kenneth, Mary Lynn

Contents

Acknowledgements

In addition to our 13 contributors, we would like to acknowledge those scholars whose work helped to shape the focus of this collection: Joan Melville Corcoran (Columbia University), William Crisman (Penn State University, Altoona), Stefanie Dojka (Lakewood Community College), Donna A. Gessell-Frye (Case Western Reserve University), Jean E. Graham (University of Akron), Mary Ann Hoberman (Yale University), Lillian O'Neal Manning (Southern Illinois University—Edwardsville), Lorie Roth (Armstrong State College), and Anne D. Wallace (University of Southern Mississippi). We thank the many, many people who responded to our calls for papers and who expressed their interest in our work.

In November 1991, we moderated a special session at the Midwest Modern Language Association Conference in Chicago entitled "The Significance of Sibling Relationships in Nineteenth-Century Novels by Women." We acknowledge our panelists, William Crisman, Stefanie Dojka, and Julia Waddell, for their participation in that lively discussion, as well as the Midwest Modern Language Association for accepting our proposal.

The perceptive comments of Kay Puttock and Louisa Smith (Mankato State University) helped us to make specific suggestions for revisions.

Pat Browne, Director of the Bowling Green State University Popular Press, and her staff—particularly Kathy Rogers Hoke—have been most helpful with timely suggestions and feedback.

For their help with typing envelopes and various other clerical tasks, we thank the Department of English secretarial support staff at Mankato State University, especially Jason Nado for proofreading the manuscript.

We thank Dan Ward for child-minding when we needed to have some "quality" work time.

Most of all, we thank the 13 contributors whose ideas form the chapters of this anthology. The greatest personal benefit of editing an anthology, regardless of the topic, is the opportunity of meeting and collaborating with interested and interesting scholars from the various institutions represented in this anthology. Without them, this book would not have been possible.

Introduction

We have long been intrigued with the broad topic of relationships with and among individuals in our respective families, as those relationships are formed by biological or marital ties. As we and our contributors explored in *Joinings and Disjoinings: The Significance of Marital Status in Literature*, in many ways our very sense of self is determined and sustained by our continuing and broken ties with others. Marital bonds, as we all know, are made and unmade; one becomes joined, one becomes disjoined.

Blood ties, however, can never be put asunder. We are reminded of Antigone's words before she is led away to the cave which will be her tomb: "If my husband had died, there would have been another man for me; I could have had a child from another husband if I had lost my first child. But with my mother and father both hidden away in Hades, no other brother could ever have come into being for me. For it was thus I saw the higher law." In summarizing the importance of Antigone's story, Christine Downing points out in *Psyche's Sisters*, "Her integrity as a human being is for her entirely dependent on her *being* a sister....The brother and sister come from the same womb; together they reenter the womb of earth" (74). The sibling bond is unique, irreplaceable. With our siblings we share the greatest possible degree of similarity (based on the randomness of the gene pool, on shared family history, and so on), plus since in the natural order of things our parents die before we do, it is a relationship that cannot be replicated. In fact, in some ways one of the reasons for Oedipus' horror at learning that he has fathered children with his own mother is that his sense of identity (as either a father or a brother to the children) is skewed. Perhaps incest is such a universal taboo because one should not have both a vertical and a horizontal blood relationship.

The first sibling relationship, according to the Old Testament account, is that between Cain and Abel. Cain, after killing Abel out of jealousy that only Abel's offering was accepted by God, responded to God's question with the challenge, "Am I my brother's keeper?" (Genesis 4:9). Thus, we find the first brother-brother bond, as well as the first murder, in the Judeo-Christian tradition. In *Uses of Enchantment* Bruno Bettelheim comments about the Cain and Abel story: "there is no sympathy in the Bible for the agonies of sibling rivalry—only a warning that acting upon it has devastating consequences" (52).

Sibling rivalry is also the foundation for the story of Esau and Jacob. Jacob, son of Isaac, was the twin brother of Esau. Because Esau was the eldest (Jacob born clutching his heel), he was the heir. As described in Genesis 25-27, their mother, favoring Jacob, helps him to disguise himself as Esau, thus obtaining Isaac's blessing and Esau's birthright. As a consequence, Esau threatens to kill Jacob, so Rebekah contrives to send him to their uncle Laban.

2 The Significance of Sibling Relationships

Clearly, two important ideas relate this story to that of Cain and Abel—one son is obviously favored over the other, and that favored son is the second born.

Interestingly, the first Old Testament mention of a sister-sister bond does not occur for many generations after the story of Cain and Abel, and since it is not as well known, we discuss it in some detail. The relationship between Leah and Rachel, both daughters of Laban and both wives of Jacob, is an important parallel to that between Cain and Abel. After laboring for seven years in order to marry Rachel, Jacob is tricked by Laban into accepting Leah (and her handmaid) instead: "What is this thou hast done unto me? Did not I serve with thee for Rachel? Wherefore then has thou beguiled me?" (Genesis 29:25). (This substitution is perhaps poetic justice for Jacob's own duplicity when he swindles his twin brother Esau from his inheritance.) In any event, Laban tells Jacob that if he will stay with Leah for a week, he will also give him Rachel (and her handmaid), provided that Jacob work for him seven additional years, which is exactly what happens.

Not surprising given this Old Testament patriarchial society, Jacob seems to have found himself in an enviable position (in spite of his 14 years of labor), but he loves Rachel more. God, however, causes Leah in quick succession to conceive four sons, and Rachel becomes envious. When she says to Jacob, "Give me children, or else I die" (Genesis 30:1), Jacob becomes angry at her; in order to pacify him, Rachel send in her handmaid Bilhah, who eventually bears Jacob two sons. This impregnating by proxy, as it were, seems to have pleased both Jacob and God because Rachel eventually bears two sons to Jacob. Leah, meanwhile, decides that it is time not only to send in her own handmaid Zilpah but also to resume bearing children, which she does. As Leah comments, seemingly in understatement, "A troop cometh" (Genesis 30:11).

And family sibling rivalry continues into the next generation. Rachel's first son Joseph is loved best by Jacob, who gives him a coat of many colors. His 11 brothers, jealous over Joseph's pampered status, conspire to kill him but place him in the bottom of an empty well instead; passing merchants pull him out and sell him into slavery. Sibling jealousy, then, takes a violent turn among Jacob's sons, yet another example of brotherly rivalry gone too far.

What is significant about the sister bond between Leah and Rachel, especially as compared to the relationships between Cain and Abel, between Esau and Jacob, and between Joseph and his brothers, is the way in which the women deal with their jealousy. They don't resort to violence, one doesn't murder or even swindle the other; instead, as the story continues, they eventually work together to help Jacob and his large family of children to prosper, even against their own father Laban. And, as one can't help but note, the situation that forms the basis of their jealousy is their wanting to be mothers and the fact that God had given Leah children but not Rachel (just as God previously accepted only Abel's offering). Is there something in the sister-sister bond that ultimately transcends masculine machinations and needs? If we look at the first examples of brothers and sisters in Judeo-Christian literature, the answer must be yes.

Also related to the jealousy exemplified by these sets of siblings is the significance of birth order: Cain feels that he should not have been "bettered" by his younger brother, Esau is rightfully upset with his twin Jacob, Jacob can't marry Rachel until after her older sister is taken care of, and Joseph's older brothers resent his special status. Thus, our relationships with our siblings are interrelated to another important aspect of our sense of self—birth order. In fact, in planning this anthology the significance of birth order was originally our focus, but soon we realized that birth order is predicated upon the facts that one either has or has not siblings, and that one's siblings may be older, younger, or as in the case with multiple births, the same age. (Though as JoAnna's nephews are aware, even in the case of twins, only one person can have been born first.) The family unit has always been altered by the introduction of half-and step-siblings, as well as, of course, adopted and fostered siblings, but contemporary society, with our more common serial joinings and disjoinings, complicates these variations upon the theme in the formation of blended families.

The individual's "place" within the family unit is a major influence in development of self-identity. Several studies, beginning in the nineteenth century, provide more information about the importance of birth order on the individual's development. For example, Sir Francis Galton found in 1875 that a preponderance of eminent English scientists were first-born and single-born sons (Fishel 62). Alfred Adler, a pioneer in depth psychiatry, claims, "The position in the family leaves an indelible stamp on [the individual's] style of life" (qtd. in Leman, *Growing Up* 32; see also Downing 117ff). Psychologist Karl Konig posits that the "family constellation" determines our social behavior. "Even the choice of a husband or wife is deeply influenced by the facts of the family-constellation" (qtd. in Leman, *Growing Up 32*). Birth Order affects our career path. A study by Margaret Hennig and Anne Jardim (published in 1977) showed that 25 percent of the successful American businesswomen in their study were single-born or firstborn with female siblings (Fishel 62).

What contributes to who we are, as mentioned earlier, has long been an especial interest, and we have often talked about our respective families, particularly our siblings. Just for the record, JoAnna is the oldest of three females, the youngest being only five years younger than she. Janet has one sibling, a brother who is 12 years older. We are both firstborns. JoAnna's status as firstborn is obvious, but Janet is also a firstborn because, as Kevin Leman explains in *Growing Up Firstborn*, there is more than five years between her older brother and her, a relationship compounded because they are different sexes (15; also *The Birth Order Book* 35). It seems, then, that family "place" is of two-fold importance—the order in which we were "introduced" to our parents and family, and which of our siblings were boys and which were girls. For JoAnna, being the oldest of three girls implies (correctly) a great deal of childhood competition. And it is perhaps not surprising that we are all very different adults—in terms of marital status, in the decision to have children or not, in our political stances, and in our professions. Kevin Leman would not be surprised to know that JoAnna, the oldest, is a university professor, the middleborn identifies herself as a mother of three, and the lastborn recently opened her own guitar shop and school (see also Hoopes and Harper, *Birth Order Roles* 36-37).

Birth order—and gender—play a role in Janet's relationship with her brother. Growing up on a farm in central Illinois meant two important things—they were isolated from other children, and they grew up with traditional family values. Compounding the situation of the first-born being male is the 12 years between them; Janet was only five years old when her brother left for college, so they never really had a shared childhood. Because of this age gap, as adults they both manifest first-born attributes in spite of their gender difference; both are independent in personalities and successful at their different professions. Since this Introduction is intended to focus upon the following collection of essays, we will end our personal reflections here. For those interested in pursuing general reading about sibling relationships, may we suggest Kevin Leman's books, available in paperback bookstores, Elizabeth Fishel's *Sisters*, and Margaret M. Hoopes and James M. Harper's *Birth Order Roles*. Also important is *The Sibling Bond* by Stephen P. Bank and Michael D. Kahn, a study to which many of our contributors make connections in their discussions of literary siblings.

Our interest in and discussions about the significance of sibling relationships in our own lives led us eventually (and, as English teachers and scholars, quite naturally) to ponder the various kinds of literary sibling relationships. Our conversations brought us to the formation of this anthology of essays which explore manifestations of the significance of sibling relationships in literature—and most particularly, the way in which that sibling bond has been articulated by women writers. Response to our calls for papers indicated that this topic was of interest to many others as well. Choosing the essays which form the chapters of this anthology was very difficult because the topic, though seemingly narrow, offered a wide range of ways in which critics could approach a variety of texts. We are proud to include the essays that follow because they represent the best of some very fine ideas. We have organized them according to the various types of sibling relationships—the only born, brothers and sisters, twins, and sisters. Our hope is that, taken together, they will provide a continuing dialogue on the importance of birth order and the significance of sibling relationships in the formation of the individual.

We begin with an often-neglected aspect of the sibling paradigm—in this case the lack of a sibling. Rosemary M. Colt explains how the single child, who is at once an object of pity and of power, struggles to survive in the adult world. Her chapter, "Innocence Unleashed: The Power of the Single Child," connects James's *What Maisie Knew* and Bowen's *The Death of the Heart* by showing how the use of single-born females compels us to examine the choices open to women in corrupt societies. *Jane Eyre* is one of the first major single-born females to emerge in novels, a character perhaps made stronger because she must fight her battles alone. Colt, using Jane Eyre as her touchstone, compares the struggles of Maisie and Portia and discusses the significance of being an only-born as it helps us to understand their struggles. The single child, manifesting many of the attributes of firstborn children, has a vulnerable place in the family hierarchy.

Sibling relationships are often defined not only by the individual's birth place within the family but also by the gender of siblings. Our contributors in the second section of our anthology focus on several ramifications of the brother-sister bond. The half-sibling connection, a variation of the brother-sister relationship, includes literature of the legendary and mystical realm in Debra A. Benko's "Morgan Le Fay and King Arthur in Malory's *Works* and Marion Zimmer Bradley's *The Mists of Avalon:* Sibling Discord and the Fall of the Round Table." Although much has been written about the various works (inside and outside the canon) which discuss the King Arthur legend, even those authors who have included the character of Morgan le Fay have not emphasized her half-sibling relationship with Arthur. Benko explains how exploring the sibling relationship of Morgan and Arthur is an integral part of an attempt to analyze their roles in Arthurian legend. Malory, for example, casts Arthur as victim and Morgan as aggressor in her attempted physical and spiritual fratricide. Bradley, on the other hand, by exploring the early childhood bond that existed between Arthur and Morgaine, not only fosters the reader's sympathy for Morgaine but also shows the complexity of this sibling relationship. Ultimately, Benko puts her discussion of Arthur and Morgan into the larger framework of family rivalries and gender relationships.

Elisabeth Rose Gruner anchors her discussion, " 'Loving Difference': Sisters and Brothers from Frances Burney to Emily Brontë," upon political reform models (the French Revolution) and shows why Fanny Burney, Jane Austen, and Emily Brontë all propose and reject "the sister-brother relation as a model for marriage, for female self-development, even for potential social reform." *Camilla*, says Gruner, "participates in the eighteenth-century negotiation between seeing the family as a network of affiliation and as a privatized domestic unit." *Mansfield Park* may appear to resist this oppressive order but only a better position develops, not a new order. The relationships between the sisters—and the men with whom they are involved—provide the image by which both Burney and Austen make their political statements. Finally, Gruner points out that *Wuthering Heights* adds another dimension to this type of male-female relationship by using the brother-sister bond as the basis of the struggle with the "masculine principle of oppression."

Julia Waddell adds another dimension to the topic of sibling relationships in the nineteenth century novel. In "Women Writers as Little Sisters in Victorian Society: *The Mill on the Floss* and the Case of George Eliot," she posits that the relationship between Maggie and Tom Tulliver not only reflects the relationship between Marian and Isaac Evans, but also symbolizes the "little sister" position that women writers had with male authors during the nineteenth century. Thus, claims Waddell, as an adult Marian Evans "filled the role of second child in the opposite way from Maggie," becoming independent of her older brother. In a larger realm, Eliot is but one example of the ways in which women writers were deemed less-valued little sisters in the world of *belles lettres*. This historical knowledge is a necessary part of our reading of Victorian novels by women writers.

6 The Significance of Sibling Relationships

Deanna Madden points out in "Ties That Bind: Identity and Sibling Relationships in Anne Tyler's Novels" that Tyler's first sentence of her first novel, *If Morning Ever Comes*, mentions a brother-sister sibling relationship, one that portrays a sentimental picture of an only male in a household of females, and her second novel *The Tin Can Tree* focuses on a brother-sister relationship. In many ways Madden's chapter parallels both Gruner's above and Connie R. Schomburg's discussion of Toni Morrison's novels below, as it traces the importance of sibling relations in nine of Tyler's novels. In several novels, siblings occur in pairs, such as the three sibling bonds in *The Tin Can Tree* which show siblings at three different life stages; one of the triad is a brother-sister bond. Madden explores Tyler's half-brothers in *Searching For Caleb* and a surviving sibling in *Saint Maybe*. While marriages and families form the focus of Tyler's novels, sibling relations "illustrate the connectedness" between people.

Teresa Mangum, in "Sex, Siblings, and the Fin De Siecle," presents an often-ignored sibling relationship, that of opposite-sex twins. Sarah Grand's *The Heavenly Twins*, according to Amy Cruse, "created one of the greatest sensations of literature," causing great excitement to Feminists and Anti-Feminists alike. As children Angelica and Diavolo exchange clothing, causing comic misunderstandings, but the novel explores this simbiotic sibling relationship in more meaningful ways. Clothing becomes a "metonomy for gender positioning," which is just one way in which *The Heavenly Twins* parallels Brontë's *Wuthering Heights*, but because their relationship is comic, the twins can absorb change rather than "dooming themselves to fantasizes of regression" as do Brontë's characters. In particular, Angelica's disguises, as she becomes whatever gender she wishes, reveal Grand's theme that "patriarchy disciplines women through sexual exploitation." At the turn of the century, as women took to bicycles and protest marches and men's clothing became more foppish, "opposite-sex twins," claims Mangum, "embodied the confusion, the potential liberation, and the dangers of resisting sexual polarities."

In "The Circles of Ran and Eugene Maclain: Welty's Twin Plots in *The Golden Apples*," Allison Pingree explores the importance of identical twin brothers, a special sibling bond that biologically is even closer than the brother—sister twin relationship in *The Heavenly Twins*. While many readers note Eudora Welty's use of identical twins as part of her larger motif of duality, few critics, says Pingree, have seen the bond shared by the twins in *The Golden Apples* as something distinct. Paradoxically, what makes this relationship different is the twins' indistinguishability. Identical twins raise questions about our basic assumptions concerning individual identity. Using the circle motif which forms the basic structure of the novel, Pingree shows how circularity also leads to the fusion of the twins' identity throughout the novel until they are presented as comprising a single unit.

Relations between twin sisters in the eighteenth-century British novel provides the focus of Michael Cohen's discussion of plot-significant sisters. In "First Sisters in the British Novel: Charlotte Lennox to Susan Ferrier," Cohen maintains that (male novelists) Defoe, Richardson, Fielding, Sterne, and

Smollett use no sisters in their plots, and it is not until the work of Charlotte Lennox in the 1760's that "sisters begin to come into their own as plot movers and as representatives for all women's relation to each other." Often, authors would continue the tradition of using sisters to present "paired" behavior, with one sister being "good" in contrast to the "bad" one. As a result neither sister is portrayed as an individual. In the latter part of the eighteenth century, sisters are more than "opposed poles of a duality" and the idea of sisters transcends biological ties, involving cousins (Fanny Burney's *Camilla*) as well as sisters-in-law. Cohen's discussion centers on Susan Ferrier's *Marriage* in which two sets of twin sisters behave differently more as a result of their differing education than their genetic identity. Thus, Cohen intertwines his discussion of twins with the rise of the novel of education, showing how this sibling relationship contributes to the development of the genre in the eighteenth century.

Cohen's essay bridges our final section on the sister—sister bond. Perhaps it is not surprising that Cinderella, the best-known and best-liked fairy tale (Bettelheim 236), is about sisters. While daughters (like sons) take many cues for life-planning from their parents, "channels of communication between sister and sister are often more open and accessible, less guarded and defended against than the lines between parent and child" (Fishel 114). Ironically, the sister—sister relationship has been noticeably ignored in depth psychology, even twentieth-century studies, perhaps because it does not include the male (Downing 115). But in recent years, it has gained the attention of literary and social critics. Studies such as Nina Auerbach's *Communities of Women* and Carroll Smith-Rosenberg's *Disorderly Conduct* (to name only two of several important books) expand the idea of sisterly relations into the realm of sisterhood. And that is what the chapters in this section of our anthology accomplish.

Karen J. Hall explores a sister—sister relationship with a macabre twist in "Sisters in Collusion: Safety and Revolt in Shirley Jackson's *We Have Always Lived in the Castle.*" This Gothic novel, long considered in the genre of juvenile fiction, illustrates what can happen with adult women who are victims of childhood abuse and competition. The novel opens years after the death by arsenic poisoning of all of the Blackwood family members except Uncle Julian and the two sisters. Constance, the older sister, assumes the role of "little parent" of this dysfunctional family, whereas Merricat copes by violent outbreaks and frequent splitting with reality. Hall presents their relationship in its resistance to patriarchal order but finds little that is liberating in the sisters' final self-containment.

In Eva Rueschmann's chapter, "Sister Bonds: Intersections of Family and Race in Jessie Redmon Fauset's *Plum Bun* and Dorothy West's *The Living Is Easy*," relationships between sisters transcend apparent racial boundaries. Fauset and West, both black women writers of the Harlem Renaissance, not only portray in their novels the "narrative and psychological significance of sisters in the development of a sense of self in black women," but also "problematize the individual's relationship to the black community" through the sister bond. *Plum Bun* is a novel about two sisters in 1920s America, one of whom "passes" for white, causing a crisis of identity that goes beyond the search for individual and family to encompass one's racial identity. *The Living is Easy* focuses on Cleo Judson, the oldest of four sisters. While Cleo does not "pass" for white, as does Angela Murray in *Plum Bun*, she embraces white middle class values. The sister relationships in these two novels show the consequences of disowning one's cultural heritage. Thus the sister bond, claims Rueschmann, takes on "a particular power for black women whose culture and identity have been denied by the larger cultural milieu."

In the nineteenth century, the home was the sanctuary, the place where females provided stability and purity against the "outside" world. The daughter—uncontaminated and undefiled—was the "purest element in the architectonics of the family," says Leila S. May. In her chapter, " 'Eat me, drink me, love me': Orality, Sexuality, and the Fruits of Sororal Desire in 'Gob(b)lin(g) Market' and *Beloved*," May shows how Christina Rossetti reveals the facade of the family structure as "a hidden locus of repressed feminine desire." Rossetti's surreal vision of sisterhood challenges the authority of the nineteenth-century patriarchy. The poem ends on the image of motherhood, a relationship that forms the basis of Toni Morrison's *Beloved*. Denver's relationship with the ghost of her sister, and the ways in which that relationship changes the family structure, serve as May's points of comparison with "Goblin Market." In these works by Rossetti and Morrison, claims May, an "unspeakable spectre of sisterhood and sororal desire" is what "results from the external masculine intervention creat[ing] forces which, if unleashed, could undermine the very social structures which promoted the intrusion." Thus her chapter bridges Connie R. Schomburg's study by pairing not only examples from British and American literature, but also of the nineteenth and twentieth centuries—as well as the bourgeois Victorian and the post-slavery African-American family.

In Toni Morrison's novels, as Schomburg demonstrates, the lives of black women form a larger community, one based on "sisterhood" that transcends biological bonds. "To Survive Whole, To Save the Self: The Role of Sisterhood in the Novels of Toni Morrison" encompasses Morrison's first five novels, all of which demonstrate the importance of different kinds of sibling relationships. *The Bluest Eye* has as its focus two biological sisters whose bond is similar to that shared by the two friends, Sula and Nel, in *Sula*. *Song of Solomon* and *Tar Baby* show what happens to an only child in the absence of sustaining sibling relationships. Finally, in *Beloved* Morrison "brings to fruition" the possibilities for fulfilling relationships among siblings, as Denver forms a sisterhood with the women in her community. This connection, this identification with the sisterhood of black women, claims Schomburg, is particularly important as it shows sibling relationships in their fullest sense.

Our final chapter goes beyond the British and American experience related in previous discussions to deal with contemporary German short stories. (Interestingly, in German "the word for sibling, *Geschwister*, is an intensification of the word for sister, *Schwester*" [Downing 116]). In " 'Fly, little sister, fly': Sister Relationship and Identity in Three Contemporary German Stories," Helga G. Braunbeck posits that recent feminist criticism has idealized the bond of sisterhood, emphasizing trust, mutual care, solidarity. However, as she points out, often sister relationships are fraught with competitiveness, rivalry and hostility. In Marie Luise Kaschnitz' short story, "Das dicke Kind," the narrator's negative response when she meets a fat girl reminds her of her own childhood competition with an older sister. The extreme emotional dependence in the sister relationship depicted in Botho StrauB' short story "Marlenes Schwester" leads finally to death when the sisters are separated. Death is the central concern in Angelika Jakob's "Flieg, Schwesterlein, flieg!," told from the perspective of the older, surviving sister. Her bond with her younger sister submerges into a mother-daughter relationship when the biological mother dies. Each of these narratives, as Braunbeck points out, shows one sister who is perceived by the other as an ideal, causing a schism.

It was our intent to assemble a collection of essays which explore the many variations and ramifications of the topic of sibling relationships. Our organization, loosely based upon the types of sibling relationships explored at the beginning of this Introduction, encompasses variations of the sibling paradigm—the single child, brothers and sisters, twins (same sex and opposite sex), and sisters and sisterhood. Literary siblings is our focus, but as our readers will note, each discussion is placed within the parameters of cultural and social commentary. Sibling relationships is an intriguing and potentially addictive topic—intriguing because it brings together two important influences on our lives, family connections and literary studies, and addictive because one idea seems to lead to another and then another. It's hard to stop.

As editors, we became aware as we sifted through literary and related studies that we need to focus our collection to keep it within reasonable bounds. After looking through the many ideas submitted to us, we decided that focusing on the ways in which women writers presented the dichtomy of sibling relationships would provide some parameters to help develop a Table of Contents. More importantly, however, it soon became clear to us that women writers provide a range of perspectives, a variety that we hope will become apparent as our readers explore the essays offered here.

We hope that two ideas become evident: Study of sibling relationships (and birth order) helps us better to understand ourselves as individuals, and women writers offer a variety of perspectivess which illuminate our search for self-knowledge. The essays, all written solely for this collection, give voice and shape to a continuing dialogue which brings together the best of the studies in the field of social and family therapy, psychological research, and literary criticism. The essays included in *The Significance of Sibling Relationships in Literature* not only illustrate the various ways in which this topic is explored, but also provided a framework for future study. May this collection serve, then, as the springboard for exploration of ourselves and of our connection with our siblings.

JoAnna S. Mink and Janet D. Ward

Works Cited

Auerbach, Nina. *Communities of Women: An Idea in Fiction*. Cambridge and London: Harvard UP, 1978.

Bank, Stephen P., and Michael D. Kahn. *The Sibling Bond*. New York: Basic Books, 1982.

Bettelheim, Bruno. *The Uses of Enchantment: The Meaning and Importance of Fairy Tales*. New York: Knopf, 1985.

Downing, Christine. *Psyche's Sisters: Re-Imagining the Meaning of Sisterhood*. San Francisco: Harper & Row, 1988.

Fishel, Elizabeth. *Sisters: Love and Rivalry Inside the Family and Beyond*. New York: William Morrow, 1979.

Hoopes, Margaret M., and James M. Harper. *Birth Order Roles & Sibling Patterns in Individual & Family Therapy*. Rockville, MD: Aspen, 1987.

Leman, Kevin. *The Birth Order Book: Why You Are the Way You Are*. New York: Dell, 1985.

_____. *Growing Up Firstborn: The Pressure and Privilege of Being Number One*. New York: Dell, 1989.

Mink, JoAnna Stephens, and Janet Doubler Ward. *Joinings and Disjoinings: The Significance of Marital Status in Literature*. Bowling Green: Bowling Green State University Popular Press, 1991.

Smith-Rosenberg, Carroll. *Disorderly Conduct: Visions of Gender in Victorian America*. New York: Knopf, 1985.

Sophocles. *Antigone*. Trans. Shaemas O'Sheel. *Ten Greek Plays in Contemporary Translations*. Ed. L.R. Lind. Boston: Houghton, 1957.

Innocence Unleashed:
The Power of the Single Child

Rosemary M. Colt

Behavioral geneticists now theorize that children may have the ability to organize around themselves the psychological environment they need, but some novelists have always known that environment serves the genes. For instance, there are those novels about single female children who against great odds gain control over their destinies. Vulnerable but resiliant, they are lone innocents in a world scornful of or threatened by their presence. Earlier novelists defined innocence as freedom from evil, often portrayed as sexual knowledge, but since the mid- to late-nineteenth century innocence has more often been portrayed as the absence of worldly knowledge, although sexual passion is part of this. Thus we are told that although innocence will inevitably be lost, it may be replaced by wisdom and moral integrity. By protecting the child from the world, innocence allows her to prepare for adulthood. This fictional association of the single child with innocence amidst corruption is a dominant theme in Henry James's *What Maisie Knew* (1897) and Elizabeth Bowen's *The Death of the Heart* (1938), two novels in which lone innocent girls gain power over a dissolute and disordered adult world in order to establish lives for themselves.[1]

To lay the groundwork for this discussion, I look briefly at the passive and martyr-like innocence of children in the work of Charles Dickens, and argue that in *Jane Eyre* (1847) Charlotte Brontë offers a contrasting model of the single child. I am not suggesting that later writers deliberately copied Brontë, rather that by breaking free of the traditional codes of the sentimental novel, she established a pattern of rebellious self-interested innocence. Novelists like James and Bowen echoed Brontë rather than Dickens by creating youthful protagonists who go on living despite (or because of) the loss of innocence. Next, contrasting single children in fiction to those with siblings, I look at how first James and then Bowen, often linked as master and pupil, portray lone female innocents confronted with sexual passion and corruption. As both novelists show, such figures, like Jane Eyre before them, discomfit the adult world. Their innocence challenges contemporary life as their respective creators saw it.

James and Bowen seem both to have realized that while it is true that literary children traditionally serve as commentators on the adult scene, their role is more pronounced when they are alone. As novelists have discovered, single children are in a good position to observe their elders and to make them uncomfortable. Further, they may act as mouthpieces for a novel's prevailing point of view by offering moral commentary from positions that however vulnerable, are also privileged by the traditional nature of childhood. For example, the Lamb children in Ivy Compton-Burnett's *Manservant And Maidservant* (1947) act, as Penelope Lively says in an introduction to the novel, "as a kind of Greek chorus, commenting, with unswerving accuracy, on the actions of their elders" (ix). They also have a considerable impact on the plot of their story. Then look at two more recent examples of lone children, the boy Tarwater in Flannery O'Connor's *The Violent Bear It Away* (1955) and Dot in Louise Erdrich's *The Beet Queen* (1986). Tarwater, the burning glass that concentrates the tensions in the novel between ignorance and revelation, is the vehicle for O'Connor's urgent spiritual message. Dot is the focal point of the energies and desires of the adults around her, so that finally, the novel turns out to be her story, not theirs. Each of these children stands alone, a potent symbol of the vulnerability and the power of the child, qualities not so apparent when, as in Compton-Burnett's novel, brothers and sisters band together.

Significantly, Bowen and James's use of female lone children compels us to ask if they reach different conclusions about the choices open to women in morally compromised societies. And if so, can one generalize about the differing ways in which a man and a woman novelist depict the fate of the single child, especially the female child? At the very least, the comparison suggests that Bowen's is the more realistic view of childhood innocence in its recognition of the drive for endurance of young women burdened by their elders' desires, which Maisie defines when she reflects that she knows as well that a "person could be compromised as that a person could be slapped with a hair-brush or left alone in the dark, and it was equally familiar to her that each of these ordeals was in general held to have too little effect" (129). In conclusion, both novelists perceive the price of defying social codes, of innocence if you will. For both James and Bowen, the single child uniquely embodies a major novelistic theme. Finally, their use of such characters is suggestive of the role of gender in fictional choice.

In his biography of Charles Dickens, Peter Ackroyd notes that "*Oliver Twist* is the first novel in the English language which takes a child as its central character or hero" (216). A radical development, it went unnoticed at the time because of the existence of " 'factual orphan tales' " and the "ancient but healthy tradition of 'rogue literature,' " which in part chronicled the dramas of lost or abandoned children" (216-17). *Oliver Twist* was published in 1837-38, and Dickens went on to write other works featuring memorable juveniles, many of them single or orphaned, such as David Copperfield, Esther Summerson, Pip and Little Nell in *The Old Curiosity Shop* (1840-41), in which Dickens creates the ideal innocent child as heroine. Nell, however, dies before she can experience the loss of innocence and the (male) narrator's attitude towards her is epitomized by the closing words of the first chapter. Haunted in his dreams by Nell, he thinks of her "in the midst of...decay and old age, the beautiful child in her gentle slumber, smiling through her light and sunny dreams" (I, 15).

Relating Nell's grim history, the narrator always stresses her passivity and innocence. Ever the willing victim, she dies untouched by evil and is eulogized as "Dear, gentle, patient, noble Nell" (II, 140). Thus when we hear of the dead child's pet bird, "a poor, slight thing the pressure of a finger would have crushed," in its cage (140), Nell too seems like a caged bird. The thin glory of martyrdom not withstanding, her innocence has been useless to the point of self-destruction.[2]

Dickens is arguably the quintessential Victorian novelist who both reflects and shapes the prevailing myths of his times, one of which was the image of the innocent female child he made famous with Little Nell, whose plight is emphasized by her solitude. Later, in young women like Esther Summerson, Little Dorritt and Sissy Jupe, Dickens portrays innocence acting against evil although he never resolves the contradictions in their characters. Esther, for example, moves from action to passivity and back again with dizzying speed. Another Victorian novelist, Charlotte Brontë, does imagine a bold female child, and a single one at that, whose innocence advances her in the world. But first a word about the significance of single children in literature, lonely creatures who confront adults on their own with neither the comfort nor the distraction of siblings. Children with siblings have each other for company, and they form relationships depending on the nature of the enemy. Thus Florence comforts Paul Dombey, while the children at Thrushcross Grange combine and recombine with each other according to Heathcliff's changing status. Celia blunts Dorothea Brooke's sharp edges, and Maggie Tulliver's conflict with her parents occurs in the context of her relationship with her brother Tom. Thus when she cuts off her hair early in the novel, she is aided and abetted by Tom. Greeted by the horrified derision of her family, she thinks not of them, but of Tom's triumph over her disgrace. Maggie's obsession with Tom, which eventually causes her death, thus weakens the thrust of her struggle with her family for her own identity. Much later, in the last section of Virginia Woolf's *To the Lighthouse* (1927), Cam and James Ramsay unite against their father. On their way to the lighthouse they respond in unison to his threatened recital of poetry by the collective thought that "if he did, they could not bear it; they would shriek aloud; they could not endure another explosion of the passion that boiled in him" (305). Just as Maggie's love for Tom sets the limits of her freedom, so the Ramsay children's concern for each other circumscribes their ability to overcome their father; two are not stronger than one and they remain passengers in the boat of his ultimate victory. To recognize the significance of siblings one has only to imagine how different their stories would be if Maggie and Cam were only children.

It is equally difficult to conceive of Jane Eyre with brothers or sisters. Forced to live by their wits, children like her develop the powers of observation that give them power over adults. For instance, Jane's understanding of the dynamics of the Reed household serves her well in her battles with Mrs. Reed. This may not be immediately obvious, but it is, after all, her flying into a temper that forces Mrs. Reed to save Jane by sending her to school. Shut up in the red room, Jane questions her existence at a place where she is "like nobody there"

(12). Yet on her deathbed Mrs. Reed tells Jane that she herself had " 'felt fear, as if an animal that I had struck or pushed had looked up at me with human eyes and cursed me in a man's voice' " (210). Often, as with Mrs. Reed, Jane wins out by reacting to events rather than initiating action, but armed with the lonely courage of her convictions, she nevertheless progresses towards self-definition. Innocence in particular serves her well, saving her not only from the madwoman in the attic, but from Rochester himself.

Most importantly, Jane's innocence is active and not passive, like Little Nell's. It thus helps her to control first herself, and then others. Her strength prophesies those later novelists who depict similarly lone female children. For them as for Jane, innocence in the traditional sense is not an option. As Tony Tanner says of Nanda in James's *The Awkward Age* (1899), in her this quality is

. . . something far other than the surface blush of a fruit which, tendered never so carefully often proves to be rotten before half ripe. It is a quality of response to inevitable experience: it can be exposed and submerged in a corrupt and complex medium but need not be contaminated or undermined. (301)

Tanner could be talking about Jane, but the active innocence he champions is an even more essential quality for women in the unstable Edwardian world of *The Awkward Age* and *What Maisie Knew*. Tanner is comparing Nanda to Aggie in that novel, a girl who might well be Little Nell in Edwardian dress. Similarly, Nanda could be an older Maisie, a child whose beleaguered innocence is a useful weapon in her struggle against her parents and stepparents. The resolution of Maisie's history, however, casts doubt on the quality of her future. The ending of the novel is seen, for instance, by Joseph Hynes as "concerned with the process, the shape, and the value of renunciation" (528); unlike Jane, she may lose as much as she gains, at least from the perspective of anyone but James, who trusts in the redemptive imagination. He may not kill off Maisie, but her projected life is painfully narrow.

Whatever its end, the beginning of Maisie's life is horrific. Six when the novel begins and twelve or so when it ends, Maisie is the luckless only child of Ida and Beale Farange, whose acrimonious divorce has just been finalized. Her helplessness and isolation are stressed by the narrator, when, for example, he says how clear it was to "any spectator...that the only link binding her to either parent was this lamentable fact of her being a ready vessel for bitterness, a deep little porcelain cup in which biting acids could be mixed" (13). A "mite of an infant in a great dim theatre" (15), she is "the little feathered shuttlecock they could fiercely keep flying between them" (19). Maisie's story would be less effective if she were not alone; it is essential, as in *Jane Eyre*, to focus the reader's attention on her consciousness of events. James depicts Maisie experiencing her parents' remarriages—her father's to Maisie's ex-governess—and their sporadic efforts to use her as a weapon. To complicate matters, her stepmother Mrs. Beale and stepfather Sir Claude become lovers. Ultimately Maisie faces a Solomon's choice that forces her to renounce the one person she loves, Sir Claude. Maisie chooses instead her sometime governess,

Mrs. Wix, and goes off to start a new life.

Rather irrelevantly—it does not seem the primary issue—Maisie's critics have concentrated on her innocence, or lack thereof. They fall roughly into two groups, those who believe that she retains it and those who argue that Maisie becomes no better than those around her.[3] James states in his Preface to the 1907 New York edition that some readers might find it "disgusting...to attribute to Maisie so intimate an 'acquaintance' with the gross immoralities surrounding her" (9), and then dismisses this by noting her ability to make people "portentous." She makes, for example, her mother "concrete, immense and awful" (8). In other words, Maisie's vision grounds others in reality by lending them "a precious element of dignity" (7). James, then, evades the issue of her relative innocence or corruption in favor of the livelier one of Maisie's capacity to endow her world with meaning. It is this that gives her a moral power denied anyone else in the novel and that will comfort her in exile with Mrs. Wix.

Maisie's situation is a paradox. Powerless because she is innocent and alone, she survives by exploiting her seeming disadvantages to gain her independence. For example, early on she learns to exaggerate her innocence by pretending stupidity. Realizing "that she had been a centre of hatred and a messenger of insult, and that everything was bad because she had been employed to make it so, Maisie decides to "forget everything, repeat nothing" (20). Her parents find her dull, while she, on the other hand, sees enough to make life if not fun, at least interesting. But existence is still like "a long, long corridor with rows of closed doors," doors at which it "was wise not to knock" (33). In her loneliness Maisie transfers her ignorance to her doll Lisette, whose "questions" convulse Maisie just as she herself makes her mother's friends laugh. Not surprisingly, Maisie also keeps secrets. She does not, for instance, speak to her stepfather of the other man at her mother's side. In doing so, she acquires both a sense of "freedom to make out things for herself" (79) and "an odd air of being present at her history in as separate a manner as if she could only get at experience by flattening her nose against a pane of glass" (85). Thus solitude gives her freedom, but it also alienates her from herself.

The process by which Maisie learns to employ her innocence to survive is best shown by her behavior towards Sir Claude and Mrs. Beale, who have the gall to say that she has brought them together. In fact, they talk of her power to save them, bantering with each other in her presence in a way that is all the more appalling for being heard through Maisie's ears. Adoring Sir Claude, she is delighted to see him so cheerful, although she admits that being with the happy pair is "like being perched on a prancing horse" (102). There are two scenes about halfway through the novel that reveal this precarious perch. In the first of these Maisie and Sir Claude encounter her mother with a lover; in the second, she and Mrs. Beale unexpectedly meet Beale Farange and the dusky American "Countess" who is his current amour. Each scene teaches Maisie a brutal lesson about the limits of her authority, and at the same time shows her that she is not helpless because each parent, and Sir Claude, tries to use her and fails. When she leaves her stepfather unsatisfied at the end of the first scene— she won't tell him about her conversation with her mother's lover—she feels the same "sweet sense of success that...she had had at a crisis when, on the stairs, returning from her father's, she had met a fierce question of her mother's with an imbecility as deep and had in consequence been dashed by Mrs. Farange almost to the bottom" (121).

This grim vignette suggests the disturbing side of Maisie's suffering innocence. James implies that her pain is balanced by a gain in sensibility, but the second of the previous scenes reveals the cost of an advantage that remains of little practical use. After they meet, her father asks Maisie to go with him to America. Longing to accept, she thinks to herself that to give him something "here on the spot was all her desire" (138). Because she also intuits that he wants her to refuse, Maisie, caught between her own wishes and his, becomes the parent, her father the child. The narrator notes the pathos "on the child's part of an innocence so saturated with knowledge and so directed to diplomacy" (139). Wise beyond her years, Maisie sees that "this was their parting...and that he had brought her there for so many caresses only because it was important such an occasion should look better for him than any other" (141).

Innocence thus becomes knowledge, and even power. By refusing to acknowledge the true nature of the relations between her elders, just as Jane Eyre denies the existence of Bertha Rochester, Maisie escapes their world. The price paid out in suffering in return for this triumph is made concrete in the last section of the novel. Sir Claude has taken Maisie across the channel to France, where they are joined by Mrs. Wix, the governess who shares her charge's love for Sir Claude and who envisions them living together as a *ménage à trois*, Mrs. Beale having been conveniently sidetracked. Maisie now knows that she is "morally at home in atmospheres it would be appalling to analyse" (155), and as before, she deliberately chooses not to do so. She is also running out of choices. For instance, before leaving England Maisie bests Mrs. Ida by unconsciously provoking the latter's temper, a victory as ambiguous as her tumble down the staircase. The interview is described as "the occasion of Maisie's life on which her mother was to have the most to say to her" (163), but what she says is that Maisie is a " 'dreadful dismal deplorable little thing' " (170). Ida then stalks off, leaving her daughter to stare "at the image her flight had still left standing" (170), but also leaving her free to go with Sir Claude.

Maisie thus gains her freedom by losing her mother, just as she has earlier "lost" her father by granting him his wish. She is, then, ready for the decision that will lead to her gravest loss, and in making it, she exercises for the first time authority over others. Mrs. Beale and Sir Claude, having decided to live together on the Continent, ask her to join them, a choice complicated by Mrs. Wix, who has been summoned by Sir Claude and invited to join the proposed household; she refuses on moral grounds. Sir Claude then asks Maisie to give up Mrs. Wix, telling her that she is the " 'best thing' " that he and Mrs. Beale have ever known (247), that they need her innocence to maintain the propriety of their relationship. Maisie responds that she is being asked to betray Mrs. Wix. Afraid of her longing for Sir Claude, she sees, however, that he is in turn afraid of her and of his own weakness. Her fear vanishes and she tells him that she will give up Mrs. Wix if he will give up Mrs. Beale. As Joseph Warren

Beach has said, "In asking no less than heroism from him she becomes herself heroic" (233). It is a triumphant moment, prepared for equally by Maisie's studied ignorance of the passion that dominates Sir Claude's love for her stepmother and her consciousness that because she has nothing to lose, she has supremacy. The novel ends with Maisie's departure for England in the custody of Mrs. Wix. She has rejected the world of her elders for Mrs. Wix, whose virtue is her love for Maisie. Not knowing exactly what she has lost, but associating it with the confused lives of her parents and stepparents, Maisie instinctively knows what to do. She controls this last scene because she has been driven by her innocence and solitude to great resourcefulness, and wisely, she has used what she possesses to gain her independence. In doing so, she loses the person she loves most in the world and knowingly abandons him and her stepmother to a lesser life.

Is Maisie's costly victory deplorable? Is she forced to choose Mrs. Wix because like Nanda after her, she is too good for the only world she knows? Philip Weinstein thinks so, and says that "clearsighted, deprived, and uprooted, Maisie is left with little more than dubious Mrs. Wix and her own imaginative capacities" (96). For James this may be enough, but others may wish Maisie a less solitary fate. A similar plot with a kinder ending is offered by Elizabeth Bowen in *The Death of the Heart*. Her protagonist is, like Maisie, a lone child caught in a web of adult intrigue; however, Bowen suggests that Portia Quayne, while equally dependent on innocence and solitude, is not forced to choose a lesser life. Portia exploits her tenuous position to shame her elders into recognizing her existence and more importantly, her emotional needs.

The formal and thematic similarity between these two novels has been recognized by critics, as has the literary relationship between James and Bowen. For instance, Hermione Lee writes that like *What Maisie Knew, The Death of the Heart* is "an educative novel which surrounds the child with carefully balanced influences" (117). In a 1964 review of Bowen's *The Little Girls* Anthony Burgess cites the novel as an example of the faults of women writers: "they chatter, they are deficient in moral values, they are too empirical, they fall in love with the accident and miss the essence . . ." (254). Thus while Burgess names James as Bowen's "true progenitor," he claims that he "articulates a whole culture" while Bowen merely "conserves a particular place at a particular time" (254). Ironically, it may be her acknowledgment of the accidental specific that leads Bowen to foresee a more hopeful future for her protagonist. For instance, the rackety charm of Waikiki in the second part of *The Death of the Heart* implies that the world has its pull; it has no counterpart in Maisie.

It may also be that Bowen, an only child herself, needed to imagine ways of escape for children similarly placed in lonely and isolated situations. It is not then surprising to find in her fiction girls who disturb adults by railing against their own solitary innocence. In the short story "Sunday Afternoon," for example, the girl Maria annoys her elders at an Irish country house by behaving like "some difficult pet animal" (617), and announcing that " 'About what is important...it seems that no one can tell one anything. There is really nothing, till one knows it oneself' " (618). She, like Portia, has an angry air of suspension lacking in Maisie, who wants but dreads to "know." This is partly due to their age difference—Maisie is only six, after all. It also suggests that youthful innocence is a trap best escaped, a notion that James finds more problematic judging by Maisie or by Nanda in *The Awkward Age*. True, Aggie's imprisonment in innocence is a disaster, but neither is Nanda's fate totally positive—it is at best a compromise. From one perspective, then, Maisie merely exchanges one prison for another while Portia may win actual freedom. In an early Bowen novel, *The Last September* (1929), an orphaned nineteen-year-old girl longs to connect: " 'I like to be related; to have to be what I am. Just to be is so intransitive, so lonely' " (142), but at the end of the novel she is still alone, still intransitive. Bowen said of the novel that it was closest to her heart of all her work, perhaps because it evokes so vividly the heroine's suspended state which she may herself have known and pitied in retrospect.

In *The Death of the Heart*, however, a young girl breaks free of intransitive innocence. Granted, the quality of her future is open to debate, but the suspended indeterminacy with which the novel ends is less stifling than the abrupt closure of Maisie's life with Mrs. Wix. Moreover, to reinforce the necessity of escaping innocence, it is represented not just by Portia who like Maisie, is genuine, but by Eddie, in whom it is calculated. The narrator asserts "that innocence so constantly finds itself in a false position that inwardly innocent people learn to be disengenuous....They exist alone....Their singleness, their ruthlessness, their one continuous wish makes them bound to be cruel, and to suffer cruelty. The innocent are so few that two of them seldom meet—when they do, their victims lie strewn all round" (128-29).[4]

In theory this is true of both Eddie and Portia, but the difference between them is that Eddie, Portia's first love and the sometime Platonic lover of her sister-in-law Anna, embodies innocence as self-consciousness, which in Portia it is not. The orphaned offspring of the father of Anna's husband Thomas and the feckless Irene, Portia has come to live with the Quaynes in London. Their house is described as "without any life above-stairs, a house to which nobody had returned yet, which, through the big windows, darkness and silence had naturally stolen in on and begun to inhabit" (27). And despite Anna's pretty decorations, the house remains as empty as the Quaynes' marriage. Eddie, the innocent *manqué* is "the brilliant child of an obscure family" and as "clever as a monkey" (75-76). After an erratic career at Oxford he has written a semi-successful novel and now works, thanks to Anna, for Thomas's advertising firm. Eddie is her "first troubadour" (80), welcome at Windsor Terrace until he tries to kiss Anna, who loathes physical contact. As the novel opens he is flirting secretly with Portia, an "innocent" preying on a true innocent. Thus Bowen lets us know right off that innocence is a potential trap for Portia.

The character of the trap is inherent in the novel's division into three sections with headings that reflect the temptations to which innocence is subjected: "The World," "The Flesh," and "The Devil." In each of them, Portia's innocence meets new challenges and in turn, threatens the adult world. For example, initially it is Anna who protests, calling Portia " 'more like an animal' " (10) than a child because her room is untidy. Later, she wonders if

Portia is "a snake, or a rabbit?" (57). Guilty about episodes in her past, especially an old love affair, Anna feels "bound up with her fear, with her secret, by that enwrapping look of Portia's: she felt mummified" (60). Portia meanwhile reflects Anna's feelings by recognizing that she has "stepped over" people to meet with Eddie, and envisions all whom she has "sacrificed" (129). (In fact, there are hints that Anna in her own lone youth was like Portia—the danger is that Portia will become Anna.) Stubbornly, Portia pursues Eddie because like other Bowen heroines, she is desperate to experience life: "...she could not doubt people knew what they were doing...She could not believe there was not a plan of the whole set-up in every head but her own" (72-73). Eddie is the handiest clue to the puzzle, and so she seizes upon him. Portia controls the novel from the beginning. By responding to Eddie she sets the plot in motion, and she makes the other characters revolve around her by ignoring the sexual undercurrents that hold them together, and apart. She is able to do this because her innocence permits her to remain ignorant of Eddie's true nature and of the power of the emotions she is unleashing.

Even in the novel's second section when she is overwhelmed by both a new setting and new faces, Portia's innocence and solitude are disconcerting. While the Quaynes are on holiday she goes to stay at Waikiki (an ill-named house) with Mrs. Heccombe, Anna's former governess. There she joins in the sexually charged social life of Daphne and Dickie, Mrs. Heccombe's stepchildren and it is at their parties that she first senses the importance of passion. When Eddie visits, Portia sees him holding Daphne's hand in a darkened movie theatre and this, her first conscious experience of betrayal, adds to her new sense of sex. Emboldened, she challenges the usually unflappable Daphne to explain herself. Daphne responds by saying that " 'if you'll excuse my saying so, a person might almost take you for a natural. Have you got no ideas?' " (248). She is right; Portia's lack of guile makes her idiotic at both Waikiki and Windsor Terrace—like Maisie with her mother. One begins to understand why Anna finds her presence (and Eddie her innocence) so unsettling. Earlier, Eddie tells Portia that she makes him feel guilty—just as she does Anna. Alone, she has more power than the two of them. It is limited in the sense that innocence itself is limited; it serves as a refuge for just so long, but that is long enough.

Still, despite the way in which she threatens him, at the end of the second section Eddie asks Portia not to change. His reliance on her as a symbol of purity—he wants her never to grow up—is belittling, and Portia shows that she cannot go on as she has by asking if " 'is there something unnatural about us? Do you feel safe about me because I'm bats? What did Daphne mean about ideas I hadn't got?' " (257). Portia is still relatively innocent but it is obvious that she cannot remain so. Like Maisie, torn between innocence and experience, she must find her own balance, on her own. Flirted with by Daphne's boyfriend, she wonders if he has "behind that opaque face...the impulse that made Eddie write her that first note?" (205). Portia pretends to find this an appalling thought, just as Maisie does when she ignores the affair between Sir Claude and Mrs. Beale, but plainly the truth about adult sexual complicity is dawning on her. In the first section, Portia inhabits the middle ground between childhood and adolescence, keeping, for example, an extensive small animal collection much scorned by Anna. But then she is recently orphaned, and for the last years of her mother's life lived a vagabond life in second-class Continental hotels; Portia remembers them making tea on bedside tables and sharing chocolate bars in bed like two schoolgirls. She is thus torn, anxious for life and yet attracted by seclusion and separateness. Like Maisie with her doll, she hangs onto childhood; challenged by sexual knowledge, Portia wills her ignorance while at the same time moving eagerly towards experience.

Yet whatever she may will, the world beckons Portia, and in the last section she undergoes the ultimate betrayal of her innocence and isolation. Alerted to its existence by her friend St. Quentin, Anna finds and reads Portia's diary. St. Quentin tells Portia, warning her that although what she writes is silly, " 'all the same, you are taking a liberty. You set traps for us. You ruin our free will' " (301). One sees what he means—girls like Maisie and Portia antagonize their elders by inhabiting alternative worlds. Portia protests that she simply writes what happens, and is accused in turn of spying: " 'Another offence is, you have a loving nature; you are the loving nature in vacuo' " (301). St. Quentin thus identifies precisely why Portia threatens Anna and Eddie: innocently, she loves without qualification, simply for the sake of loving. Thus in a final confrontation with Eddie he tells her that she expects " 'every bloody thing to be either right or wrong, and be done with the whole of oneself' " (339). For him, and for everyone in the loveless world of the novel, this is intolerable. More importantly, it won't do for Portia either.

The final episode of the novel, although it foretells little of Portia's future, suggests that there is hope for her if she will learn from the experience of betrayal. Escaping from the Quaynes after the discovery of the diary, Portia finds refuge at the Karachi Hotel with Major Brutt, a kindly retired Army man down on his luck who has been nice to her. Portia lets him know that Anna views him with scorn, thus shattering the Major's illusions about his status at Windsor Terrace by hurting him as she has been hurt. He calls the Quaynes and dares them to do the right thing for Portia, whatever that may be. They send Matchett, the proverbial old family retainer inherited from Thomas's mother who has been Portia's ally. After deciding that this is "right thing," Anna is for once honest. Asked how she would feel if she were Portia, Anna answers " 'Contempt for the pack of us, who muddled our own lives then stopped me from living mine' " (376). It is a rare moment of honesty; as Anna says, " 'Though she and I may wish to make a new start, we hardly shall' " (377).

We never see Portia again, only Matchett on the steps of the Karachi, but the narrator speaks of "intimation of summer coming" that fills the air, a season that is "the height and fullness of living" (384). If she can translate the innocence of spring into the fullness of summer, perhaps Portia too will gain happiness. Of course it is equally conceivable that she will become like Anna, embittered and passionless. Whatever her fate, she does not, like Maisie, go off to live a separate life—this is somehow unimaginable. Like Maisie, she leaves behind victims, Major Brutt in his lonely hotel room and the Quaynes and Eddie in the drawing room at Windsor Terrace. As San Quentin says, " 'This evening the pure in heart have simply got us on toast' " (374). For them, as for Mrs. Beale and Sir Claude, life will never be the same now that innocence has passed through it.

In summary, Bowen as a woman novelist imagines if not a happy ending for Portia, at least an open one, a chance for a life that leaves innocence behind but remembers its uses. Burgess accuses women novelists of focussing on the accident rather than the essence, and perhaps Bowen does not show as James does a whole culture. Perhaps she chooses instead to recreate a particular place at a particular time. But if it is the accidents and the particulars that dominate women's lives, then Bowen is writing what she knows to be true. Portia shows how innocence becomes a handicap when it blinds one to reality, as it has Eddie. It protects Portia first from her unusual childhood, then from the corruption of the Quayne household and finally, from the latent sexuality at Waikiki. But she cannot sustain it without further limiting her emotional growth, as Maisie does in choosing Mrs. Wix. In Portia's story, life keeps breaking in, whether it be in the shape of Waikiki or in the description of the Karachi Hotel. Like James before her, Bowen picks a single child to illustrate her theme because the choice makes the uses of innocence blatantly clear: alone in a hostile world, single children, especially innocent young girls, both embody their virtue and employ it to gain an end. And ultimately, single children represent all of us, only more sharply delineated. Writing about fiction that depicts the middle years of life, Margaret Gullette argues for the pragmatic value of novels, saying that "if ever we have novels that can absorb all the kinds of suffering that we know, and that can still plot survival, this is the expandable genre out of which they will arise" (172). Perhaps, but youth comes before middle age, and one must survive it first. James posits a compromised survival for Maisie that validates the lonely life of the imagination. Bowen offers instead the potential for complexity; a life that abandons the shield of innocence for the troubled richness of one committed to experience. Both do so through the medium of only children.

Notes

[1] I do not want to speculate why these figures are female and not male. Suffice it to quote Henry James in the Preface to *Maisie*: "...my little vessel of consciousness...couldn't be with verisimilitude a rude little boy; since...the sensibility of the female young is indubitably, for early youth, the greater..." (4).

[2] I am aware that *The Old Curiosity Shop* is a sentimental novel meant to be read almost typologically. Jane Tompkins makes a persuasive case for the value of this in the case of *Uncle Tom's Cabin* in her 1981 essay, "Sentimental Power: *Uncle Tom's Cabin* and the Politics of Literary History." However, in a worldly sense, Nell's death remains pointless.

[3] The first of these includes, to name only a few, Marius Bewley and F.R. Leavis in Bewley's *The Complex Fate* (London, 1952, 79-144; Joseph Warren Beach, *The Method*

of Henry James (Philadelphia, 1954), 237-42, and James Gargano, "What Maisie Knew: The Evolution of 'Moral Sense' " NCF, 16 (June 1961), 244-62. As his title suggests, a middle ground is offered by Joseph Hynes in "The Middle Way of Miss Farange: A study of James's Maisie" ELH, 32 (1965), 528-553.

⁴In *Eva Trout* or *Changing Scenes* (1968) Bowen explores the potential destructiveness of innocence in darker terms than in this novel. Both Eva, another single female, and her mute son Jeremy have a devastating effect on those with whom they come in contact—and indeed, the novel ends in murder.

Works Cited

Ackroyd, Peter. *Charles Dickens*. New York: Harper Collins, 1990.

Bowen, Elizabeth. *The Death of the Heart*. London: Jonathan Cape, 1948.

_____. "Sunday Afternoon." *The Collected Stories of Elizabeth Bowen*. New York: Knopf, 1981.

Brontë, Charlotte. *Jane Eyre*. New York: W.W. Norton, 1971.

Burgess, Anthony. Review of *The Little Girls*. Spectator 21, February 1964.

Compton-Burnett, Ivy. *Manservant and Maidservant*. Oxford: Oxford UP, 1983.

Dickens, Charles. *The Old Curiosity Shop*. New York: Thomas Y. Crowell, 1896.

Eliot, George. *The Mill on the Floss*. New York: New American Library, 1965.

Erdrich, Louise. *The Beet Queen*. New York: Bantam Books, 1989.

Gullette, Margaret. *Safe at Last in the Middle Years: The Invention of the Midlife Progress Novel: Saul Bellow, Margaret Drabble, Anne Tyler & John Updike*. Berkeley: U of California, 1988.

James, Henry. *What Maisie Knew*. Oxford: Oxford UP, 1980.

Lee, Hermione. *Elizabeth Bowen: An Estimation*. Totowa, NJ: Barnes & Nobel, 1981.

O'Connor, Flannery. *The Violent Bear It Away*. New York: Farrar, Straus, Cudahy, 1955.

Tanner, Tony. *The Reign of Wonder: Naivety & Reality in American Literature*. Cambridge: Cambridge UP, 1965.

Weinstein, Philip. *Henry James & the Requirements of the Imagination*. Cambridge: Harvard UP, 1971.

Woolf, Virginia. *To the Lighthouse*. New York: Harcourt Brace Jovanovich, 1955.

Morgan le Fay and King Arthur in Malory's *Works* and Marion Zimmer Bradley's *The Mists of Avalon*: Sibling Discord and the Fall of the Round Table

Debra A. Benko

The character Morgan le Fay and her relationship to her half-brother King Arthur are portrayed very differently when the reader compares the versions of the Arthurian legend written by Malory in the medieval period and Marion Zimmer Bradley in the twentieth century. The perspective of Marion Zimmer Bradley as a woman writer contributes to the reader's understanding of the differences in character and contributes to the study of sibling relationships in works by women writers. The sibling relationship between Morgan and Arthur merits the reader's attention because of the way in which the two characters are inextricably linked in the legend's denouement as Morgan bears Arthur to Avalon in his final moments.

Previous critics have not placed much emphasis on Morgan's relationship to Arthur as a sibling. Rosemary Morris notes that previous scholarship by L.A. Paton and others has sought explanations for Morgan's role in Malory and other Arthurian works by giving her the role of "Arthur's fairy mistress," a role Morris categorically denies exists in the medieval texts (97). Concluding that the relationship is in fact a brother-sister relationship, Morris seems to consign Morgan to relative insignificance, stating that Morgan "hovers elusively, malevolent or strangley [sic] benevolent, on the fringes of Arthur's story" (97). Perhaps Sheila Fisher, in her analysis of the marginality of Morgan in *Sir Gawain and the Green Knight*, best expresses the significance of the relationship between Morgan and Arthur when she concludes that Morgan "is always simultaneously lurking at the fringes and inescapably at dead center, related to Arthur and to Gawain" (143). Fisher's conclusion of Morgan's centrality applies to the works of Malory and Bradley as well. Exploring the sibling relationship of Morgan and Arthur is an integral part of an attempt to analyze their roles in Arthurian legend, roles which have persisted and varied for centuries. The variations and continuities in Morgan's character and role and in Morgan and Arthur's sibling relationship between Malory's and Bradley's versions of the Arthurian legend speak to changes and continuity in the perception of sibling relationships and gender roles over time and by men and women authors.

In the medieval work by Malory, Morgan is stereotyped as an evil traitor witch who uses her powers to oppose her half-brother Arthur, his wife Guinevere, and the knights of his kingdom for her own gain or out of pure maliciousness. Her greatest evil, in Malory's eyes, is her enmity toward Arthur and his knights: " 'And ever as she myght she made warre on kynge Arthure, and all daungerous knyghtes she wytholdyth with her for to dystroy all thos knyghtes that kynge arthure lovyth' " (367). Malory places his emphasis upon Morgan's conflict with Arthur; she could simply destroy good knights or knights of the Round Table, but instead, in Malory's description, she attacks the knights her brother loves. Malory's Morgan attempts physical and spiritual fratricide.

Malory casts the roles in the sibling dispute with Arthur as guileless victim and Morgan as the aggressor, and Malory's Arthurian community supports Arthur. In fact, the voices of the Arthurian community act as a Greek chorus, becoming an identical voice issuing one judgment of Morgan. For example, Palomides speaks to Dinadan: " 'So God me helpe,' seyde sir Palomydes, 'this is a shamefull and a vylaunce· usage for a quene to use, and namely to make suche warre uppon her owne lorde that is called the floure of chevalry that is Crystyn othir hethyn' " (367). Gawain's reaction when Morgan's knights and ladies attempt to entrap Lancelot and Tristram stereotypes and condemns Morgan, his condemnation, like that of Palomides, emphasizing her relationship to Arthur, " 'Fy for shame...that evir such false treson sholde be wrought or used in a quene and a kyngys systir, and a kynge and a quenys doughtir!' " (315). The members of Malory's chivalric world call Morgan " 'the false sorseres and wycche moste that is now lyving' " (270). Throughout the portions of the text in which Morgan appears, the entire community unites in expressing outrage at Morgan's betrayal of Arthur. Thus, Morgan becomes a touchstone for or a precursor to the eventual betrayals of Arthur which bring about the ultimate tragedy.

In the brother-sister relationship Malory portrays, Arthur is the innocent, trusting victim, and Morgan is the selfish enchantress who puts her lover Accolon and her desires for political power before her brother the King and her husband Uriens. Morgan replaces the scabbard that prevents Arthur from losing blood and the sword Excalibur, both of which he has entrusted to her for safekeeping, with an enchanted imitation and sends Accolon with the real sword and scabbard into battle against Arthur, who is saved from death by the magic of the Lady of the Lake, which allows him to retrieve the true sword and scabbard from Accolon (Malory 49, 87-88). As Accolon explains Morgan's motives of passion for him and desire to be queen at his side, he includes evil's spite for the good as well when he states that " 'kynge Arthure ys the man in the worlde that she hatyth moste, because he is moste of worship and of prouesse of ony of hir bloode' " (Malory 88). Arthur vows revenge upon Morgan and the enmity and discord between the two siblings is sealed until the closing moments of the saga.

In Malory, any suggestion of a prior sibling relationship in which the two were congenial relations is found only in Arthur's response to Morgan's acts of betrayal. Arthur says, " 'God knowyth I have honoured hir and worshipped hir more than all my kyn, and more have I trusted hir than my wyff and all my kyn aftir' " (Malory 88). Malory here suggests that there has been a previous time in which the sibling relationship was loving and amicable, but no details are provided to us other than Palomides' mention that Arthur had given her a castle and later regretted it " 'a thousand tymes, for sytthen kynge Arthure and she hath bene at debate and stryff' " (367).

If the reader finds any hint of mitigating explanation or even sympathy for Morgan in Malory's description of the Accolon episode, it is when Arthur has his revenge by sending Accolon's body to Morgan as " 'a present' " with the message that he has the real Excalibur and the scabbard in his possession again, and Malory states that "whan quene Morgan wyste that Accolon was dede, she was so sorowfull that nye hir herte to-braste, but because she wolde nat hit were knowyn oute, she kepte hir countenaunce and made no sembelaunte of dole" (90-91). Morgan mourns the death of Accolon out of love for him. Here the reader finds that Morgan may have acted more out of her love for Accolon than for her own interests. Be that as it may, Morgan has through her actions against Arthur declared herself his rival, and the sibling rivalry continues when Morgan answers Arthur's revenge by seeking him as he lies sleeping recovering from his wounds and taking the charmed scabbard, declaring before she throws it into a lake to disappear forever, " 'Whatsoever com of me, my brothir shall nat have this scawberde!' " (91-92). Morgan can thus be held responsible for Arthur's death at Mordred's hands since, when the day of his battle with Mordred comes, he does not have the scabbard.

Morgan and Arthur are enemies in Malory's text from the Accolon episode onward until the denouement. Morgan saves the life of Accolon's cousin and Arthur's knight Manessen and bids him tell Arthur she did it " 'nat for the love of hym, but for the love of Accolon, and tell hym I feare hym nat whyle I can make me and myne in lyknesse of stonys, and lette hym wete I can do much more when I se my tyme' " (93). Here Morgan implies that she might have once acted for the love of her brother. Malory notes that in spite of her challenge to Arthur, she reinforces her castles and towns "for allwey she drad muche kyng Arthure" (93). Arthur's answer to Morgan's action is his own challenge laced with sarcasm, " 'Well,' seyde the kyng, 'she is a kynde sister! I shall so be avengid on hir and I lyve that all crystendom shall speke of it' " (Malory 93). Malory nevertheless treats Arthur's reactions to Morgan as justified responses while, as previously discussed, Morgan bears the blame and condemnation of Arthurian society for her actions.

Scholars have offered various reasons for Malory's portrayal of Morgan as evil and opposed to Arthur. Katharine Rogers terms Malory's portrayal of Morgan "ruining men" misogynistic (59). Myra Olstead tells us that "Malory's chief emphasis is upon heroic life and the affairs of men" (128). In Olstead's view, Malory's portrayal of both Morgan le Fay and the Lady of the Lake "opposes their magical skills in so forthright a manner, they become more clearly than ever symbolic embodiments of evil and good" (133). Malory has typed Morgan le Fay by choosing to make her, according to Henry Morgan, "the single character throughout the work whose actions are consistently evil" (165). While all of these explanations have validity, they do not fully account for the implications created by Morgan's sibling relationship with Arthur.

Perhaps Henry Morgan discusses the implications of the brother-sister relationship in Malory's work in greater depth than previous scholarship:

Malory found in the Arthur and Accolon story the perfect opportunity to establish the theme of disloyalty and its tragic consequences, for not only does it represent the first attempt against Arthur's life, but it emphasizes that the attempt is made by his sister, a fact which deepens the nature of the trust which is being explored. (158)

According to Henry Morgan, Malory's Morgan is "the symbol of the weakness in loyalty which is the ultimate downfall of the society" and she "is seen...sowing the seeds of distrust in the court of Arthur and bringing ever closer the ultimate downfall of the Arthurian society (166). However, in Henry Morgan's analysis, he appears, like Malory, to perceive Morgan le Fay as the sole root of distrust instead of viewing Morgan and Arthur as sibling rivals with both parties sharing blame. Morgan is narrative impetus, not human equal, according to Malory as narrator and Henry Morgan as critic.

Eugène Vinaver states in his notes to his second edition of Malory's *Works*:

The final catastrophe was to Malory a human drama determined from first to last by the tragic clash of loyalties. With remarkable consistency he emphasized throughout the work the ties of friendship and affection between his protagonists—Gawain and Lancelot, Lancelot and Guinevere, Lancelot and Arthur. (773)

Although Vinaver does not include Morgan in this discussion (773-774), his noting of the tragic clash of loyalties and the eventual deathbed or graveside reconciliations suggests that in a study of Malory's portrayal of Morgan, the reader may conclude that Malory's emphasis upon her betrayal of Arthur is an example of the breakdown of the closest and most long-standing of loyalties— the loyalty between sister and brother, not as suggested by Henry Morgan, merely a symbolic one-sided failure on Morgan le Fay's part to retain the trust her brother has placed in her. Indeed, through juxtaposition, Malory links Morgan to other causes of and players in the Arthurian tragedy. For example, Morgan comes with Igraine to Arthur's court immediately following Merlin's prophecy that Arthur will die at Mordred's hands (29-30). Merlin's repetition of his prophecy regarding Mordred occurs in the text immediately following his advice to Arthur to protect the charmed scabbard and Malory's narration of Arthur's entrusting the scabbard to Morgan and her creation of the imitation (49). In another example, Lamorak wins a battle to end the custom of Morgan's castle in which her knights lay in wait to fight Arthur's knights (369). It seems a telling juxtaposition that, shortly afterward, Lamorak must leave Arthur's court because Gaheris and his brothers are seeking revenge against him for lying with Morgause, who is murdered by her own son Gaheris (Malory 377-78).

Morgan's threat to Arthur's court is one against which the knights may unite; once her threat has been removed, they turn to arguments among themselves which wreak havoc among the members of the Round Table.

The final appearance of Morgan and Arthur together shows a loyalty, friendship, and love that remain despite jealousy, magical powers, or treasonous acts and despite Malory's stereotyping of Morgan. Olstead states, "Perhaps we accept the violent wrenching of Morgan's character because blood is thicker than water. Perhaps tradition decrees it....Perhaps we merely feel the merging of the Lady of the Lake and Morgan le Fay..." (137). Olstead's alternatives, while giving some weight to Morgan's blood relationship to Arthur, do not account satisfactorily for the previous importance of the sibling relationship, antagonistic though it is, as a measure of the extent to which Malory values loyalty, as complex as loyalties may be in family and society. Morgan has power over life as well as death. Her brother lies with his head in her lap, and she mourns, " 'A, my dere brothir! Why have ye taryed so longe frome me? Alas, thys wounde on youre hede hath caught overmuch coulde!' " and that Arthur finds some peace with her is implied in his words to Bedivere, " 'Comforte thyselff...For I muste into the vale of Avylyon to hele me of my grevous wounde' " (716). Whether or not Malory intended to grant Morgan power over life and death, Morgan's contribution to Arthur's death and his possible return to life exists underneath Malory's stereotypically evil traitor-witch. Morgan appears finally as loyal, beloved sibling and healing goddess to Arthur.

In *A Room of One's Own*, Virginia Woolf's comments on literature prior to Jane Austen speak to the difference between Malory and Bradley as authors and between their characterizations of Morgan and her relationship with her brother Arthur:

But almost without exception they [women characters] are shown in their relation to men. It was strange to think that all the great women of fiction were, until Jane Austen's day, not only seen by the other sex, but seen only in relation to the other sex. And how small a part of a woman's life is that; and how little can a man know even of that when he observes it through the black or rosy spectacles which sex puts upon his nose. Hence, perhaps, the peculiar nature of woman in fiction; the astonishing extremes of her beauty and horror; her alternations between heavenly goodness and hellish depravity.... (Woolf 86)

In *The Mists of Avalon*, Marion Zimmer Bradley does what the medieval Malory could not have imagined doing by portraying the Arthurian legend through the perspective of the women, making Morgaine (Morgan le Fay) her main narrator, and recasting the sibling relationship between Morgaine and Arthur into a relationship between two complex human beings, not a witch and a hero.

Bradley explores the early childhood history of Morgaine and Arthur to a depth that comments upon their adult relationship. As in Malory, the sibling relationship between Morgaine and Arthur is significant in terms of both their eventual enmity and their eventual reunion during Arthur's dying throes, but

Bradley provides the reader with a much fuller history of their relationship and consequently a deeper understanding of both characters as human beings. Morgaine is a fully realized person, not a wicked enchantress. She has desires and ambitions, but she also makes sacrifices and considers others. She uses her powers as a priestess of the Goddess for good and/or with good intentions in addition to individual or selfish motives. Bradley's focus upon the Arthurian women allows the reader to understand Morgaine's perspective.

Bradley describes Morgaine the child as her half-brother Arthur's caretaker. Psychologists Stephen Bank and Michael Kahn have noted the profound effect such a relationship has on both individuals, stating, "Such caretaking dominates the life of both caretaker and charge to good and bad effect" (113). Bank and Kahn conclude:

Any sibling who must in some extraordinary way, care for a brother or a sister, has been to some extent abandoned by a parent. The rage that the child...feels toward that parent can be temporarily assuaged by a variety of defense mechanisms in the sibling relationship. By loving and looking after a sibling, one can sublimate anger both at the depriving parent and at the bothersome brothers or sisters. (134)

Bradley portrays a Morgaine who through her narration of recollections of her early childhood relationships reveals both the love for and anger at Arthur that Bank and Kahn describe in caretaker siblings. Igraine directs Morgaine to be responsible for her brother (Bradley 109). Morgaine remembers thinking, "Igraine has forgotten both of us, abandoned him as she abandoned me. Now I must be his mother, I suppose" (Bradley 110). When Morgaine goes to Avalon to be reared a priestess of the Goddess, her attachment is such that "her heart hungered for her own small brother" (141). The impact of Morgaine's early sibling relationship with her brother permeates her life: "She had never known what it was to be happy, not since she was a small and heedless child; happiness was something she dimly remembered before her mother had burdened her with the weight of her little brother" (Bradley 154). Bradley fosters the reader's sympathy for Morgaine through her portrait of her childhood.

The significance of the sibling relationship to Bradley's portrayal of Morgaine is revealed in the Prologue. The first role Morgaine mentions for herself is "*sister*" and the first context in which she mentions Arthur is as "*my brother*" (Bradley ix). The elements of estrangement and reconciliation between siblings present in Malory are present even more vividly in Bradley as Morgaine says, "*But the strife is over; I could greet Arthur at last, when he lay dying, not as my enemy and the enemy of my Goddess, but only as my brother, and as a dying man in need of the Mother's aid, where all men come at last*" (x).

According to Mildred Day, Bradley dramatizes the "conflict for power between the devotees of the Great Goddess of Avalon and the adherents of Christianity in Arthur's court," which ensues in tragedy for both court and Avalon (27). We come to know Morgaine through this pagan-Christian conflict. The differing beliefs of the adult Morgaine and Arthur contribute greatly to their discord in Bradley's version of the Arthurian saga. By placing their discord in terms of a larger battle between ideologies, Bradley makes Morgaine's treason against Arthur, if still wrong, more justifiable.

In contrast to Malory, Bradley depicts Morgaine's relationship with Arthur such that her betrayal of him through Accolon comes late in the narrative, rather than near the beginning. Consequently, the Morgaine the reader sees in this episode is one the reader has seen design the scabbard, which Arthur receives with the sword of Avalon, sewing the spells that will protect Arthur in battle into it; Morgaine realizes "it was she, also of the sacred line of Avalon, who must fashion the spell-scabbard of his safety, guarding the royal blood" (Bradley 198). Bradley here emphasizes Morgaine's relationship to Arthur when she functions as his protector, not just when she becomes his enemy.

The reader follows Morgaine as she casts herself out of her Avalon home, home of her aunt Viviane (the Lady of the Lake) and the other priestesses of the Goddess, because she resents bearing Arthur's child, conceived in the ritual Great Marriage with the Land of Britain Arthur participates in as future king, in which neither Morgaine nor Arthur knew the other until the act was completed, for Viviane's purposes (Bradley 230). Morgaine shows concern for Arthur and his Christian belief that incest is sinful when she conceals the fact of their child from him. Later, when she must tell him, she tries to defend him against Gwenhwyfar's (Guinevere's) desire that he confess this sin to the priests, even though he committed it unknowingly (Bradley 551-52).

Bradley's Morgaine changes and struggles with complexities of the heart and mind throughout the novel. Eventually she is no longer the young woman whose own Christian upbringing before she went to Avalon to be schooled as a priestess, along with her belief that Viviane is manipulating her, leads her to deny her Goddess for a time (Bradley 28). At first Morgaine's knowledge that she has betrayed Avalon keeps her from assuming her powers as a priestess when she might have yet had some influence over Arthur, to keep him ruling for Avalon and keep him from betraying his oath to revere the gods of Avalon just as he reveres the Christian God (Bradley 438). Bradley calls the reader's attention to the silences that can exist between adult siblings as she reveals Morgaine's thoughts about talking to Arthur about her concern over his breaking his oath to rule for the people who worship the Goddess as well as the Christians:

She could speak with him—but no, he would not listen to her; she was a woman and his sister—and always, between them, lay the memory of that morning after the kingmaking, so that never could they speak freely as they might have done before. And she did not carry the authority of Avalon; with her own hands had she cast that away. (438)

Bradley underscores the patriarchy of the Arthurian court, which contrasts with the matriarchy of Avalon, in Morgaine's recognition of her place within the hierarchy of man over woman and brother before sister.

In Bradley's version of the Arthurian legend, Morgaine's rebellion against Arthur is to a certain degree a rebellion against the patriarchal hierarchy. Once

Morgaine has renewed her priestess vows, she dedicates herself almost uncompromisingly to doing the will of the Goddess as she sees it. Consequently, Morgaine will let no other person or even her own misgivings deter her from committing treason against Arthur after he lets the sword of Avalon be used as a symbol of the Christian cross. Morgaine believes that with actions like these, the Christians leave no room for the Goddess, for any recognition of many gods rather than just one. Kevin Harper (the Merlin) challenges Morgaine's assertion that she does the will of the Goddess, asking her if instead she acts according to " 'your own will and pride and ambition for those you love' " (Bradley 728). Indeed, Morgaine's love for Accolon and her wish to rule as Queen so that the people's minds might be "free" from the restrictions of the priests do play a role (Bradley 734). Morgaine finally admits to herself, in her grief over Accolon's death, that her failure to remove Arthur from his throne occurs because she is not a Queen but a priestess (Bradley 757).

Even in the midst of what may be Morgaine's fanaticism, Bradley still characterizes her as a human being who realizes the consequences of her actions in sending Accolon to fight Arthur: *"Whatever comes of this day, she thought, never again, never again shall I know a moment's happiness, since one of those I love must die"* (734). Bradley's Morgaine contemplates killing Arthur herself with her dagger but realizes that because he is her brother, she cannot, even if he is a traitor to Avalon: *"We were born from a single womb and I could not face my mother in the country beyond death, not with the blood of my brother on my hands....Morgaine...took the scabbard. This at least she had a right to take—with her own hands she had fashioned it"* (749). Morgaine cannot slay her brother, but she rationalizes taking the scabbard, making her ultimately responsible for his death, as in Malory.

Bradley brings Morgaine to an ultimate reconciliation with her Goddess, with a world in which Christianity appears to have triumphed over paganism, with her own humanity, and with her brother Arthur. As Morgaine bears the dying Arthur to Avalon, he asks, " *'Morgaine, was it all for nothing then, what we did, and all that we tried to do?'* " and she answers that he brought peace to Britain so that some part of civilization might survive the chaos that is upon them (Bradley 867). Morgaine ultimately realizes, *"No, we did not fail. What I said to comfort Arthur in his dying, it was all true. I did the Mother's work in Avalon until at last those who came after us might bring her into this world"* (Bradley 876). Thus, in spite of the very human differences Bradley has portrayed between Arthur and Morgaine, Bradley, like Malory, reconciles them at last.

Malory says of Arthur that "here in thys worlde he chaunged hys lyff" (717). If Arthur changes his life in this world by remaining a part of the spirit of legend, so does Morgan. They are a literary tribute to the strength of the sibling bond. Morgan, either enchantress or human being, is the healer and sister who brings Arthur home and who will send him forth again in the promised denouement of almost all the versions of the Arthurian legend. Of real siblings, Bank and Kahn say, "Still—whether one celebrates or denies the sibling bond— as long as one has a brother or a sister alive there is always another human being who has known one as a child, who has experienced one in a unique and intimate way..." (336). The differing yet similar literary portrayals of Morgan and Arthur by Malory and Bradley suggest the existence of subconscious rivalries and loyalties which remain constant within families throughout history and suggest the ultimate significance of gender relationships between not only men and women in general but also brothers and sisters in particular.

Works Cited

Bank, Stephen P., and Michael D. Kahn. *The Sibling Bond*. New York: Basic, 1982.

Bradley, Marion Zimmer. *The Mists of Avalon*. 1982. New York: Del Rey-Ballantine, 1984.

Day, Mildred L. Rev. of *The Mists of Avalon*, by Marion Zimmer Bradley. *Avalon to Camelot* 1.1 (1983): 27.

Fisher, Sheila. "Leaving Morgan Aside: Women, History, and Revisionism in *Sir Gawain and the Green Knight*." *The Passing of Arthur: New Essays in Arthurian Tradition*. Ed. Christopher Baswell and William Sharpe. New York: Garland, 1988. 129-51.

Malory, Thomas. *Works*. Ed. Eugène Vinaver. 2nd ed. 1971. Oxford: Oxford UP, 1981.

Morgan, Henry Grady. "The Role of Morgan le Fay in Malory's *Morte Darthur*." *The Southern Quarterly* 2 (1964): 150-68.

Morris, Rosemary. *The Character of King Arthur in Medieval Literature*. Arthurian Studies 4. Cambridge: Brewer-Rowman, 1982.

Olstead, Myra. "Morgan le Fay in Malory's 'Morte Darthur.' " *Bibliographical Bulletin of the International Arthurian Society* 19 (1967): 128-38.

Rogers, Katharine M. *The Troublesome Helpmate: A History of Misogyny in Literature*. Seattle: U of Washington P, 1966.

Woolf, Virginia. *A Room of One's Own*. San Diego: Harvest-Harcourt, 1929.

"Loving Difference":
Sisters and Brothers from
Frances Burney to Emily Brontë

Elisabeth Rose Gruner

Who or what is a sister, in nineteenth-century England? In conduct literature, Romantic poetry by men, and novels by Scott, Dickens, and Thackeray, women cast as sisters are self-sacrificing helpmates to heroic men—or even solipsistic reflections thereof. Dorothy Wordsworth, *David Copperfield*'s Agnes Wickfield, and *Pendennis*'s Laura Bell are notable examples of this tendency. The sister is the extreme version of the relational self: a woman who, as Mary Howitt says of her children's book heroine Mary Leeson, "cannot be taken apart" from her family and friends (10). Howitt—like her fellow conduct writers Sarah Ellis and Charlotte Yonge—promotes a model of sisterly self-sacrifice for all women. Sarah Ellis memorably terms women "relative creatures" in *The Women of England*, taking (what seems to a twentieth-century reader) the extreme position that—unlike men—"women, considered in their distinct and abstract nature, as isolated beings, must lose more than half their worth" (123). In a later conduct book, Charlotte Yonge's *Womankind* (first published in 1876), the author advocates "giving up" to family members, following the model of "our great Elder Brother," Jesus (142, 143); Yonge's model for sisterhood is more self-denying and self-effacing than even a Mary Howitt or a Sarah Ellis could want. But other models also prevailed among women writers, models which modify and even challenge this notion of purely relational selfhood.

In 1848, a new novel by the Swedish novelist/abolitionist/millenarian Christian Frederika Bremer appeared in English, translated by children's book author Mary Howitt. The novel, *Brothers and Sisters: A Tale of Domestic Life*, is deservedly forgotten today. Nearly plotless, and almost unbearably didactic, it details the lives of a family of orphaned siblings as they struggle to come to terms with their responsibilities to each other and to the greater world around them. While many of the siblings marry and some even have children before the novel ends, the determinative relationship for all of them is between brother and sister. All are paired in opposite sex couples early in life, and the eldest two, who never marry, are finally represented as the "patriarchs" of the family and indeed the larger community (v. 3, 255). The sibling bond, Bremer's novel argues with unrelenting conviction, is deeper, stronger, and more meaningful than any later relationship. It can serve as a preparation or substitute for marriage—but at its best, it becomes a model for a new socio-political system.

32

The eldest pair become the founding "parents" of a new fraternal community—a "Swedish Lowell" (v. 3, 254, 131) in which workers live in harmonious unity with each other.

Of course, Bremer did not invent the metaphor of siblinghood for progressive political order. It was already well-established, for example, when the French Revolutionists adopted *"liberté, egalité, fraternité"* as their motto. Siblings' supposed lack of hierarchy, shared interests, and united opposition to fathers have long been recognized as models for reform or revolutionary movements.[1] Bremer's model differs from the standard political one in several respects, however. First, hers is an explicitly Christian vision, in which familial relations ultimately expand to include the rest of humanity in the shared parenthood of God. While the metaphor of Christian brotherhood is even older, perhaps, than that of political brotherhood, reform movements after the French Revolution usually privileged the latter. The abolition movement, however, of which Bremer was a part, but which rarely sought wholesale political reform, is an important exception. Second, she includes sisters. The seeds of political reform are sown in the home, and in Bremer's household sisters reign. It is this aspect of Bremer's novel which most interests me: a woman novelist, she seems to me to be reworking an important (male) Romantic revolutionary trope—sibling solidarity as the model for the reform of the world—while carefully skirting another Romantic icon—the sister as solipsistic reflection of the male poet/revolutionary. The spectre of incest, which haunts male Romantic writers, haunts Bremer as well, and her novel raises in crude form issues which troubled several of her more accomplished predecessors and contemporaries in fiction writing: what is the relationship between family life and political life? What are the right relations between men and women? What can sisterhood teach us—about reform, about love? What is the relationship between sisterhood and female selfhood?

British women writers from Burney to Brontë took up many of Bremer's questions about siblings, and for different reasons, *Camilla, Mansfield Park,* and *Wuthering Heights* all both propose and reject the sister-brother relation as a model for marriage, for female self-development, even for potential social reform. As I hope to make clear, the brother-sister relation is thus essential to understanding a particular aspect of the nineteenth-century heroine—the self-sacrificing, desexualized "angel"—and to understanding some writers' resistance to that model. Nineteenth-century women writers use the relationship—newly important because of the growing separation of spheres[2]—to mount buried challenges to the patriarchal order but also to reinscribe women's position within it. In the brief analyses which follow, I will examine the specific aspects of the relation which most engaged each author.

Frances Burney's third novel *Camilla* (1796) is explicitly concerned with the complexity of familial relations and female participation in the (variously defined) world. Camilla Tyrold begins and ends the novel "in the bosom of her respectable family," but in the intervening nine hundred pages she must negotiate a web of familial and social relations that simultaneously constrain and empower her; in the process, the novel tries to redefine what family is (8). It also continually long-circuits plot: that is, the courtship "thread" on which the plot hangs becomes attenuated as Edgar, time and again, hesitates. By repeating the same plot device over and over—Edgar's misunderstanding or misinterpretation of an innocent action of Camilla's, and his subsequent hesitation about speaking—Burney calls into question the very concept of the courtship plot. And if, as many critics argue, marriage in the novel is usually "a metaphor recognizing the heroine's internal growth," then Camilla's quasi-incestous marriage represents her growth only into her previously-defined domestic role, a role defined more by a father and an uncle than by a husband (Yeazell 37; see also Kennard; Boone 48).

Or, Camilla's growth may lie in recognizing that her true family obligations lie in filial loyalty; her marriage to Edgar, ward of her father and "brother" to her sisters, represents a reunion with her father and with the fatherly institutions of the church and the landed gentry which support both men. The novel is, however, riven with contradictions which call filial loyalty into question just as much as the false sibling loyalty which the novel only barely rejects. Camilla must discover or defend her necessarily domestic identity in the context of a family falling apart, for her story, *Camilla*, participates in the eighteenth-century negotiation between seeing the family as a network of affiliation and as a privatized domestic unit.[3] Camilla's two "brothers," Lionel and Edgar, help focus that negotiation. Lionel clearly participates in the affiliational model of family. His manipulations of his uncle and sisters demonstrate his need to establish networks beyond his immediate family for financial gain. Edgar, by contrast, promotes domesticity and privacy. In the context of a shift from kin networks to a domestic unit, Edgar represents the "modern" family, the private, nuclear family. But no such ideological change can really be as clear-cut as this dichotomy implies. While Burney never calls into questions the sincerity of Edgar's attachment to Camilla, and while he is clearly superior to Lionel as a brother, let alone a husband, many aspects of the "new" family simply replicate the old. The novel's somewhat confusing ideological stance—critiquing mercenary marriage, for example, while still representing such marriages as rewarding, or drawing parallels between family life and prisons, but still celebrating Camilla's enmeshment in her family— derives from the shifting parameters of "family" and "household" which the novel tries to represent.

Camilla's two "brothers," Lionel and Edgar, together represent aspects not only of the family, but specifically of the father. As often happens in Burney's novels, brothers are made to carry much of the negative ideological weight of fatherhood. With Macartney in *Evelina* and Lord Melbury in *The Wanderer*, Burney plays with the eighteenth-century convention of unwitting sibling incest to explore the debauched and implicitly violent nature of the heroine's unacknowledging fathers. (See Wilson for a further discussion of this convention.) Macartney almost kills his father—perhaps also acting out Evelina's buried anger towards him—as his father has "killed" both his and Evelina's mothers. In *The Wanderer*, Lord Melbury's proposition to his unknown sister, Juliet, reenacts their father's (and, in this novel, most men's) exploitation of helpless women. But these brothers are quickly restored to favor and work with, not against, their sisters. In Camilla's brother Lionel, however, Burney most fully explores the familial exploitation of women implicit in the mercenary marriage system. Lionel's prank in misleading Dubster about his sister's expectations turns serious when he imprisons his sisters in Dubster's house, and even more dangerous when he accepts Sir Sedley's money. In a scene which Austen replays in *Mansfield Park*, the brother's acceptance of a suitor's gift implies an obligation which the heroine is unwilling to accept. Fanny Price's brother, however, is no manipulator: William Price does not even seem to recognize the implications of accepting Henry Crawford's gift of his commission, planning instead a future for *himself* with his sister. Unlike William, Camilla's brother recognizes that a sister may be bought. He sees the two hundred pounds from Sir Sedley as implicit payment for his sister, whom he immediately addresses as "My sister Clarendel...my dear Lady Clarendel" when he receives the money (505). Clearly Lionel believes that women can be exchanged for money—and should, for his benefit. Her feelings in the matter are irrelevant, compared to his being "freed from all [his financial] misfortunes at once" (505).

Lionel's crimes against women reach their peak in his manipulation of Camilla. He forces her to borrow two hundred pounds from their uncle, takes all of her own money at the same time (thus forcing her into obligations to Sir Sedley, Mrs. Arlbery, and Mrs. Mittin), and finally maneuvers her into accepting the two hundred pounds from Sir Sedley. The debts which she contracts because she has given up her money to Lionel ultimately force her father into prison, just after he has relinquished his own small fortune to his brother, also burdened by a mercenary heir-presumptive in his nephew Lynmere. Thus Lionel, through his manipulations of his sisters' money and his own and their potential inheritance, precipitates the crisis which leads to Camilla's madness and near-death.

If Lionel, the threatening prankster, is the brother/father as controller and exchanger of women, Edgar is the brother/father as mentor and, finally, lover. Inappropriate anger at the father who misleads, manipulates, or abandons his daughter is thus redirected at Lionel (as, in *Clarissa*, it is redirected at James Harlowe); inappropriate desire for the man who teaches and loves his daughter is safely redirected to Edgar, "whom she delighted to consider as a younger Mr. Tyrold" (742).

Edgar is first substituted for Lionel when the scene of Lionel's disgrace (over his extortion) is followed by one of Edgar's devotion and incorporation into the Tyrold family. Mrs. Tyrold's "affection nearly maternal to [Edgar's] person" is increased by his proposal to accompany her to Lisbon, prompting her to claim him as "the true son of [his] guardian" (230, 231). As Edgar begins to replace Lionel, however, his relationship with Camilla becomes more complicated. Although he claims that this near-familial relationship should "permit [him]... honestly to speak" to Camilla, they are both repeatedly silenced by their closeness (235). Whereas Lionel's speech with his sisters is free, open, and easy, Edgar continually second-guesses himself and Camilla, often closing off their conversation before it can really begin. The new version of domesticity which Camilla embraces with Edgar too often entails her silence, especially with him and with her father. The incestuous overtones of Camilla's union with Edgar are double: he represents both a father and a brother. Camilla's marriage thus completes her enmeshment in domesticity and redefinition of family as domestic unit—married to her father's ward, she ends the novel as she has begun it, happily ensconced in the narrow circle of Etherington, Cleves, and Beech Park, "rarely parted...from her fond Parents and enraptured Uncle" (913).

While Burney explicitly represents Camilla's marriage to Edgar as a happy ending, important questions remain as to the viability of a domestic identity. Women like Mrs. Arlbery and Mrs. Mittin, unconstrained by familial relations or aspirations to domesticity, represent a mobility and a freedom (of speech and action) which Camilla can never attain; while Miss Ussin and Eugenia expose the dangers of domesticity which may continue to threaten her. While the shift from manipulator to loving protector—Lionel to Edgar—is positive, Camilla's fortunes, both literal and metaphoric, are still tied to a man, her mobility severely circumscribed, her desire safely channelled inward.

In *Northanger Abbey*, Jane Austen lets her readers know what to think of John Thorpe the first time they meet him by revealing his inability to read Frances Burney's *Camilla*. "Such unnatural stuff!" he exclaims, "An old man playing at see-saw!" (49). What Thorpe misses is almost his own portrait in *Camilla*—he's another Lionel, manipulating appearances, misleading people about expectations, attempting even to engineer a sister's marriage for his own benefit. Thorpe passes out of *Northanger Abbey* rather quickly, but with his portrait in her first completed novel Austen signalled an interest in the brother-sister relationship that would recur in her later work, especially in *Mansfield Park*.

Mansfield Park is a novel in which nature and nurture are at war, family affection gives way to greed masked as duty, and the private, domestic arena is a contested site. While Burney proposes domesticity as a substitute for the mercenary values which mar the affiliational family, Austen's critique is different. Domesticity is still a positive value, but blood relationship and, especially, memory imbue domesticity with significance for *Mansfield Park*'s conservative heroine. Fanny Price, unlike her cousins Maria and Julia Bertram, defines herself primarily through her family relationships: she appears to exemplify the relational identity analyzed by Nancy Chodorow and Carol Gilligan in her determined self-definition in terms of other people's needs and wants.

As Edmund turns his cousin with dizzying rapidity into first a sister and then a wife, we sense that Fanny finally comes into herself. Her desire is recognized and legitimated in a way no other female desire has been in the novel. Contrived and unsatisfying as this ending may be to readers, it's clear that Fanny has gotten exactly what she wants. But why? Why does this most passive of heroines finally get her man, and what does it mean for "sisterly regard" to be "foundation enough for wedded love" (470)? The brother-sister relation provides the context for Fanny's self-development in opposition to the patriarchal system which controls Mansfield Park; her marriage to Edmund represents patriarchy's ironic ability to assimilate her challenge.

While Chodorow's version of a relational identity begins with an attachment to the mother, other attachments follow. And, according to analysts of sibling relations, brothers and sisters may indeed "use one another as major influences, or touchstones, in the search for personal identity" (Bank and Kahn 19). Clearly, her brother William serves this purpose for Fanny. William, "her constant companion and friend; her advocate...in every distress" (15) supplies for Fanny what her mother does not: an "internal sense of the presence of another who is caring and affirming"—a necessary component, according to Chodorow, of the "central core of the self" (10). But William exercises his influence *in absentia*: the siblings meet only once in the ten years between Fanny's arrival at Mansfield Park and the central action of the novel. While Edmund fills in for William in many ways, from his first ruling Fanny's lines for her to his gift of the chain for William's cross, William himself remains a constant presence in Fanny's life, through his letters, and primarily through memory.

Memory is the impediment to Henry's courtship of Fanny, and the glue which binds her to William. When Henry first decides to "make Fanny Price in love with [him]" (229), the narrator suggests that he cannot succeed, in part because Fanny "had by no means forgotten the past" (232)—specifically, his earlier flirtations with her cousins. Later in the same chapter, the narrator makes clear how important remembrance is to Fanny as she rhapsodizes over her reunion with William:

with [him] (perhaps the dearest indulgence of the whole) all the evil and good of their earliest years could be gone over again, and every former united pain and pleasure retraced with the fondest recollection. An advantage this, a strengthener of love, in which even the conjugal tie is beneath the fraternal. Children of the same family, the same blood, with the same first associations and habits, have some means of enjoyment in their power, which no subsequent connections can supply. (235)

Here, as in Henry Crawford's later musings over Fanny, Austen moves into indirect discourse; Fanny's valorization of memory has authorial sanction. The modern Mary Crawford, by contrast, finds nothing to value in memory, her own or anyone else's. The traditions at Sotherton mean nothing to her, nor can she even derive present value from a past connection, such as that with her uncle, the Admiral. (Alistair M. Duckworth's *The Improvement of the Estate* offers the most comprehensive discussion of the role of innovation and "improvement" in *Mansfield Park* [see esp. ch. 1, pp. 35-80].) Perhaps the most pressing argument against the kinds of improvements Henry proposes for Sotherton and Thornton Lacey is that they "forget" the original purpose of many aspects of the estates. Innovation—anathema to Fanny—is all the rage with the Crawfords.

But it is not just the remembrance of his misdeeds that keeps Fanny from accepting Henry. For a woman who participates in the marital exchange system must forget her own past, forget her family to join another; and this, Fanny cannot do. Certainly the Ward sisters have forgotten each other, in all but the most superficial ways; Fanny is pained, on her return to Portsmouth, to find "scarcely an inquiry made after Mansfield," so that she believes "Mansfield forgotten" (382). Although the Prices have forgotten the Bertrams and even herself, Fanny has forgotten no one. And while Edmund represents the strengthening of memory and familial association, Henry can only loosen those ties—and such, despite his plan for settling in Northamptonshire, is his express desire. Recognizing the way the marital exchange system works, Henry plans to replace Sir Thomas and Edmund in Fanny's life—and fancies himself an improvement (297). For Fanny, however, no "stranger" can ever replace her first affections. Fanny Price is the only Austen heroine whose childhood we share; Austen introduces us to Fanny as a child, I suspect, in order that we, too, shall not forget her childhood associations.

As we have seen, her connections with William and Edmund provide Fanny with a sense of identity her cousins and Mary Crawford lack; her refusal to be a counter in the marriage game is strengthened by her sense that marriage (at least to Henry Crawford) would dilute her identity and her most important connections. By marrying Edmund, then, Fanny valorizes her self-identity and subverts one of the central props of the patriarchal system: the exogamous exchange of women. And the novel may offer a further challenge to patriarchy by focusing, like a fairy tale, not on the eldest son and heir, but on a younger son (and a daughter). But this fairy-tale quality may work both ways: like Cinderella, Fanny is rewarded for her acceptance of a subordinate role by entrance into the system which has oppressed her. Should we, then, see her final situation at Mansfield as subversive or supportive of that system?

Fanny prefigures Anne Elliot, another out-of-favor daughter who does not marry a landowner. Although Edmund Bertram's position is less precarious than Captain Wentworth's, he is, finally, only a steward for both Thornton Lacey and his final living at Mansfield. But Fanny and Edmund are finally far more conservative than Austen's later pair. Alistair Duckworth implicitly contrasts Edmund with Rushworth when he recognizes that Rushworth "has utterly no awareness of his duty as a trustee" (49). Edmund does. Land-ownership—a central prop to patriarchal power—clearly conveys no special moral position in this novel. In fact, the characters (Fanny and Edmund) whose identities seem *not* to be tied to possession are the mainstays or unacknowledged backbones of the system which *does* tie identity to possession. Both Sir Thomas and his heir are bad trustees—but instead of falling into bankruptcy or dying, they continue to live comfortably with the support of the previously-neglected Fanny. Sir Thomas, rather than changing his ways, comes only to "the high sense of having realised a great acquisition in the promise of Fanny for a daughter" (472). Like a fairy tale, *Mansfield Park* offers the illusion of resistance to an oppressive order—but the reward for that resistance is not a new order, but simply a better position in the old one. Fanny does become a wife, a daughter, a Bertram, and a mother. (While many critics have seen Fanny and Edmund's "incestuous" marriage as implicitly sterile, their acquisition of the Mansfield living "just after they had been married long enough to begin to want an increase of income" seems to imply children [369].) Susan replaces Fanny at Mansfield Park just as Fanny has replaced Mary Crawford in Edmund's affections; finally, she is "an acquisition" to Sir Thomas—almost as interchangeable as any other woman.

While Fanny and Edmund may seem to provide, in their relationship, a model for social change, it is nonetheless a fundamentally conservative model which continues to locate women's primary value within the home and family—institutions of which the novel is otherwise critical. The patriarch—Sir Thomas—is subverted, his social network diminished, his daughters replaced by poor relations, his heir debilitated, his second son not advanced by marriage. But the patriarchy continues to thrive; and the self-effacing sister—soon to be recast as the self-sacrificing sister in Dickens and Thackeray—has ensured its continuance for another generation.

In the novels I have discussed so far, a "brother" is transformed into a "husband" with relative ease, and, in Edmund Bertram's case, without passing through the difficult intervening stage of "lover": the heroine's identity as a sister, in both cases, remains constant. While both Camilla Tyrold and Fanny Price suffer silent agonies of embarrassment as they are repeatedly misinterpreted, abused, or ignored, each finally gains her man by her constancy, her sisterhood, her continuing determination to define herself and be defined by her familial relations, especially to her brother/lover. This transition is successful, I would argue, because Burney and Austen finally valorize domesticity as an essential component of identity for their heroines.

Emily Brontë's model for heroinism is more conflicted; thus Heathcliff and Catherine are unable to negotiate the same transition successfully. While they begin as pseudo-siblings in almost perfect equality—under the same oppression and neglect—Heathcliff fulfills Lionel Tyrold's promise instead of Edgar Mandelbert's: he becomes the patriarchal oppressor *par excellence*. But Catherine Earnshaw is also transformed—into a wife—and while she insists that her marriage cannot and does not change her primary identification with Heathcliff, both Edgar and Heathcliff believe that it does. In *Wuthering Heights* we see what Burney and Austen only hint at obliquely: the subversive potential of a female self conceived primarily in relation to a brother-figure, and its inevitable dangers as well.

Wuthering Heights focuses its creation of a new female self on a relationship with a brother-figure for the Catherines of both generations, but the two "brothers"—Heathcliff and Hareton—differ significantly. Heathcliff is, of course, the central brother-figure; Catherine's bedmate as well as playmate in their early childhood, he metamorphoses into the worst kind of patriarchal oppressor before his death. (In this metamorphosis, he is not at all unlike Catherine's "real" or "blood" brother Hindley, Nelly Dean's playfellow, "foster brother," and later master [see 61, 153].) If Catherine claims identity with

Heathcliff, then, is she identifying with a masculine principle of oppression, or with a brother in arms against an oppressive order? Is she stifling her development by defining herself solely in terms of a domestic relation, or is she rejecting domesticity by uniting herself with a "brother" who can move out into the world? The answer, of course, is both.

While arguments have been advanced to establish a blood relationship between Heathcliff and Catherine, Brontë carefully leaves the question of Heathcliff's paternity unsolved. (See especially Eric Solomon.) With one "blood" brother already in Hindley, Catherine forges a new relationship with Heathcliff, choosing to identify with the "gipsy brat" rather than her own rather overbred brother, "the young master" (39, 40). Nelly, on the other hand, identifies with Hindley—nursed by the same mother, they are in a sense foster siblings—and even her banishment to the back-kitchen on his return cannot efface her abiding loyalty to what she considers his legitimate authority. According to Bank and Kahn, siblings who are orphans or who experience "insufficient parental influence" are especially likely to "use one another as major influences, or touchstones, in the search for personal identity" (18, 19). Biographers of the Brontës have noted the closeness the siblings developed after their mother's death, and have connected this development to the representation of the Wuthering Heights household. Bank and Kahn find such substitutions of siblings for parents common:

A young child needs a stable, reliable environment or 'object constancy'; a child cannot be totally self-reliant. In our view, a brother or sister close at hand becomes a likely candidate to be that warm and reassuring important external object....The child who can fuse and merge with another person, will feel more whole, more integrated, and less vulnerable to the vagaries of an uncertain world. This blending of aspects of oneself with those of another makes any child feel that he or she is more complete. (31)

Viewed in this light, Catherine's identification with Heathcliff can be seen as a replacement for the lost mother (see Homans ch. 3, Hirsch 58); or, more simply, as a survival strategy in a chaotic and unwelcoming world.

Heathcliff clearly sees himself as a means to Catherine's survival and even escape—even, perhaps, as the metaphoric "whip" which he became in his entry into the Earnshaw family. And identification with a boy who is also an equal is a way—perhaps the only way—out of patriarchal oppression for girls. Catherine teaches Heathcliff whatever she learns from the curate, providing him access to the tools of culture from which Hindley shuts him out. But Heathcliff equally provides Catherine access to otherwise inaccessible modes of behavior: primarily, he is her conduit to the moors. In the first diary extract Lockwood reads, Catherine is writing to pass away the time; "but my companion is impatient and proposes that we should appropriate the dairy woman's cloak, and have a scamper on the moors" (27). As when he promises to break the Lintons' windows, Heathcliff here helps Catherine get out—out of writing, out of domesticity, out of "culture." But Heathcliff's "outside," while it may be a place for nearly genderless children, is not a place for a young woman entering adolescence—Catherine must negotiate an entrance into the domestic, and Heathcliff cannot join her.

Like all brothers, Heathcliff has the capacity to become a "father," a patriarch. Carole Pateman, in *The Sexual Contract*, characterizes modern masculinist society as "fraternal patriarchy." Pateman argues that in a capitalist world governed by contract, masculine power is still patriarchal (that is, still involves male control of female sexuality and selfhood) even though it is no longer explicitly tied to paternity. Her discussion of fraternity is particularly helpful:

A very nice conjuring trick has been performed so that one kinship term, fraternity, is held to be merely a metaphor for the universal bonds of humankind, for community, solidarity or fellowship, while another kinship term, patriarchy, is held to stand for the rule of fathers which passed away long ago. (78)

The bond of equality which Catherine and Heathcliff share, which is a "fraternal" bond, must then finally dissolve into a patriarchal one, since Catherine can never really be a "brother," a member of a fraternity. Thus I think it is significant that the first rebellion mentioned in *Wuthering Heights* is against the brother, Hindley, not the dead father. In *Wuthering Heights*, as in *Camilla*, the worst aspects of fatherhood are displaced onto brothers: first Hindley, then Heathcliff, is the patriarchal oppressor in this text. (Edgar Linton does, of course, become a fatherly oppressor in the second half of the novel—but neither Nelly nor his daughter ever openly characterizes his rule as oppressive.) Earnshaw's authority—"legitimate" paternal authority—is not the subject of Nelly's story, although it may be of Brontë's; Nelly Dean's story is the story of a "cuckoo," a usurper, and she carefully distinguishes between the "rightful" authority of the master and Heathcliff's unearned and, in Nelly's eyes, undeserved power (37). But any brother can "usurp" a father's power—Catherine's early characterization of Hindley as "a detestable substitute" for her father alerts us to the theme before Nelly ever articulates it (26). Nelly, in her overidentification with the sources of power (despite her upbringing at the Heights, she calls the Lintons "us"), cannot see that the system of power—indeed, the construction of the family—is arbitrary. As Jay Clayton says, "the arbitrariness of this system is brilliantly underlined by the novel, for Heathcliff learns to turn all the forms of society...against the 'rightful,' which is to say the hereditary or biological, owners of Wuthering Heights" (89). If anyone can manipulate the system, it cannot really be based on biology or "legitimacy." Brontë's juxtaposition of the children's escape from the tyranny at the Heights with the first description of the Grange makes it clear that both kinds of power are really the same: the patriarchal family is always a prison, and the difference between a jail like the Heights and a low-security "detention center" like the Grange is less important than their basic similarity.[4]

For Catherine, Heathcliff represents the limitless power of childhood; in her past, she can fantasize, they were the same: two oppressed children, equally neglected and equally free. Limitations always set in for the Romantic child; for

Catherine, however, they include the limitation of femaleness. Heathcliff, then, represents the self she was before she learned she was only a girl. To be Heathcliff, as she claims she is, would be to be masculine, to be powerful, to be uncircumscribed by femaleness: to be "half savage, and hardy, and free" (107). To define oneself in relation to a brother-figure is a radical move for Catherine because it implies an external focus, not the domesticity of the conventional self-in-relation. To identify with Heathcliff allows Catherine the fantasy of male power: the two stand as equals against patriarchal authority. It also seems to promise that her future will not be her mother's: will not end in childbirth and death. But the identification is illusory: Catherine is *not* Heathcliff, *is* "only a girl," and will be a mother. Even her attempt to internalize Heathcliff fails. She says on her deathbed: "That is not *my* Heathcliff. I shall love mine yet; and take him with me—he's in my soul" (134). But the "real" Heathcliff does not go with her; her "double character" finally splits in two and she dies.

While Catherine Earnshaw Linton is finally destroyed by domesticity, her daughter Catherine Linton (Heathcliff) Earnshaw seems to revel in it. As the reversal of names suggests, the second Catherine reverses her mother's progress from Heights to Grange and in so doing manages to create a domestic future and a more positive version of selfhood for herself. It seems unlikely that the second Catherine would be able to develop a positive self-in-relation, given the isolation in which she is reared. In fact, life at Thrushcross Grange during "the happiest [years] of [Nelly's] life" (155) sounds in many ways like a Chodorowian nightmare. With a patriarchally identified mother-figure in Nelly Dean, and a patriarchally distant father who "reiterate[s] orders that she must not wander out of the park" in Edgar Linton (157), she seems predestined to become the passive, over-dependent, reactive woman of Chodorow's worst-case scenarios (see esp. ch. 12).

Ironically, Catherine Linton Heathcliff comes into her (relational) self in the prison of the Heights, reversing and qualifying her mother's history as she passes through her names. She must lose the internalized sense of class and gender markers that her mother gained, finally recreating and revising her mother's preadolescent identification with Heathcliff in her postadolescent relationship with Hareton. She revises both parents' history as she teaches Hareton to read, re-enacting her mother's relationship with Heathcliff and her father's with her; in return, Hareton helps her cultivate a garden which replaces the fiercely patriarchal Joseph's currant bushes. Together, they reclaim the inheritance which Heathcliff has deprived them of, reuniting the Earnshaw and Linton holdings in a marriage of mutual regard, trust, and love.

This is, of course, a rather optimistic reading of the ending which other critics have called "attenuated" at best (Macovski 379), and at worst have lamented as a failure of Brontë's will, intention, or art. Thomas Moser, for example, is famous for his assertion that the "creation of the second generation serve[s] chiefly to mar the structure" of the novel, misogynistically complaining that "all Wuthering Heights *suffers* feminization" with the Cathy/Hareton union (182, 194; my emphasis). Moser continues: "Under Cathy's tutelage Hareton clears out Joseph's black currant trees for a flower bed while she puts primroses in her beloved's porridge" (194). While I am at a loss to identify the masculinity of black currant trees, Sandra Gilbert and Susan Gubar crucially misidentify them as wild blackberries (black currants are cultivated fruits) in order to include their loss in a litany of Catherine's crimes of domesticity. "Domesticity," like Moser's "feminization," is clearly pejorative in their usage. They call the second Catherine "virtually an angel in the house," "all of whose virtues are in some sense associated with daughterhood, wifehood, motherhood" (300, 299). Expanding on Moser, they continue: "Catherine II nurses Linton (even though she dislikes him), brews tea for Heathcliff, helps Nelly prepare vegetables, and replaces the wild blackberries at Wuthering Heights with flowers from Thrushcross Grange" (299). Many of these acts, however, are rebellious in context: Heathcliff prefers to withhold medical attention from his son; making tea and preparing vegetables indicate a softening of her class-conscious insistence on being served rather than serving; and replacing anything that belongs to Joseph could usefully be seen as an anti-patriarchal act. In many ways, this Catherine's domesticity seems a parody of domesticity, not the wifely submission Gilbert and Gubar see [5]. But, like many parodies (one thinks of Austen's homage to the gothic in *Northanger Abbey*), Catherine's parodic domesticity retains many of the values of the original in its mockery.

What Catherine learns in her brief, forced marriage to Linton Heathcliff is essential to the development of the new relationship with Hareton; having tried "loving difference" and failed, with Hareton she forges a relationship based on resemblance, on similarity. And Catherine and Hareton are strikingly similar. As Nelly Dean says, they resemble each other physically in only one regard: "their eyes are precisely similar, and they are those of Catherine Earnshaw" (254). But they are also, and more importantly, united in an oppression like that which united their predecessors: united, perhaps, in an ungendered siblinghood. Catherine and Hareton's love first makes itself known to Heathcliff when she challenges him, on her own and Hareton's mutual behalf:

"You shouldn't grudge a few yards of earth for me to ornament, when you have taken all my land!"
"Your land, insolent slut? you never had any!" said Heathcliff.
"And my money," she continued, returning his angry glare, and, meantime, biting a piece of crust, the remnant of her breakfast.
"Silence!" he exclaimed. "Get done, and begone!"
"And Hareton's land, and his money," pursued the reckless thing. "Hareton and I are friends now; and I shall tell him all about you!" (252)

Unlike her predecessors, the second Catherine can confront her oppressor and articulate her awareness of oppression. In other words, she learns and grows—unlike her mother, who can only regress, returning in death to her preadolescent childhood rather than face the (separate) reality of her adult life. Catherine gets what her mother never has: a second chance, and—more centrally—a second marital choice.

And yet—this adult relationship of equals is also a cousin-marriage, even an uncomfortably close, almost incestuous cousin-marriage. And while, as we have seen, incest could be said to be subversive of patriarchal order, refusing as it does the orderly exchange of women and property, this marriage—this "curiously narcissistic union of Earnshaw with itself"—does serve property interests as well (Bersani 199). The property Catherine fights for will still, ultimately, be Hareton's: she simply returns to him his own patrimony, after teaching him how to read his name over the door and recognize it. So is the marriage a reform, a new marital order, or a regression after all?

Brontë leaves this tension between reform and regression unresolved by leaving the marriage in the unnarratable future of the novel. For Nelly, it has almost already occurred; she predicts the marriage before she even narrates the death of Heathcliff. Her interests are clearly vested in the return of the Earnshaws; she sounds like the bride herself as she gloats, "The crown of all my wishes will be the union of those two; I shall envy no one on their wedding-day—there won't be a happier woman than myself in England!" (250). Heathcliff's death is almost an afterthought to the courtship tale she has just finished telling. Lockwood, on the other hand, returns to the first generation to finish his story, walking home past the three graves of Catherine, Edgar, and Heathcliff, and refusing to "imagine unquiet slumbers for the sleepers in that quiet earth" (266). With this bifurcated ending, Brontë clearly leaves the imagination of a future up to her readers. The ideal self-in-relation which Catherine and Hareton seem to have achieved may be swallowed up in the forms of patriarchal marriage and property ownership, as Catherine and Heathcliff's relationship was; or it may continue to grow and change, as the ghosts of Catherine and Heathcliff watch over the moors. If it is a version of the "sibling marriage" we have seen in Burney, Austen, and Bremer, it is more conflicted, more problematic—and more sexually aware. Certainly this second Catherine seems more in control of her life, less of a domestic "angel" than her predecessors, Camilla Mandelbert and Fanny Bertram. But the family looks more naturalized in this novel than the earlier ones: blood relationships have an unquestioned and unchanging determinative ability, and expulsion of Heathcliff's "other" seems the simplest solution to domestic tragedy. The cousin-marriage which ends *Wuthering Heights* avoids the question of sibling incest raised by Bremer while still creating what seems a partnership of domestic equals: but can it survive outside the home, or even outside Nelly Dean's self-satisfied fiction? As the self-sacrificing sisters of Dickens and Thackeray prove, Brontë's parody sounds no death knell for the domestic heroine. But her sophisticated awareness of the importance and complexity of the sibling bond still has much to teach us today.

Notes

[1]See, for example, Freud's theory in *Totem and Taboo* that a united brotherhood establishes "social organization...moral restrictions, and...religion" by the overthrow of the father (142).

[2]Davidoff and Hall offer a useful caution against a too-literal acceptance of the

nineteenth-century ideology of the separate spheres (33). Nonetheless, they trace in middle-class conceptions of family an increasing tendency to equate family, domesticity, and femininity in the early to mid-nineteenth century.

[3]See Stone for the most thorough discussion of this shift—which he characterizes as a move toward "affective individualism." Davidoff and Hall provide a useful corrective to Stone's often class-blind analysis, while still remaining generally within his framework.

[4]Many arguments about *Wuthering Heights* work off an assumption of difference between the Heights and the Grange: Gilbert and Gubar, for example, claim that "at every point the two houses are opposed to each other, as if each in its self-assertion must absolutely deny the other's being" (273). They go on to characterize the particular difference between the two houses as the difference between nature and culture. William R. Goetz also sees the novel as enacting the transition from nature to culture, embodied in the movement from Heights to Grange. Both Gilbert and Gubar and Goetz thus follow an early review by G.H. Lewes, who claimed of Catherine that "Edgar appeals to her love of refinement, and goodness, and culture; Heathcliff clutches her soul in his passionate embrace" (Allott 292). Even Terry Eagleton's sophisticated Marxist analysis of the novel depends in large measure on an opposition between feudal yeomanry (the Heights) and "the progressive forces of agrarian capitalism" (the Grange) (114; but see 112-116). While these oppositions are important to an understanding of the novel, I find most persuasive Leo Bersani's view that "the contrast between Grange and Wuthering Heights is a false, or at least an insignificant, one....To go from Wuthering Heights to the Grange is not to go from nature to society; it is to go from the strong children to the weak children, or, more precisely, from aggressively selfish children to whiningly selfish children" (201).

[5]Gilbert and Gubar's reading then seems somewhat like Lockwood's when he insists on identifying the surly and unhelpful Catherine as a "beneficent fairy." I am indebted to members of Anne Mellor's UCLA seminar on Romanticism and Feminism, Spring 1990, for the idea that Catherine's end is somehow parodic. Members of the seminar, qualifying my sense that the ending is optimistic, called it a parody of a Jane Austen novel. While it is unlikely that Emily Brontë read Austen—her sister Charlotte didn't do so until soon before Emily's death—the suggestion is nonetheless provocative, and has qualified my original reading considerably.

Works Cited

Allott, Miriam, ed. *The Brontës: The Critical Heritage*. London: Routledge Kegan Paul, 1974.
Austen, Jane. *Mansfield Park*. 1814. London: Oxford UP, 1934, rpt. 1966.
_____. *Northanger Abbey*. 1818. London: Oxford UP, 1934, rpt. 1966.
Bank, Stephen P., and Michael D. Kahn. *The Sibling Bond*. New York: Basic Books, 1982.
Bersani, Leo. *A Future for Astyanax: Character and Desire in Literature*. Boston: Little, Brown, 1976.
Boone, Joseph Allen. *Tradition Counter Tradition: Love and the Form of Fiction*. Chicago: U Chicago P, 1987.
Bremer, Fredrika. *Brothers and Sisters. A Tale of Domestic Life*. Trans. Mary Howitt. London: 1848.
Brontë, Emily. *Wuthering Heights*. 1847. New York: Norton, 1972.

46 The Significance of Sibling Relationships

Burney, Frances. *Camilla; or, A Picture of Youth*. 1796. Oxford: Oxford UP, 1983.

Chodorow, Nancy. *The Reproduction of Mothering: Psychoanalysis and the Sociology of Gender*. Berkeley: U California P, 1978.

Clayton, Jay. *Romantic Vision and the Novel*. Cambridge: Cambridge UP, 1987.

Davidoff, Leonore, and Catherine Hall. *Family Fortunes: Men and Women of the English Middle Class, 1780-1850*. London: Hutchinson, 1987.

Duckworth, Alistair M. *The Improvement of the Estate: A Study of Jane Austen's Novels*. Baltimore: Johns Hopkins, 1971.

Eagleton, Terry. *Myths of Power: A Marxist Study of the Brontës*. London: Macmillan, 1975.

Ellis, Sarah Stickney. *The Women of England: Their Social Duties, and Domestic Habits*. New York: 1839.

Freud, Sigmund. *Totem and Taboo: Some Points of Agreement between the Mental Lives of Savages and Neurotics*. Tr. James Strachey. New York: Norton, 1950.

Gilbert, Sandra M., and Susan Gubar. *The Madwoman in the Attic: The Woman Writer and the Nineteenth-Century Literary Imagination*. New Haven: Yale UP, 1979.

Gilligan, Carol. *In a Different Voice: Psychological Theory and Women's Development*. Cambridge: Harvard UP, 1982.

Goetz, William R. "Genealogy and Incest in Wuthering Heights." *Studies in the Novel* 14 (Winter 1982): 359-76.

Hirsch, Marianne. *The Mother/Daughter Plot: Narrative, Psychoanalysis, Feminism*. Bloomington: Indiana UP, 1989.

Homans, Margaret. *Bearing the Word: Language and Female Experience in Nineteenth-Century Women's Writing*. Chicago: U Chicago P, 1986.

Howitt, Mary. *A Pleasant Life*. London: Gall & Inglis, n.d.

Irigaray, Luce. "When the Goods Get Together." *New French Feminisms*. Ed. Elaine Marks and Isabelle de Courtivron. New York: Schocken, 1980: 107-10.

Irigaray, Luce. *This sex which is not one*. (1977) Tr. Catherine Porter with Carolyn Burke. Ithaca, NY: Cornell UP, 1985.

Kennard, Jean. *Victims of Convention*. Hamden, CT: Archon, 1978.

Macovski, Michael S. "Wuthering Heights and the Rhetoric of Interpretation." *ELH* 54 (Summer 1987): 363-84.

Moser, Thomas. "What is the Matter With Emily Jane? Conflicting Impulses in Wuthering Heights." *NCF* 17 (June 1962): 1-19. Rpt. in *The Victorian Novel: Modern Essays in Criticism*. Ed. Ian Watt. London: Oxford UP, 1971. 181-199.

Pateman, Carole. *The Sexual Contract*. Stanford, CA: Stanford UP, 1988.

Solomon, Eric. "The Incest Theme in Wuthering Heights." *NCF* 14 (June 1959): 80-83.

Stone, Lawrence. *The Family, Sex and Marriage in England, 1500-1800*. (Abridged Ed.) New York: Harper & Row, 1979.

Wilson, Daniel W. "Science, Natural Law, and Unwitting Sibling Incest in Eighteenth-Century Literature." *Studies in Eighteenth-Century Culture* 13 (1984): 249-270.

Yeazell, Ruth Bernard. "Fictional Heroines and Feminist Critics." *Novel* 8 (Fall 1974): 29-38.

Yonge, Charlotte. *Womankind*. 1876. 2nd ed. New York: Macmillan, 1890.

Women Writers as Little Sisters in Victorian Society: *The Mill on the Floss* and the Case of George Eliot

Julia Waddell

In their preface to *The Madwoman in the Attic*, Sandra M. Gilbert and Susan Gubar explain their rationale for focusing on the woman writer in Victorian times. The nineteenth century, they aver, was the first one in which a significant number of women took up the pen with the intention of creating *belles-lettres* (xi). Prior to the nineteenth century, women had written eloquently but privately, in the forms of unpublished journals, diaries, and letters. It is not so much the fact that women were writing, but rather the facts that they were striving to write "literature" and that they sought and achieved publication that distinguish the nineteenth century in terms of women's history.

In coming upon the literary scene as writers at this late date, Englishwomen confronted the thriving body of *belles-lettres* written in English almost exclusively by men since the time of the Anglo-Saxons. As Gilbert and Gubar point out, the woman writer did *not* experience in relation to that literature the phenomenon which Harold Bloom names "the anxiety of influence," that Oedipal struggle of male writers from each new generation to carve out their own creative space by symbolically carving up (i.e., by misreading) the works of their forefathers (46-48). An Englishwoman's male peers may have wrestled with the past, but she had to wrestle with the present, with the daunting task of establishing a right which male writers took for granted: the right to one's own authorial voice. She had to establish this right in the teeth of her culture's opposition, opposition voiced most strongly by male literary critics and male authors—in other words, her peers, or, to retain Bloom's useful family model, her brothers.

Just as Bloom's Oedipal analogy provides insight into the struggles of male writers, I propose a sibling analogy as a way to enlarge our understanding of the struggles of female writers, particularly in the Victorian era. In this analogy male Victorian writers occupy the position of older brother to female Victorian writers, considered collectively here as younger sister. Bonded to earlier writers by gender, male Victorian writers were psychologically older than their female counterparts, for the gender bond meant, to some extent, a shared experience. In contrast, the female writer, with no available roster of great literary foremothers, faced a blank sheet: women's experience was yet to be written. A sense of novelty, itself inducing anxiety, pervaded the whole enterprise of daring to write and publish as a woman. Women's literary history was yet in its infancy. As we enlarge our understanding of this history, the

47

sibling analogy should prove helpful, for, as we shall see, Victorian women writers shared key personality traits with the typical second sibling in a family, as this role is described by modern psychologists. By comparing the behavior of these two groups—Victorian women writers and second siblings—we should gain a more accurate grasp of the plight of our literary foremothers, thereby enabling us to bring deeper understanding and fresh insight to the literature they created.

As a case in point, let us consider George Eliot. Eliot's fiction, from *Scenes of Clerical Life* to *Daniel Deronda*, records the author's struggle to establish an authoritative narrative voice. This voice, that of the Victorian sage, first appears in Eliot's third book, *The Mill on the Floss*. The very existence of such a voice bespeaks the author's struggle to overcome in her own life the plight in which she places the book's protagonist, Maggie Tulliver. Marian Evans (the real name of "George Eliot") wrote no autobiography, but in *The Mill on the Floss* she brings us her life story dressed in the clothes of fiction. By her protagonist's failure to claim the right to her own "voice," her individuality, Eliot shows what happens when a gifted young woman tries to live within her culture's sexist constraints. In the novel these constraints are represented in memorably stifling form by Maggie's older brother, Tom. Marian Evans also had an older brother, Isaac, who thwarted her at every opportunity, and she came to realize that Isaac represented the cultural constraints under which she suffered. The challenge to both author and protagonist was to break through this oppression by casting off the older brother (real as well as metaphorical) and laying claim to her own uniqueness, her own conscience, her own world view.

In his standard biography, *George Eliot*, Gordon Haight notes some of the remarkable similarities between the sibling relationship in Evans's life and that portrayed in *The Mill on the Floss*:

Isaac and Mary Anne [or "Marian," as she later called herself[1]]...became inseparable playmates. There is good reason for reading autobiography in the childhood of Tom and Maggie Tulliver, who were born in the same years as they [1816 and 1819].... The dominating passion of her childhood was her love for her brother Isaac.... Her delight in seeing him again when he came home from Folehill for the holidays is clearly reflected in *The Mill on the Floss*.... (4-6)

Not only were Maggie and Marian born in the same years; they also shared the same birth order. Both girls were the youngest child in their respective families. The comparison runs even deeper: both girls held the position of second child in the family. As psychologists are discovering, birth order often plays a crucial role in the development of personality. Each birth order role from the first to the fourth sibling carries its own personality traits. Now Maggie is clearly the second child in the Tulliver family, but Marian was her father's sixth child.[2] However, according to family therapists Margaret M. Hoopes and James M. Harper, "After the fourth sibling, the position patterns begin to repeat, with the responses taking into consideration the increased complexity of the family" (29). Hoopes and Harper also assert, "The sex of the sibling affects the way in which a role is performed rather than what the role is" (30). If this theory is correct, Isaac Evans, the fifth sibling, should demonstrate the personality traits found in the first sibling's role, and Marian, the sixth sibling, should fulfill the second sibling's role. Likewise, Tom and Maggie should exhibit the behavior patterns of the first and the second sibling, respectively. As we shall see, Hoopes and Harper's role explanations hold true in all four cases.

As Hoopes and Harper explain:

Part of the role assignment for the first child is to be responsible for everyone else in the family.... [F]irst children represent the explicit parental standards of responsibility, success, and social decorum.... Interpersonally, first children work to keep individuals within families functioning within the rules and parental values.... Sometimes, however, they seem to be rule-bound, rigid, and inflexible in trying to get others to comply with their interpretation of the rules. (30, 36-37)

The above is a textbook description of the personalities of Tom Tulliver and Isaac Evans, as Isaac's personality comes down to us in the biographies and letters of his sister.

First, both Tom and Isaac take on responsibility for everyone else in their families. Tom feels so responsible for the welfare of his family that when Mr. Tulliver loses Dorlcote Mill in his reckless lawsuit against Mr. Wakem, Tom determines to win back the Tulliver holdings single-handedly. In particular, he feels responsible for Maggie. As the narrator wryly notes, Tom "was very fond of his sister, and meant always to take care of her, make her his housekeeper, and punish her when she did wrong" (40). Likewise, Isaac felt responsible for his siblings, though he waited until his parents' deaths to exercise the authority he felt incumbent upon him over his adult sisters, the pliant Chrissey and the uncontrollable Marian. Having received the bulk of his father's estate simply by virtue of his masculinity, Isaac held financial power over his sisters. When Chrissey's husband suddenly died, leaving her with six children to raise, "Isaac agreed to let her live rent free in the house at Attleborough, once her own, and tried to be kind to her, 'though not in a very large way'.... Isaac's help was far from generous" (Haight 125-26). As for Marian, Isaac maintained tight control of the annual income his father had allotted her. Rather than allowing the family solicitor to make payments to Marian, Isaac insisted on handling them himself; all her life Evans worried that her income would not be available when she needed it. Further, as head of the family (in his view) after his father's death, Isaac considered himself responsible for determining what would become of Marian's life. That Tom Tulliver wants to make Maggie his housekeeper is perfectly in line with Isaac's view of Marian's function in life, though not in regard to himself: a married man by now, Isaac had his own housekeeper. But the widowed Chrissey had six children to care for; who better to keep house for Chrissey than the unmarried Marian? Indeed, as soon as she heard of the death of Chrissey's husband, Marian herself dropped her editing work for the *Westminster Review* to stay with her sister. However, after a week Chrissey agreed that Marian could do more good by providing financial help than by keeping house, so Marian decided to return to London. At this news Isaac threw a fit:

> Isaac, however, was very indignant to find that I had arranged to leave without consulting him and thereupon flew into a violent passion with me, winding up by saying that he desired that I would never "apply to him for anything whatever"—which, seeing that I have never done so, was almost as superfluous as if I had said that I would never receive a kindness from him. (*Letters* 2: 75)

Besides taking on responsibility for their families, Tom and Isaac both represent within their own persons their respective families' standards of success and social decorum. Tom determines to be a success in the one way his father will understand. As Elizabeth Deeds Ermarth points out, "In response to Mr. Tulliver's loss of his mill and home, all Tom can think of is to regain the property and to avenge the family on Wakem" (82). And not only on Wakem, we might add, but also on Wakem's innocent son, Philip, just as Mr. Tulliver has insisted. In desiring vengeance against the innocent, Mr. Tulliver demonstrates a sense of justice straight out of the Old Testament: "I the Lord your God am a jealous God, visiting the inequity of the fathers upon the children to the third and the fourth generation of those who hate me..." (Exod. 20: 5). Fittingly, in a dramatic scene at the end of Book III, Mr. Tulliver commands Tom to write and sign an oath of vengeance against Wakem and his offspring within the sacred pages of the family Bible, and Tom eagerly does so. The remainder of the novel finds Tom laboring to regain the Tulliver property and nursing his hatred of Philip.

However much Tom has internalized his father's standards of success, his veneration of social decorum stems from his mother. Mrs. Tulliver is the stupidest of the four Dodson daughters, who share a ridiculous pride in their name. As Elizabeth Weed has noticed, "[T]here is no living Dodson in the book.... [A]ll of the Dodson women belong to men...; the Dodson name is part of a paternal hegemony..." (122). Accordingly, Tom feels no pride in the Dodson name, but time and again the narrator alerts us to Tom's identity as a Dodson in essence, if not in name. Tall, blond, handsome, he resembles the Dodsons physically as well as sharing their stupidity, as we see in his difficulties at school. Most importantly, like the Dodsons, Tom strives to maintain socially correct behavior: "He would provide for his mother and sister, and make everyone say that he was a man of high character" (225). Tom cannot conceive of his actually having a high character apart from everyone else's thinking so. When he spurns Maggie, he cannot imagine the truth that she and Stephen Guest are innocent of a sexual affair; St. Ogg's society has condemned Maggie, so she must be guilty. Still worse than his inability to exercise independent judgment is his cruel refusal to let Maggie into the Tulliver home. Even Aunt Glegg, the most pompous ex-Dodson, offers Maggie a place to live. In Aunt Glegg's view, a family must stand by its members. In contrast, Tom's self-pride outweighs his family loyalty. As owner now of Dorlcote Mill, he casts Maggie out, lest kindness to her sully his own reputation. In so doing, he exceeds even the Dodsons' concern with social correctness.

As with Tom Tulliver, so with Isaac Evans. Success and social decorum were Isaac's gods. His love of wealth prevented him from aiding his nearly destitute sister, Chrissey, beyond providing a pittance. Ina Taylor reports that he even suggested that Chrissey send her two youngest children to the Infant Orphan Asylum (118). By increasing his own wealth and controlling two properties—his own home and Chrissey's—Isaac capitalized on his inheritance to earn the reputation of a man of importance in his provincial community in Warwickshire. As Walter Allen notes of St. Ogg's, Isaac's community was "a society in which generosity itself is a vice" (57). This emphasis on money is of course crucial to the Dodson identity in *The Mill on the Floss*: "The Dodson badge was to be not only rich but 'richer than was supposed' " (Fisher 75-76). Thus, it is hardly surprising to find that Isaac's middle name, Pearson, shares its final syllable with "Dodson," or that "Pearson" was the maiden name of Isaac's mother.

Because he valued social decorum as much as success, Isaac, like Tom, renounced his "ruined" sister. Some three years after the fact, Marian Evans wrote her brother that she was living with George Lewes, whom she called her husband. Ferreting out the truth that no wedding ceremony had actually occurred, Isaac renounced Marian and insisted that Chrissey and his half-sister, Fanny, do the same. Although Chrissey repented of such harshness two years later on her deathbed, Isaac never relented until after Lewes's death. When the 60-year-old Marian Evans married the 40-year-old John Cross, Isaac sent her a note of congratulations, his first communication with his sister in 23 years. Like Tom, Isaac conflated morality with social decorum. For this reason he had been unable to accept Evans's claim that she and Lewes were ethically, if not legally, married.[3]

We have seen how Tom and Isaac shared key personal traits and that these are typical traits of a child in the first birth order role in a family. Now we turn to Maggie and Marian. According to Hoopes and Harper:

Second children can live totally for someone else or they can be totally independent. In the former case, they do not assert their wishes, and...they are unable to separate their feelings from those of the other person.... [They] take on the pain of other people through the melding process.... They tend to feel and act as though they are extensions of other people; their sense of joy, sorrow, and failure depends utterly on the experience of others. (50-55)

From the above remarks it should be clear that a second sibling's struggle for autonomy is first and foremost the struggle for her right to her own identity. Never developing a strong sense of self, Maggie Tulliver is saved only by a *deus-ex-machina* flood[4] from the anguish of continued existence in a world where she knows she will always fail to fulfill others' expectations. Conversely, Marian Evans developed a secure identity and found fulfillment in her personal life. Still, she could never completely project that identity into her writing. As

"George Eliot," Evans won acclaim for her novels by concealing her femininity.

At this point it will be helpful to examine specific ways in which Maggie and Marian enacted the role of second child. Typically for a second child, Maggie evinces an almost neurotic dependence upon the approval and love of other people. Eliot writes of "the need of being loved, the strongest need in poor Maggie's nature" (37). To her anguish, Maggie learns that others will love her only if she behaves contrary to her nature. Tom, for instance, in a stance typical of a dominant male lover, constantly threatens her with withdrawal of his love as punishment for her "bad" (i.e., independent) behavior. Realizing this oppression by Tom and, later, by St. Ogg's society as intolerable, Maggie rebels against overt and covert male domination, but her efforts are doomed. As a child, she cuts her hair rather than submit to the onerous curling iron that would control her wild black locks. When this attempt ends in derision (Maggie's jagged haircut arouses the jeers of her extended family), she runs away to the gypsies (another futile effort), and, as a young woman, she runs away with Stephen (to the utter ruin of her—but not his—reputation). But revolt is for naught: Maggie's conscience remains enslaved to her sexist upbringing. To the detriment of her personality, Maggie accepts Tom's moral judgments of her actions, even as her world view widens. As she matures, Maggie knows that she can never share the narrow world view of Tom and St. Ogg's, that she is temperamentally unfit for provincial life. As Gillian Beer writes, "For Maggie, there can be no accommodation with society, because the community in which she has grown up, and the culture of which this is an expression, will accord her nature no recognition" (92). Nevertheless, instead of asserting her right to her own conscience, Maggie castigates herself for behaving improperly. Indeed, in her greatest moral crisis as a young woman, Maggie melds her conscience with Tom's, so identifying with him that she craves his harsh words as a moral tonic: "In her deep humiliation under the retrospect of her weakness…she almost desired to endure the severity of Tom's reproof…. [His] looks and words would be a reflection of her own conscience" (483-84). And after hearing Tom disown her, Maggie is "too heavily pressed upon by her anguish to discern any difference between her actual guilt and her brother's accusations, still less to vindicate herself" (485). Hating herself, she wants Tom to constrain her so that she will be "good": "I want to be kept from doing wrong again" (485).

Although Tom's reproofs substitute for her own unique conscience, Maggie melds with others than Tom during the course of the novel. As we have seen, melding is typical behavior for a second child. For instance, Maggie tells Stephen Guest that she cannot marry him because doing so would hurt Lucy Deane and Philip Wakem: "I feel their trouble now: it is as if it were branded on my mind" (478). When Stephen counters—as well he might—that her refusal is hurting *him*, Maggie will not allow herself to be sympathetic because, if she were, she might marry him and be happy at Lucy's and Philip's expense. In order to be unselfish, thereby fulfilling her society's feminine ideal as a martyr, Maggie rejects Stephen—never mind the misery to Stephen and herself. As Eliot writes, "She had made up her mind to suffer" (474).

A warped personality, this Maggie Tulliver, and yet she seems admirable because she tries so hard to be good. Alas, like Marian Evans herself, Maggie has learned that whatever she wants is invariably wicked in the eyes of the world. Unlike her creator, however, Maggie believes in the world's morality, so she relies on it, particularly as represented in Tom, to guide her conscience and her feelings. Yet, unable to stifle independent thoughts and feelings completely, she rides an unending merry-go-round of individual expression followed by repentance. In a succinct reading of this novel, Mary Ellen Doyle, S.C.N., explains:

Part of Maggie's problem is that she is predominately "Sister Maggie"; she always turns to Tom for salvation.... [Maggie] remains fundamentally compulsive and insecure...a girl damaged beyond repair, *not* spiritually wise or psychically sound, to be greatly pitied but not glorified. (58-59)

And yet Eliot's rhetoric *does* glorify Maggie. As Sister Doyle later remarks, the narrator is unable to maintain his[5] tone of ironic detachment toward Maggie once she becomes an adult. Hence, we assume that both narrator and author approve of Maggie's sacrifice. However, there are a few places in which the narrator steps back from Maggie, seemingly in disapproval: "She had made up her mind to suffer" is one example. Still, most of the time we confront a paradox: the narrator's rhetoric glorifies Maggie, but Maggie's thoughts, emotions, words, and actions show that she is more to be pitied than praised. In a curious passage, the narrator himself seems aware of the ambiguity of his stand on renunciation:

The great problem of the shifting relation between passion and duty is clear to no man who is capable of apprehending it: the question whether the moment has come in which a man has fallen below the possibility of a renunciation that will carry any efficacy, and must accept the sway of a passion against which he had struggled as a trespass, is one for which we have no masterkey that will fit all cases. (497)

Besides the moral relativism of this passage, what is striking about it is its rejection of responsibility for judging a character's behavior—most unusual for this narrator and, truly, for this author. Despite the glorifying rhetoric and the occasional implied criticism of Maggie in the last two books, Marian Evans simply does not know whether Maggie should have renounced Stephen or not. And the reason for this ambivalence, I believe, lies in the author's own enactment of the role of second sibling.

As we have seen, besides melding with others, the other option for second children is to be totally independent. In her personal life Evans achieved this independence, taking the drastic step of living with her own "Stephen Guest," but she always winced from the pain of what that decision had cost her: the loss of her good name and the subsequent alienation from her family and polite (i.e., patriarchal) society. As a married man, legally unable to divorce his wife despite her continuing adultery, Lewes was even more morally forbidden to Evans than Stephen was to Maggie. In asserting her moral right to marriage with Lewes when legal marriage was impossible, Evans was claiming a high moral ground for herself and Lewes contrary to Victorian standards. As she had foreseen, her family and most of her and Lewes's acquaintances rejected them both. Only when "George Eliot" had become famous did visitors crowd her salon—and even then, truly respectable people stayed away.

In the other major decision of her life, to become a writer, Evans showed less self-assertion. Her reviews for the *Westminster Review* were unsigned, and although she was editing the journal, she agreed with John Chapman, the journal's owner, that he should nominally remain editor, lest a female name in that position damage the journal's reputation. So great was the prejudice against "bluestockings" that when she submitted her first book of fiction, *Scenes of Clerical Life*, Evans again concealed her femininity. Ironically, her forthrightness in openly taking a lover all but necessitated concealment of her authorship, lest her books be condemned not only as silly, because written by a woman, but also as immoral, because written by a woman living with a man "in sin."

Evans's ambivalence about her decisions comes through in some of her letters. On the one hand, she was proud of her choice to live with Lewes rather than conducting a surreptitious affair: "Light and easily broken ties are what I neither desire theoretically or could live for practically. Women who are satisfied with such ties do *not* act as I have done—they obtain what they desire and are still invited to dinner" (*Letters* 2: 214). In addition, she credited her "marriage" with nudging her toward creative writing:

Under the influence of the intense happiness I have enjoyed in my married life...I have at last found out my true vocation.... I have turned out to be an artist.... One whom you knew when she was not very happy and when her life seemed to serve no purpose, has been at last blessed with the sense that she has done something worth living and suffering for. (*Letters* 3: 186)

On the other hand, in her review of Geraldine Jewsbury's *Constance Herbert*, Evans equates renunciation with "moral heroism," explaining, "And it is this very perception that the thing we renounce is precious, is something never to be compensated to us, which constitutes the beauty and heroism of renunciation" (*Essays* 321). To Herbert Spencer, whom she loved before she met George Lewes, Evans wrote, apologetically professing love, "I have struggled—indeed I have—to renounce everything and be entirely unselfish, but I find myself utterly unequal to it" (*Letters* 8: 56). Thus, Evans did value renunciation, but she chose not to renounce the men she loved—neither Herbert Spencer, who rejected her; nor George Lewes; nor, after Lewes's death, John Cross. Yet any guilt over this failure to be "entirely unselfish" seems to have been compensated by her belief that, thanks to Lewes's encouragement, she was doing something noble with her life.

As a result of the above evidence, we may say that in her personal life as an adult, Marian filled the role of second child in the opposite way from Maggie: unlike Maggie, Marian became independent of others, forming her conscience apart from her society's constraints. Although her society rejected her, she had rejected it first by leaving home and living an unorthodox private and professional life. Of course, Evans always hoped for a reconciliation with her brother, and her abiding affection for him shines forth in Maggie's love for Tom. Yet, in a practical sense, Evans did not allow this affection to constrain her. As she wrote to her friend Sara Hennell shortly after mailing the bombshell to Isaac about her living arrangement with Lewes, "I dare say I shall never have further correspondence with my brother, which will be a great relief to me" (*Letters* 2: 364). Professionally, however, Evans displayed "melding" behavior, making her novels palatable to male reviewers by pretending to share their gender. While admiring her artistic achievement, we may also, I think, regret the historical conditions that made such subterfuge necessary.

Evans's wisdom in adopting a male pseudonym is borne out by an incident in her own lifetime. In a letter that foreshadows the fate of her first novel, *Adam Bede*, Evans wrote the following about "Evangelical Teaching," one of her *Westminster Review* pieces: "The article appears to have produced a strong impression, and that impression would be a little counteracted if the author were known to be a *woman*" (Haight 193). Later, after *Adam Bede* had won laudatory critical reviews as well as popular success, Lewes explained to Barbara Leigh Smith Bodichon (co-founder of Girton College, Cambridge) that Marian had chosen a masculine pen name "in order to get the book judged on its own merits, and not prejudged as the work of a woman, or of a particular woman. It is quite clear that people would have sniffed at it if they had known the writer to be a woman, but they can't now unsay their admiration..." (Haight 290). But some *did* unsay their admiration. For instance, on 26 Feb. 1859, the *Athenaeum*, in an article by the novelist Geraldine Jewsbury, had praised *Adam Bede* as "a work of true genius...a novel of the highest class...a book to be accepted, not criticized" (Haight 276). However, when rumors circulated that "George Eliot" was in fact the woman whom novelist Charles Kingsley called "Lewes's concubine" (Ashton 80), the *Athenaeum* reversed itself. On 2 July 1859, in its Weekly Gossip column, in a paragraph by William Hepworth Dixon, the *Athenaeum* declared, "The writer [of *Adam Bede*] is in no sense a 'great unknown'; the tale, if bright in parts, and such as a clever woman with an observant eye and unschooled moral nature might have written, has no great quality of any kind" (Haight 290). Dixon also seemed outraged by Evans's garnering of praise for her fiction by duping honest critics (like himself) into believing she was a man: "No woman of genius ever condescended to such a *ruse*,—no book was ever permanently helped by such a trick" (Haight 291).

In fact, an extraordinary amount of Victorian literature was authored by women who felt pressured into assuming pen names either explicitly male or androgynous but male-sounding, or who used the initials of their first names instead of the full-length, feminine first names. Besides George Eliot, famous examples include Currer, Ellis, and Acton Bell (Charlotte, Emily, and Anne Brontë, respectively), E. OE. Somerville (Edith Oenone Somerville), and Martin Ross (Violet Martin). Another tactic to garner favorable criticism was simply to remain anonymous and choose the erudite language that supposedly

would mark one out as masculine. For example, Harriet Martineau, not daring
to sign her criticism, "deliberately tried to make her articles 'look like a man's
writing' in the *Edinburgh Review*" (Haight 268). Still another tactic, while
revealing femininity, permitted one partially to redress this drawback by
advertising one's married status, thereby assimilating oneself into patriarchy by
omitting one's feminine first name—e.g., Mrs Humphry Ward (Mary Augusta
Arnold Ward) and Mrs Gaskell (Elizabeth Cleghorn Stevenson Gaskell). Even
Elizabeth Barrett, having already established a name for herself as a poet, at
once added "Browning" to her name in signing all poetry composed after her
marriage. Of course, "Elizabeth Barrett Browning" was indeed her legal name;
yet one cannot help but notice the female Victorian writer's penchant for
gaining respectability by advertising her married status.

I believe all such behavior can be viewed under the same sibling
paradigm by which I have "read" *The Mill on the Floss* and the life of its author.
In other words, the typical Victorian woman writer behaved like a second
sibling, a younger sister, toward her male peers, her older brother, melding with
him as much as possible. Though regrettable, this decision is understandable
and pragmatic: for every Robert Browning, encouraging a Marian Evans with
such comments as "the noblest and most heroic prose-poem that I have ever
read" (Browning's criticism of *Romola*) (Haight 367), there existed a Robert
Southey, then Poet Laureate, chastising a Charlotte Brontë that "Literature
cannot be the business of a woman's life, and it ought not to be" (Gilbert and
Gubar 545).

Thankfully for us, many women *have* made literature the business of their
lives. As more women write, fewer feel the need to disguise their femininity.
That such a need was felt in the previous century is part of the historical
knowledge we should bring to our readings of Victorian novels authored by
women. As the medievalists long ago discovered, a medieval work, read by
itself, may be indecipherable; only with an understanding of shared cultural
assumptions do the stumbling blocks become stepping stones. While Victorian
literature, written as it is in Standard Modern English, entails no comparable
linguistic enigmas, we shall nevertheless find our understanding and
appreciation of it greatly deepened by our knowledge of Victorian culture and
history. Woman's claim to her own authorial voice is an important part of that
history.

Notes

[1]Baptized "Mary Anne" in 1819, Evans began spelling her name "Mary Ann" in
1837 and changed both spelling and pronunciation to "Marian" in 1850. She remained
"Marian" throughout her fiction-writing career, but in the last year of her life, 1880, she
reverted to "Mary Ann." In consideration of her career as a writer, I refer to her in this
essay as "Marian Evans."

[2]Robert Evans's first wife, Harriet Poynton, died shortly after giving birth to their
third child. Robert's second wife, Christiana Pearson, gave birth to Chrissey, Isaac, and

Marian.

³This "marriage" could never have been legalized because Lewes was unable to obtain a divorce from his wife, Agnes, who was carrying on a long affair with Lewes's ex-business partner, Thornton Hunt. This affair produced four children, whom Lewes was obligated to support as his own.

⁴This *deus-ex-machina* device is quite literal: "some wooden machinery" capsizes Maggie and Tom's boat (521). In terms of the plot, wooden machinery indeed. As Barbara Hardy remarks, "What we are prepared for is the struggle between the energetic human spirit and a limited and limiting society: such struggles are not settled by floods" (47).

⁵Seemingly of indeterminate gender as the novel begins, the narrator subtly assumes masculine characteristics as the novel continues.

Works Cited

Allen, Walter. "*The Mill on the Floss.*" *Modern Critical Views: George Eliot*. Ed. Harold Bloom. New York: Chelsea House, 1986.

Ashton, Rosemary. The Mill on the Floss: *A Natural History*. Boston: Twayne Publishers, 1990.

Beer, Gillian. *Key Women Writers: George Eliot*. Bloomington, IN: Indiana UP, 1986.

Doyle, Mary Ellen, S.C.N. *The Sympathetic Response: George Eliot's Fictional Rhetoric*. London: Associated University P, 1981.

Eliot, George [Marian Evans]. *The George Eliot Letters*. Ed. Gordon S. Haight. 9 vols. New Haven, CT: Yale UP, 1954-78.

_____. *The Mill on the Floss*. Ed. Gordon S. Haight. Oxford: Oxford UP, 1980.

_____. *Selected Essays, Poems, and Other Writings*. Ed. A.S. Byatt and Nicholas Warren. London: Penguin, 1990.

Ermarth, Elizabeth Deeds. *George Eliot: Twayne's English Authors Series*. Boston: Twayne Publishers, 1985.

Fisher, Philip. *Making Up Society: The Novels of George Eliot*. Pittsburgh: U of Pittsburgh P, 1981.

Gilbert, Sandra M., and Susan Gubar. *The Madwoman in the Attic: The Woman Writer and the Nineteenth-Century Literary Imagination*. New Haven, CT: Yale UP, 1979.

Haight, Gordon S. *George Eliot: A Biography*. Oxford: Oxford UP, 1968.

Hardy, Barbara. "*The Mill on the Floss.*" *Critical Essays on George Eliot*. Ed. Barbara Hardy. New York: Barnes & Noble, 1970.

Hoopes, Margaret M., and James M. Harper. *Birth Order Roles & Sibling Patterns in Individual & Family Therapy*. Rockville, MD: Aspen, 1987.

May, Herbert G., and Bruce M. Metzger, eds. *The New Oxford Annotated Bible with the Apocrypha*. New York: Oxford UP, 1977.

Taylor, Ina. *A Woman of Contradictions: The Life of George Eliot*. New York: William Morrow and Co., 1989.

Weed, Elizabeth. "The Liquidation of Maggie Tulliver." *Modern Critical Views: George Eliot*. Ed. Harold Bloom. New York: Chelsea House, 1986.

Ties That Bind:
Identity and Sibling Relationships
in Anne Tyler's Novels

Deanna Madden

Anne Tyler has written so often about families in her novels, that the subject is clearly special terrain for her. Marriages interest her, the growth and deterioration of intimate relations between men and women, love and its ability to transform lives. For her the family is the natural outcome of people's yearning to make meaningful connection with others, to step outside the prison of self. At the same time every adult was once a child with a family that influenced, for better or worse, the person he became. In Tyler's novels, family is the crucible in which identity is forged. Her characters' identities are the result of inherited traits, childhood experiences, upbringing, and interaction with parents and siblings. Whether they love or hate their families, they define themselves in relation to them.

While critics have frequently pointed out the importance of the family in Tyler's work,[1] studies have rarely singled out the sibling bond for attention. Examining what Tyler has to say about sibling relations illuminates an important aspect of her work. Her interest in sibling relations is evident in the number of opening sentences in her novels which focus on sibling bonds:

When Ben Joe Hawkes left home he gave his sister Susannah one used guitar, six shelves of *National Geographic*, a battered microscope, and a foot-high hourglass. (*If Morning Ever Comes* 3)

After the funeral James came straight home, to look after his brother. (*The Tin Can Tree* 5)

My brother Jeremy is a thirty-eight-year-old bachelor who never did leave home. (*Celestial Navigation* 1)

In her portraits of families Tyler has shown a progressive tendency to look deeper into the nature of sibling bonds and their effect on identity. Growing up with siblings, she suggests, is a complex experience with both positive and negative aspects. It is an experience that can both nurture and damage.[2]

This ambivalent view of the family appears in her first novel, *If Morning*

Ever Comes. The Hawkes family, a household of one brother, six sisters, a mother and a grandmother, is a warm, loving home, full of life. Ben Joe Hawkes, the sole male in this largely female enclave,[3] at age 25 feels torn between the need to leave the home nest and his desire to remain in it. Compared to the familiar security of the past, the future seems insecure and bleak. Away from his large family, studying at a college in New York, he feels lonely and displaced so he returns home, seeking the comfort and sense of belonging that he sorely misses. At home he is no longer alone; he belongs to a group. Because of shared genes and the shared experience of growing up together, he feels a deep affinity with his sisters, whom he perceives as being like himself. Yet at the same time he also feels alienated from them. He is bothered by the fact that he cannot know what goes on inside their heads, that they harbor secrets he cannot fathom. He laments his family's failure to communicate, the barriers that prevent complete merging of their identities into a single whole. He also feels alienated from his sisters by his gender. As the only male, he feels responsible for the welfare of this household of females. He idealizes his sisters and fantasizes that he is their caretaker; however, this fantasy is mocked by reality:

"When I am away from Sandhill, sometimes the picture of it comes drifting toward me— just the picture of it, like some sunny little island I have got to get back to. And there's my family. Most of the time I seem to see them sort of like a bunch of picnickers in a nineteenth-century painting, sitting around in the grass with their picnic baskets and their pretty dresses and parasols, and floating past on that island. I think, I've got to get back. I think, they need me there and I have got to get back to them. But when I go back, they laugh at me and rumple my hair and ask why I'm such a worrier." (199-200)

Ben Joe's strong feelings for his family are ambivalent: "He hesitated with his hand upon the gate and found himself swinging between loving that house and hating it, between rushing into the sleepy darkness of it and turning away and shrugging off its claim on him forever" (214). He yearns to freeze his sisters at some perfect moment in time all under one roof, safe from time and change. However, the futility of this impulse is seen in his sisters' tendency to wander outside the house at night. It is the nature of things that life will change, children will grow up, leave home, and start new families of their own. This is the lesson Ben Joe learns, and when he leaves for New York, he takes with him a bride, ready to launch a new family of his own.

While his large family may fail to fulfill Ben Joe's ideal of what a family should be, Tyler's first novel gives a highly sentimental portrait of the large family. Ben Joe's family seems bathed in the golden light of nostalgia. Any bickering which occurs is minor. The family is a source of love, warmth, and security, a haven which nurtures. When Ben Joe leaves home, the girl he chooses to take with him is not a radical leap into difference. She is Shelley Domer, an old girlfriend and a native of his hometown, Sandhill, North Carolina, and hence like him in many ways. He imagines her waiting for him in their New York apartment "like his own little piece of Sandhill transplanted" (265). His choice to marry Shelley Domer, thus, is not an embrace of otherness, so much as it is a way of perpetuating likeness. As Petry has pointed out, marriage to Shelley is "an attempt to contain or prevent change" (42). Shelley is practically a sister.

In *Searching for Caleb*, the ingrown quality of large families and their tendency to insulate the individual from the outside world becomes more obvious. The Pecks are a large extended clan of bland, conservative-minded conformists. For siblings Justin II, Sarah, Daniel Jr., Marcus, Laura May and Caroline, and for their descendants, to be born a Peck means that one will partake of the Peck family identity: Pecks have blonde hair and blue eyes, prefer black V-8 Fords, practice law, avoid emotion, have good manners and view the outside world with distrust. They are a family of clones in which individuality or uniqueness is frowned upon. Whether seduced like Justine as a child by the idea of belonging to a large group, or pressured like Caleb to fit in, the individual is in danger of losing his or her separate identity, of being swallowed up by the clan. The group does not tolerate radical difference, like Caleb's proclivity for music, and thus it promotes conformity and sameness. Belonging to the clan also becomes a way of avoiding the rich variety and possibility of life. So wary of the outside world are the Pecks, that few marry. As a result the clan begins to die out. The most alive characters are those who rebel against the womb of clan—Justine and Duncan, cheerful vagabonds who refuse to live staid lives like their Peck relatives, and Caleb, who chooses to vanish rather than sacrifice his music for dreary work. However, family identity is so powerful that even those who rebel still bear sometimes hilarious resemblances to the family, quirky traits they apparently never can be rid of. Thus, Caleb as an old man, after chucking all family ties a second time, still sends the requisite "bread-and-butter" note, written exactly as his punctilious relatives would write it, even down to the same cream-colored stationery; and Duncan, who spends his life rebelling against the clan, is still a typical Peck in his inability to reveal his private thoughts and feelings.

The siblings in *The Accidental Tourist* are also like clones in their uncanny resemblance to each other. Macon Leary, his brothers Charles and Porter, and his sister Rose, are all equally inept in dealing with the randomness and chaos of life. They are like the Pecks in their desire to cling to each other and close out the rest of the world. The world beyond home looks to them threatening. Their marriages are doomed for failure because they are unable to connect with anyone outside the family. Confronted with personal crisis and the demands of adulthood, they retreat to the refuge of their childhood home and to the old ties of their sibling bonds. One by one the brothers' marriages fail and they return to their grandparents' home, where Rose, their spinster sister, who has also failed to connect with a world of strangers, cooks for and mothers them. Together the four siblings find the sense of haven they have failed to find elsewhere in their lives. But such a retreat is clearly a negative reaction to life. The sibling bond becomes a kind of death in life, a way of avoiding growth and change. Macon must break free of his identification with his siblings and discard his old family role of son and brother for a new relationship with someone unlike himself in order to grow and find happiness. Murial Pritchett, the perky and forthright young woman whom he has little in common with and whom no one in his family approves of, provides him with the opportunity to be someone new.

In several novels Tyler explores the sibling bond in families where siblings occur in pairs.[4] Her early novel *The Tin Can Tree* examines three examples of paired sibling bonds at different stages in the life cycle. Living under the same roof but in separate parts of a three-family house are 10-year-old Simon Pike and his 6-year-old sister, Janie Rose; 28-year-old James Green and his 26-year-old brother Ansel; and the Potter sisters, Miss Lucy and Miss Faye, who are in their 60s. When the novel opens, Janie Rose has just died after falling from a tractor. Her brother Simon not only mourns her loss, but must endure rejection by his grieving mother. The death of his sister creates a crisis of identity for Simon. Previously he enjoyed the status of favored child while Janie Rose was the defective or flawed child of the family. Ridden with fears, she suffered from nightmares and sometimes wore layer upon layer of underwear in an attempt to insulate herself from a cold world. She was fat, wore glasses, wet the bed and suffered from depression. Her death, however, causes her mother to be consumed by guilt for having preferred Simon, whom in her grief she now ignores. Feeling unloved and cast out, Simon runs away. His defection shocks his mother back to reality and reestablishes his place in the family. At novel's end he again feels loved and esteemed by his parents, who come to realize that life must go on.

The next pair of siblings, James and Ansel Pike, resemble the younger pair in some ways. While growing up, James, the older, was, like Simon, his parents' favorite. Like Simon, he too was a runaway. Ansel, like Janie Rose, was the child afflicted with shortcomings: "I had a runny nose from the moment I was born, I think, and pinkish eyes. One time I heard Daddy say, 'Well, if there's ever a prize for sheer *sniveliness* given, he'll take it' " (136). Ansel, at 26, is a hypochondriac, who suffers from anemia, dizzy spells and an assortment of vague complaints which he uses to draw attention to himself and elicit sympathy. Like Janie Rose, he suffers from depression. He also engages in self-destructive drinking binges intended to alarm his brother James. Most of the people around him are repelled by his insensitivity and self-centeredness, although he is patiently tolerated by his brother James, who has slipped into the role of his brother's keeper. James and Ansel are good examples of the sibling phenomenon known as mirroring, in which one sibling, usually the older, provides an audience or mirror for the other and reacts appropriately to the younger, showing for example approval or disapproval (Bank and Kahn 39). The older sibling, thus, becomes a surrogate parental figure: James takes the place of their dead mother in his solicitous care of Ansel. Together they illustrate the potentially damaging effects of the paired sibling bond. After years of living together, they have developed a symbiotic relationship that has made both unable to break free and establish independent identities. This relationship, in which James plays the role of nurturer and caretaker, fosters James's identity as strong and capable and Ansel's as dependent, weak, maimed and needy. Their identities are so intertwined that they become confused, even interchangeable, symbolized by their habit of wearing each other's clothes. The relationship threatens to stunt both brothers' growth by preventing them from forming new attachments outside the family. Ansel will not let Maisie Hammond get too close because of his attachment to James, and James will not be able to marry Joan Pike because of the responsibility of caring for Ansel. Both brothers remain trapped in roles that are left over from childhood, what Bank and Kahn call "frozen images" (73). The frozen image is, in fact, a recurrent motif in *The Tin Can Tree*, appearing especially in the form of a photograph.[5]

The third pair of siblings, the elderly Potter sisters, are barely distinguishable. They have lived together so long that they seem like clones:

> The Potter sisters always carried handbags and wore hats and gloves, even if they were going next door. They were small, round women, in their early sixties probably, and for as long as Joan had known them they had had only one aim in life: they wanted to have swarms of neighborhood children clamoring at their door for cookies.... And although no one came...they still went on baking, eating the cookies themselves, growing fat together and comparing notes on their identical heart conditions. (50)

The two sisters go everywhere together; they talk and act alike. Although they like company to visit them, they are careful to bolt their door even when visitors are present, to lock out the world and to lock themselves in (116). Their closed-off lives are symbolized not only by the bolts on their door but also by the maze of tall black screens that they have used to partition off the interior of their rooms.

The reader tends to observe these various sibling bonds through the eyes of Joan Pike, who resides with her relatives, the family of Simon and Janie Rose, and who has fallen in love with James. Joan, an only child, cannot understand James's attachment to his brother Ansel and views it as an impediment to her own relations with James. On the other hand, Joan is trapped in the identity of only child unattached to anyone, a state which looks like a lonely alternative to the sibling bond. The final scene of the novel presents James and Ansel's bond as a choice. Joan perceives that James has chosen to stay with Ansel and play the role of his brother's keeper and that this is an admirable choice demonstrating loyalty and responsibility. It is life-affirming, not life-denying. The sibling bond becomes a symbol of connectedness.

Searching for Caleb also gives prominence to a paired sibling bond, that of Daniel and Caleb Peck, half-brothers who are very different despite their shared genes. Daniel bears the blue eyes of the Pecks and shares their rigidity and practicality. Caleb bears the brown eyes of the outsider and shows his impractical and dreamy nature by his attraction to music. When they are young, they simply contrast: Daniel is the son who is approved of and Caleb the son who is not. For a while Caleb makes himself unhappy trying to be the person his family demands, but at last he chooses to discard his role as a Peck and vanish to follow his own vagabond path. As Daniel ages, he begins to regard himself and Caleb as two halves of a whole, and without his other half, he feels incomplete. Caleb, missing for 61 years, becomes the object of an obsessive search by Daniel, who is driven by the need to reconnect with this other self. In his longing to find his missing brother, Daniel epitomizes the desire to merge with sibling. But Caleb, who has made a career of running away from home and family, epitomizes the desire to separate. Once found, he soon asserts his autonomy by disappearing again.

Another paired sibling bond appears in *Saint Maybe*, which examines the effect of the death of a sibling on the survivor. As a child Ian Bedloe idolizes his older brother Danny, whom he attempts to emulate as he grows up. This identification with his older brother causes his sense of identity to be closely bound up with his brother. He even falls half in love with Lucy Dean, the pretty girl his brother marries. When he suspects Lucy may be unfaithful to his brother, he feels personally betrayed. Blurting out his suspicions to his brother, he triggers a tragic chain of events. His brother dies in a car crash, an apparent suicide. Soon after, the bereft young widow, trying to numb her grief, dies of an overdose of tranquilizers. Overwhelmed with guilt for these deaths, Ian turns to the Church of the Second Chance and becomes surrogate parent for the three children left orphaned by the tragedy. His brother's death and the subsequent atonement Ian feels compelled to undergo profoundly alter his identity. Abandoning his previous interests, goals, and even his girlfriend, he metamorphoses into a gentle celibate "saint" dedicated to raising Lucy's three children. Not until they are grown does he feel free to marry and begin a family of his own. By then he is a very different person than he was at 17 when his brother died.

The first of Tyler's novels to suggest that sometimes sibling relations can be discordant was *The Clock Winder*. This novel examines sibling rivalry and the tensions generated by the sibling bond both in terms of a sibling pair and a large family of multiple siblings. The sibling pair this time is two sisters, Elizabeth Abbott and her sister Polly. Like Daniel and Caleb, the sisters sharply contrast with each other. Polly is "the cute little sister" with blonde curls who marries and has a baby; Elizabeth is the plain sister with slack brown hair, who refuses to wear makeup, wears jeans instead of skirts, dislikes children and takes up deliberately unfeminine pursuits as a handyman and a wood carver. Polly, like Daniel, fulfills her parents' expectations; Elizabeth, like Caleb, disappoints them. In her attempt to stress her difference, Elizabeth creates an identity for herself in opposition to her family, and especially her sibling Polly. While the two sisters are not openly hostile to each other, there are no signs of closeness between them.

On the other hand, the Emersons—a large family of four brothers and three sisters—frequently quarrel but are nevertheless close. Less sentimentalized than the Hawkes, they resemble that earlier large family in many ways. Here again is the sense of belonging to a group and sharing in its identity. Their appearance, like that of the Hawkes siblings, stamps them as genetically linked: "Every one of them...had [their father's] pure blue eyes that curled like cashew nuts whenever they smiled" (108). Like the Hawkes and the Pecks, they distrust outsiders. The oldest sibling, Matthew, also bears a remarkable resemblance to Ben Joe in his gentleness and sense of responsibility, while the youngest sibling Peter, like Tessie Hawkes, is mainly distinguished by the role of youngest. Beyond these similarities, however, is an important difference. This is Tyler's first portrait of a family that squabbles. In place of the polite and affectionate exchanges of the Hawkes siblings, the Emersons bicker, compete, insult and aggravate each other. As Mrs. Emerson explains to Elizabeth, when her large family drove by, people would "never guess…behind the glass it was all bickering, arguing, scenes, constant crisis—" (15).

The first Emerson siblings Elizabeth meets are Timothy and Matthew. She finds herself attracted to both, but for different reasons. Timothy is the family "clown" who makes her laugh (59). Matthew, on the other hand, the oldest brother, is "the quiet one" (48). While Timothy never seems to be serious, Matthew always is. What Elizabeth does not realize is that Timothy's personality is more complex than it appears. The jokester is a persona he has cultivated. Underneath he hides a different sort of person, gloomy, moody and capable of violence, as when he reacts to his mother's badgering by beheading the Thanksgiving turkey Elizabeth could not bring herself to kill. As Timothy realizes that Matthew has become his rival for Elizabeth's attentions, he resorts to power tactics to win her for himself. He is not in love with Elizabeth, but the idea of losing her to his brother galls him. He locks Elizabeth in his bedroom and threatens her with a gun. When these measures fail, he threatens to shoot himself, and in fact dies when the gun goes off as Elizabeth tries to wrest it from him.

Timothy's relationship with Matthew is not his only significant sibling bond. He has an even closer bond with his twin, Andrew, although he goes to pains to deny it. He prefers to see himself as having little in common with Andrew, who is under psychiatric care far from home. Reminded of their double birthday parties as children, he remembers how even as a child Andrew had "some jerkiness of mind which I had feared a twin could catch like a cold" (52). But he is more like Andrew than he wants to admit. The whole family has worried that Andrew might commit suicide. When Timothy dies instead, his family assumes he has acted upon the suicidal impulse that both twins shared and now Andrew won't.

Andrew is the crazy sibling, the outlet for the family madness. Mrs. Emerson may give vent to the family impulse for violence when she flings an ink bottle across the room and Timothy when he beheads the turkey, but only Andrew would attempt to get revenge for Timothy's death by shooting Elizabeth. However, when he commits his act of violence, he can rest assured that his siblings will close ranks to protect him.

The three Emerson sisters are less differentiated than their brothers. At first they blur together, with names that start with the same letter. The youngest, Melissa, is a model in New York. The oldest, Mary, triggers her mother's stroke in an argument on the telephone, then dutifully nurses her out of guilt. The middle daughter, Margaret, is "moody" and prone to depression (28). At 16, Margaret eloped with a boy her parents disapproved of; however, the marriage was soon dissolved by Mrs. Emerson. Later, remarried, Margaret suffers crying jags at the memory of this first husband. From their mother's point of view, the three sisters are alike in the disorder of their lives. But at the same time each sister's identity is unique.

One scene brilliantly captures the difference in identities between Melissa and Margaret and the way they relate to each other as siblings. Margaret was planning a car trip from New York to North Carolina, ostensibly to attend Elizabeth's wedding but actually to sort through her turbulent emotions about her first marriage. Melissa insists on coming along because she wants to check out a business opportunity in Virginia. Margaret, known as the sloppy sibling in the family, is disheartened at the prospect of having to share her trip with her fastidious sister, who will insist on keeping the car windows rolled up to preserve her hairdo and will refuse to stop at Howard Johnson's, Margaret's favorite restaurant. Melissa clearly holds the power in this relationship. Margaret's thoughts revolve around how to accommodate her sister and it does not occur to her that Melissa might accede to *her* wishes.

As their trip progresses, Margaret has a marathon crying jag. However, she never does tell Melissa what she is crying about. Melissa may be her sister, but she is not the one to trust with such intimate information. In fact, Melissa's inability to sympathize seems clear in her reaction to Margaret's tears: " 'Margaret, would you *mind*?' Melissa said. 'Is this what you have planned for our whole *trip*?' " (183). The remark is wonderfully comic in the way it avoids going beneath the surface. As a sister, Melissa can be as self-centered and callous as she wishes. They do keep the windows rolled up, they eat at a restaurant Melissa approves of, and before they finish their meal, they are no longer speaking to each other.

Mrs. Emerson deplores the friction that occurs whenever her children come together. They cannot sit down together at the same table without arguing. Seemingly innocent remarks have their nasty underside and can trigger quarrels. Yet Tyler intends her readers to see the Emersons as a typical family. When Mrs. Emerson describes how her family really was behind the glass windows of the car—"all bickering, arguing, scenes, constant crisis—," Elizabeth merely responds, "I reckon *most* families work that way" (15). Matthew gives the most eloquent defense of his family in a letter to Elizabeth:

We're event-prone....Probably most families are event-prone, it's just that we make more of it. Scenes and quarrels and excitement—but that part's manufactured, just artificial stitches knitting us all together. What would we say to each other if we had to sit around in peace? I may not make scenes myself but I allow them, I go along with them....It's my way of making connection with my family. Like Andrew's peculiarities. He chose them. Every trouble he causes is just another way of talking. (153-54)

The Emersons show the paradox of the family: that siblings can feud and be loyal at the same time. It is an affirmative vision of the family that admits the dissension which so often lies beneath a surface appearance of harmony. At the same time Tyler revels in the comic aspect of family relationships, like Mrs.

Emerson's relationship with her sister Dorothy, "who was barely on speaking terms but always showed up for disasters" (110), in this case Mr. Emerson's funeral.

A darker vision of the family appears in *Dinner at the Homesick Restaurant*. When Cody, Ezra and Jenny Tull are still children, their father deserts the family. Their mother, under the strain of raising them alone, at times turns abusive. Jenny, the youngest, suffers most from this abuse. Ezra, the middle child, a clumsy, gentle boy who makes music on a whistle, is his mother's favorite. Cody, the oldest, is consumed by jealousy of his brother, whom he makes the butt of his practical jokes. Sibling rivalry gives Cody a competitive streak, a compulsive need to win, even if he has to cheat. An incorrigible troublemaker, Cody is the black sheep of the family. After they have grown up, Cody continues to be the bad son and Ezra the good son. Cody especially cannot shed his old sibling role. As a young man, he has a succession of girlfriends whom he takes from New York to Baltimore to introduce to Ezra. If they are friendly and polite to Ezra, Cody is jealous of the attention they have paid him; if they are cool to Ezra, he loses interest in them. Outwardly successful, Cody is still the same hurt sibling engaged in rivalry for his mother's love: "His ragged, dirty, unloved younger self, with failing grades, with a U in deportment, clenched his fists and howled, 'Why? Why always Ezra? Why that sissy pale goody-goody Ezra?' " (133). So rivalrous is he, that the only woman he can fall in love with is a woman Ezra loves. Ruth, a red-haired hillbilly, is not Cody's type at all, and marrying her does not make him happy. For years he avoids his family to keep Ruth away from Ezra and when he visits is suspicious and jealous of every word they exchange. Ezra's life is also devastated, since Cody's jealousy causes him to lose his one chance at love.

While *Dinner at the Homesick Restaurant* manages to end with an affirmative vision of the family, it lacks the lightness and comic tone of *The Clock Winder*. Sibling rivalry in *The Clock Winder* is a factor in Timothy's death, but the actual firing of the gun is an accident. In *Dinner at the Homesick Restaurant* the sibling rivalry that Cody feels is so consuming that it shapes his identity and drives him to marry a woman he despises just because he thinks his brother wants her too. In spite of the outer trappings of success, his life is warped by childhood resentments. He nearly wrecks his marriage and estranges his son because he cannot come to terms with the past. This is Tyler's most poignant portrait of the damaging effects of sibling rivalry.

Even when sibling relations are not the main focus of Tyler's novels, they often still play a crucial role. *Celestial Navigation* concerns the magical transformation of the life of Jeremy Pauling, gentle agoraphobe and collage artist, when love enters his life. Tyler chooses to begin Jeremy's story by describing his identity in terms of his sibling relations. The first chapter is narrated by his older sister Amanda, who along with his sister Laura, has arrived for the funeral of their mother, with whom Jeremy has lived all his life. Thus, we see Jeremy first through the eyes of his older sister, whose view of him has been molded by the sibling experience. Amanda regards her brother as a failure. She has no appreciation for his art, which she equates with a child's urge to cut and paste, something that normal people outgrow. Because he never left home, she sees him as having never grown up. He has not learned to take care of himself or to navigate in the world outside home. Relying on his mother to see to his wants, he has sealed himself away with his art and is so reclusive that he seldom leaves the house and never goes more than one block away. In contrast, Amanda considers herself "the sensible one" (2). Her personality, as it emerges, shows her to be a domineering person with a sour disposition. She is blunt, pushy and irascible. Her sister Laura, with whom she lives, is clearly accustomed to being dominated by her, but once the three siblings are reunited, Laura's allegiance quickly shifts to Jeremy, reflecting patterns of relationship established years before in childhood. Although these siblings are now middle-aged, their identities seem indelibly stamped by their sibling experience. Amanda has never recovered from the shock of being displaced by two younger siblings and as an adult continues to resent them, especially Jeremy, who was their mother's favorite. She reacted to the intrusion of the younger siblings by becoming a bully. Her sense of power resided in being the oldest. But no amount of power compensated her for feeling that she had lost her mother's love, first to Laura, "the pretty one" (26), then to Jeremy, "the youngest and smallest and weakest" (13). Laura, on the other hand, who was seven when Jeremy was born, regarded her "baby brother as some kind of super-special doll" (13). As a result, she developed an affectionate and protective attitude toward him, which carries over into adulthood. Her identification with Jeremy is clear in the way they share a whole cake for dessert, to Amanda's disgust. For her their indulgence in sweets is a sign of weak will. She fails to recognize that the roots of her barely disguised hatred of Jeremy can be traced to her own childhood resentments. She still blames him for being their mother's favorite and is still trying to exact revenge. Discovering Jeremy's agoraphobia, she promptly takes him for a walk and forces him to cross the street. She claims she is trying to help Jeremy, but of course this does not help him; it brings on an acute panic attack. Laura is not fooled by Amanda's protests that she did not mean to hurt him. According to Amanda, Jeremy has been stunted by their mother's love, which encouraged him to shelter at home and avoid the world beyond, to be a weak, dependent, needy child forever. As she remarks, "If that is what love does to you, isn't it possible that I am the most fortunate of all?" (34). But clearly she is just as stunted in her way as Jeremy is in his. As she herself admits, in all her life, she has not been loved: "I have never had a marriage proposal or a love affair or an adventure....I have been bypassed, something has been held back from me" (35).

This introductory chapter from Amanda's point of view paints a picture of Jeremy, who soon will bloom and change when he falls in love with Mary Tell. He will cease to be a lonely bachelor and become a husband and father to a lively brood of children. It also shows how empty his life could be: It could have been altogether loveless and warped, like his sister Amanda's.

Celestial Navigation is one of Tyler's few novels to have an unhappy ending. Finally Jeremy fails to sustain his new identity as husband and father.

However, the reason for this failure is not because he is an artist and must isolate himself from life in order to create art. Other artist figures in Tyler's work, like Macon Leary and Elizabeth Abbott, do connect with the Other. If Jeremy does not, the explanation lies in his sibling identity, the child he once was, the favored son of a doting mother, who singled him out as different and special.

Sibling relations have remained an abiding interest for Anne Tyler as she explores marriages and families. Even when their role is small, as in the case of Ira Moran's two dependent sisters in *Breathing Lessons*, they take on a quirky and illuminating significance. Like so many of Tyler's characters, Ira Moran has been shaped by his bond with his siblings. He has learned to be practical and competent because his sisters are not. The burden of responsibility he feels for them weighs down his life, but it also shapes him into a caring and fully human person. In the drama of human relations that unfolds in this and Tyler's other novels, sibling relations appear as one of the most basic and enduring of bonds. They illustrate the connectedness of people to the lives around them, enmeshment in the complexity and messiness of life. Brought by an accident of birth into intimate contact with his or her siblings, an individual learns the pains and joys of bonding with others.

Notes

[1]See, for example, Betts, Carroll, Gibson, Jones, Nesanovich, and Robertson.

[2]The ambivalence of the family experience in Tyler's novels has been pointed out by several critics, including Carroll (16) and Petry (27-34).

[3]Ben Joe's situation is a mirror opposite of Tyler's. She was the sole female in a family of three brothers (Tyler, "Still" 14). Like Ben Joe, she was also the oldest (Zahlan 491).

[4]As Bank and Kahn have pointed out, sibling pairs occur not only in families with two children but is a common phenomenon in multiple sibling families as well (50). In *The Tin Can Tree* James and Ansel Green, who actually belong to a family of five children, are an example of such a pair, as are Ian and Danny Bedloe in *Saint Maybe*, whose sister Claudia plays only a minor role.

[5]Tyler's use of the photograph as a symbol in this and other novels has been discussed by various critics, including Petry (46-47), Betts (32), Linton (14, 114-15) and Voelker (32-35).

Works Cited

Bank, Stephen P. and Michael D. Kahn. *The Sibling Bond.* New York: Basic Books, 1982.

Betts, Doris. "The Fiction of Anne Tyler." *Southern Quarterly* 21.4 (1983): 23-37.

Carroll, Virginia Schaefer. "The Nature of Kinship in the Novels of Anne Tyler." *The Fiction of Anne Tyler*. Ed. C. Ralph Stephens. Jackson: UP of Mississippi, 1990: 16-27.

Gibson, Mary Ellis. "Family as Fate: The Novels of Anne Tyler." *Southern Literary Journal* 15.3 (1983): 47-58.

Jones, Anne G. "Home at Last, and Homesick Again: The Ten Novels of Anne Tyler." *The Hollins Critic* 23.2 (1986): 1-14.

Linton, Karin. *The Temporal Horizon: A Study of the Theme of Time in Anne Tyler's Major Novels*. Uppsala, Sweden: Uppsala, 1989.

Nesanovich, Stella. "The Individual in the Family: Anne Tyler's *Searching for Caleb* and *Earthly Possessions*." *Southern Review* 14 (1978): 170-6.

Petry, Alice Hall. *Understanding Anne Tyler*. Columbia: U of South Carolina P, 1990.

Robertson, Mary F. "Anne Tyler: Medusa Points and Contact Points." *Contemporary American Women Writers: Narrative Strategies*. Ed. Catherine Rainwater and William J. Scheick. Lexington: UP of Kentucky, 1985: 119-52.

Tyler, Anne. *The Accidental Tourist*. 1985. New York: Berkley, 1986.

_____. *Breathing Lessons*. 1988. New York: Berkley, 1989.

_____. *Celestial Navigation*. 1974. New York: Fawcett Popular Library, 1980.

_____. *The Clock Winder*. 1972. New York: Berkley, 1983.

_____. *Dinner at the Homesick Restaurant*. 1982. New York: Berkley, 1983.

_____. *If Morning Ever Comes*. 1964. New York: Berkley, 1983.

_____. *Saint Maybe*. New York: Knopf, 1991.

_____. *Searching for Caleb*. 1975. New York: Popular Library, 1977.

_____. "Still Just Writing." *The Writer on Her Work*. Ed. Janet Sternburg. New York: Norton, 1980: 3-16.

_____. *The Tin Can Tree*. 1965. New York: Berkley, 1983.

Voelker, Joseph C. *Art and the Accidental in Anne Tyler*. Columbia: U of Missouri P, 1989.

Zahlan, Anne R. "Anne Tyler." *Fifty Southern Writers After 1900: A Bio-Bibliographical Sourcebook*. Ed. Joseph M. Flora and Robert Bain. Westport, CT: Greenwood, 1987: 491-504.

Sex, Siblings, and the Fin De Siecle

Teresa Mangum

> *"They call us the Heavenly Twins."*
> *"What, signs of the Zodiac?* . . .
> *"No, signs of the times. . . . "*
> (Grand 383)

In 1893, after leaving her husband, moving to London, and searching three years for a publisher, Frances Bellenden Clarke (who soon christened herself Sarah Grand) finally persuaded one of London's more daring publishers, William Heinemann, to take a chance on her three-volume, multi-plot novel, *The Heavenly Twins*. In the first year alone, Heinemann's reprinted the novel six times, selling nearly 20,000 copies in Britain, while Cassell's sold five times as many copies of the American edition. The novel influenced the literati as well as the paparazzi; Robert Rowlette links Grand's novel to Mark Twain's *Puddn'head Wilson*, and Stanley Weintraub notes George Bernard Shaw's tributes to Grand in his reviews as well as in his play, *You Never Can Tell*.

The three plots of the novel follow three female characters from girlhood through adolescence and into the early years of their marriages. Evadne, the heroine of the first plot, is a budding intellectual who marries an older, sexually experienced military colonel. When she learns of his promiscuous past and recognizes his mental inferiority (on her wedding day), she renounces all "conjugal" sexual duties; her wedlocked despair condemns her to life at the edge of madness. Edith, the most conventional of the protagonists, naively marries a lecherous aristocrat. Her cruel initiation into marriage builds melodramatically upon the birth of her syphilitic child and an encounter with her husband's mistress and illegitimate (and infected) child and culminates in her own horrific death. Angelica, the subject of this essay, is the protagonist of the third plot. An observer of Evadne's misery and Edith's death, Angelica characteristically elbows her way through twinship, marriage, and flirtation to politics and power. Though many professional critics attacked the novel—based either on the macabre death of Edith or the nervousness and frigidity of Evadne—Grand's "heavenly" twins diabolically won a generation of readers over to the feminist polemic that dominates this early New Woman novel.

Accounts of the twins' popularity with the public read like a Barnum and Bailey publicity campaign, and their notoriety might well be attributable to showmanship as well as literary taste. Gillian Kersley recounts several apocryphal tales in her biography, *Darling Madame*. According to one story, Grand arranged for two dolls dressed as the twins to be paraded through the streets of London, and Heinemann allegedly advised a balloon salesman to paint his wares as babies and then to offer them for twopence as the Heavenly Twins (Kersley 72).

Ironically, though angry reviewers of *The Heavenly Twins* denounced Edith's and Evadne's plots as "an allopathic pill" and "a product of hysteria and willful eccentricity" or worse (quoted in Grand's Foreword to the 1923 edition of *The Heavenly Twins*), those reviewers who praised the novel also misrepresented Grand's work, for they drowned its feminist message with deafening laughter at the twins' antics. A reviewer for the *Athenaeum* applauds characters so "humorous yet true, that one feels inclined to pardon all its [the novel's] faults and give oneself up to the unreserved enjoyment of it" (March 18, 1893, 342). Even in vituperative essays, for example "The Strike of a Sex" in the *Quarterly Review*, the characters Angelica and Diavolo are excused: "the 'Heavenly Twins' play such pranks before high Heaven, as make the serious smile with undesigned amusement" (294).

Long after the first stir occasioned by the novel subsided, the twins themselves remained popular. In an 1899 *Idler*, above the caption "Famous Book-Covers as they might have been," we find a parodic sketch of the twins by T.E. Donnison (January, 1899, 703). Still later, in 1938, Amy Cruse recalls in *After the Victorians* that

it created one of the greatest sensations of literature; it certainly caused tremendous excitement in the ranks of the Feminists and the Anti-Feminists, and the upholders of the new and the old morality. The general public read it with interest and pleasure, mainly because of the pranks of the irrepressible twins, Angela and Diavolo. These two formed the chief attraction of the story, and 'the Heavenly twins' came into common use to denote any partnership in fun and mischief. (130)

The twins do serve an important comic function in an otherwise serious political novel. However, in the best tradition of comedy, their plot is at once counterpoint and underscore to the tragic fates of Edith and Evadne. Edith's body and Evadne's intellect fall victim to the forces that determined Victorian gender roles—the family, schools, the church, and the increasingly powerful medical, legal, and political institutions. The twins' comic experiments with gender-switching, even gender-blending illustrate the power of individuals to unsettle the dichotomous logic which reproduced sexual difference as gender roles, a structuring process that, as the twins' insights make clear, benefits men. Angelica's childhood pairing with her biological twin, Diavolo, inspires her unconventionality. Later, drawing upon her experience of twinship, she also uses relationships with two other characters, the mysterious "Tenor" and the man she marries, Mr. Kilroy, in her struggle to understand not only why she experiences gender largely as prohibition but what gender is.

Though twin characters frequently appear in literature, Carolyn Heilbrun notes in *Toward a Recognition of Androgyny* that opposite-sex twins seldom appear after Shakespeare until the late nineteenth-century, perhaps in response to women's increasing visibility in traditionally male arenas. She notes the

Platonic account of opposite-sex twins which presumes "an original unit which has split, a unit destined to be reunited by sexual love, the ultimate symbol of human joining" (34-5) as well as the Shakespearean pretense that opposite-sex twins could be as easily mistaken for one another as those who were identical. In "The Lost Brother, The Twin: Women Novelists and the Male-Female *Bildungsroman*," Ellen Goodman includes "psychic" twins, such as Catherine Earnshaw and Heathcliff of *Wuthering Heights*, in her analysis of twins as a device women authors used to explore the effects of education on gender identities. She finds that the structure of the *bildungsroman* breaks down when the opposite-sex twins reach adolescence, and gender roles force the twins into different lives. The terrible loss the characters experience drives the plot toward reunion and regression as the twins search for a return to childhood (30-31). Though she suggests that women writers may have used opposite-sex twins to criticize patriarchy and the gender roles it imposes, she concludes that these plots reveal that "only art can heal the fragmentation of these characters by patriarchal society" (42).

The twins in Grand's novel raise many of these same questions and possibilities; however, the twins demand a surprising degree of control over their "gendering," by controlling how they *look*, in both senses of the word. By dictating the terms of their education, they control how they will look *at* others. Moreover, in the best Shakespearean style they put gender on and off not like, but as, clothing, thus controlling how they are looked at *by* others.

As children, Angelica and Diavolo frequently escape prescribed sexual categories by slyly slipping in and out of behaviors society labels as masculine and feminine, as a consequence of being twins. Angelica first rebels against the constraints of femininity when her parents hire a tutor for Diavolo and a governess for her. Unlike Diavolo, Angelica has an active, curious mind and a determination to learn. She receives the education Evadne and Edith are denied because she has developed such confidence from her upbringing as a twin that she holds to her convictions and demands that she and her brother continue to share life's experiences equitably. As the narrator wryly explains, "she was consumed by the rage to know, and insisted upon dragging Diavolo on with her" (126). When the twins are separated, they launch a campaign (under Angelica's direction) to break the educational barrier. True to their gender-reversed behaviors, Diavolo hesitantly asks, "Do we like having different teachers," and Angelica resolutely responds, "No, we don't" (123). First, they do one another's homework; next, they simply exchange places: Angelica appears before the tutor and Diavolo before the governess. In an 1890's revision of Catherine Earnshaw's famous speech, Angelica finally informs the tutor:

there must have been some mistake. Diavolo and I find that we were mixed somehow wrong, and I got his mind and he got mine. I can do his lessons quite easily, but I can't do my own; and he can do mine, but he can't do his.... It's like this, you see. I can't learn from a lady, and he can't learn from a man.... You don't understand twins, I expect. It's always awkward about them; there's so often something wrong. With us, you know, the fact of the matter is that *I* am Diavolo and *he* is me. (124)

Angelica's speech plays on the ambiguity of twinship. To be paired is to be split and separated, yet one cannot be a twin without "the other." When their culture (embodied by parents and friends) seeks to separate the twins along the lines of sexual difference, Angelica, often aided by Diavolo, finds increasingly daring and unconventional means to resist being positioned as feminine simply because she is female. Ultimately, parental authority gives way to cooperation. Their father, Mr. Hamilton-Wells "had recourse to a weak expedient which he had more than once successfully employed unknown to Lady Adeline. He sent for the twins, and consulted their wishes privately" (124-25). Angelica specifically states her terms, foreshadowing her determination as an adult to receive opportunities equal to men's: "it is beastly unfair...to put me off with a squeaking governess and long division, when I ought to be doing mathematics and Latin and Greek" (125). What for Evadne are silent, ineffectual conclusions become for Angelica arguments and assertions: "Men are always jeering at women in books for not being able to reason, and I'm going to learn, if there's any help in mathematics" (125). Repeatedly described as brighter, more determined, healthier, stronger, more energetic, more adventurous, and far more wicked than Diavolo, Angelica finally triumphs and joins him in his schoolroom.

Even as a child, Angelica realizes that gaining male privileges herself—in the form of a good education—may end her immediate frustrations, but will not change the world's view of women. From childhood, therefore, she assumes responsibility for Diavolo's education, according to her own lights. Most importantly, she trains Diavolo to support women's rights:

> Angelica was naturally the first to draw definite conclusions for herself, and having made up her own mind she began to instruct Diavolo. She was teaching him to respect women, for one thing; when he didn't respect them she beat him; and this made him thoughtful. (255)

Here we see one of many instances of Grand's droll humor; nevertheless, Angelica's recognition (and Grand's) that men must change before women can turn revolutionary knowledge into political practice continues to influence Angelica's relationships with men.

The novel also specifies why women require reason to see through male logic. One of the running jokes in the novel involves Angelica and Diavolo's periodic comic battles over primogeniture. When Evadne remonstrates, Angelica explains, "You see, I'm the eldest, but Diavolo's a boy, so he gets the property because of the entail, and we neither of us think it fair; so we fight for it, and whichever wins is to have it" (28). Reasoning that society believes biology is destiny, Angelica and Diavolo challenge society by unsettling destiny with disguises.

Though not specifically about twins, the recent work of critics like Judith Butler and Diana Fuss, which reconceptualizes the relation between sexuality and identity as a performance rather than a set of biologically or even socially instilled characteristics, helpfully illuminates the form of deceit—that is cross-dressing—these opposite-sex twins use to disturb the imposition of gender. Significantly, their first public gender masquerade takes place at that costume party which fixes gender as well as heterosexuality in love and in law—a wedding. To their parents' horror, the children switch clothes moments before the service:

so Angelica obtained the coveted pleasure of acting as page to Evadne, and Diavolo escaped the trouble of having to hold up her train, and managed besides to have some fun with a small but amorous boy who was to have been Angelica's pair, and who, knowing nothing of the fraud which had been perpetrated, insisted on kissing the fair Diavolo, to that young gentleman's lasting delight. (61)

In a doubled reversal, the exchange of clothing deceives the wedding party about the *sex* of each child while the exchange identifies their *gender* characteristics far more "accurately" than their "proper" clothing. In fact, the exchange reinforces the ironic reversal of the twins' characters and names; gentle Diavolo has already begun to drawl, to plead his ineptitude at mathematics, to follow the energetic and authoritative Angelica's lead. However, on the eve of Oscar Wilde's trials and Sigmund Freud's studies of infantile sexuality, the twins—because they are children—are assumed to be sexless (if not without gender), and their pranks, even Diavolo's homoerotic pleasure, amuse rather than threaten.

Grand uses the grammar of repetition to emphasize the difference between sex and gender and to address the question, is anatomy destiny? Once again the occasion is a wedding, but this time the twins, now adolescents, find that gender play no longer provides the same sense of escape and pleasure:

for the truth was that they were not as they had been. Angelica was rapidly outstripping Diavolo, as was inevitable at that age. He was still a boy, but she was verging on womanhood, and already had thoughts which did not appeal to him and moods which he could not comprehend. (150)

Though friends and family continue to treat the twins as their younger comical selves, the twins themselves experience separation in their bodies as well as their relationships. Angelica finds herself "just on the borderland, hovering between two states" (243) while Diavolo remains a child.

The crisis arises in another form of repetition, a second allusion to Emily Brönte's "psychic" twins, Heathcliff and Catherine. Once again clothing acts as the metonymic signifier of gender difference. Despite prodding by parents, aunts, and uncles, Angelica resists the marks of adult femininity: "Although she was over fifteen, she had no coquettish or womanly ways, insisted on wearing her dresses up to her knees, expressed the strongest objection to being grown-up and considered a young lady, and had never been known to look at herself in the glass" (245). Angelica's will, however, cannot subdue her body. Diavolo complains that their chief form of entertainment, fighting, is coming to an end: "you used to be hard as a nail. When I got a good hit at you it made my knuckles tingle. But now you're getting all boggy everywhere. Just look at your arms" (255). Standing before the glass together they observe their bodies: "Hers was round and white and firm...his was all hard muscle and bone" (256).

When Angelica finally concedes to her physical changes by costuming herself in adult clothes, the effect devastates Diavolo. His tutor discovers him, like Heathcliff before him, sobbing out his sense of exclusion. And, like Catherine, Angelica seeks him out in their secret retreat, significantly amidst "old books and playthings" (274) with "her hair down, and in the shortest and oldest dress she possessed" (275). True to the comic quality of their relationship, the twins analyze their differences and absorb change rather than dooming themselves to fantasizes of regression in the manner of Bronte's tragic "twins." Reassured that sexual difference does not necessitate gender division, Diavolo exasperatedly acknowledges the absurdity of the dress Angelica has outgrown.

Angelica's compromise with the changes society demands as visible symbol of her femininity reassures both twins. She decides, "Well, if I *do* wear a long one...it shall only be a disguise. I promise you I'll be just as bad as ever in it" (275). She also offers the possibility that even biological symptoms of sex difference may be disguise rather than destiny. Noting that Diavolo will also soon feel the pressures of adolescence—"You'll get a moustache in time"—she offers what we can read as a double entendre, by way of a solution: "But when it comes it will make you look as much grown up as my long dresses do me, and then we'll study some art and practice it together, and not be separated all our lives" (276). On one hand, both children have aspirations to be musicians, a form of art Angelica will later insist requires a union of both sexes in one person. On the other, the twins' experiences in cross-dressing and disguise teach Angelica the arts she'll require to survive the conflicts adolescence provokes from without as well as within.

Grand presents female adolescence as a miserable montage of moods, disappointments, confusion, and conflicts with adult authority. In itself this description sounds both normal and "realistic"; in relation to the traditional Victorian heroine, Angelica's angry awkwardness is unusual. The novel attributes Angelica's behavior to hard-won knowledge—that comes with puberty—of the dangers men pose to the female body, rather than to a failure of femininity. Elaine Showalter's essay, "Syphilis, Sex, and the Fiction of the Fin de Siecle" points out that in the popular Victorian imagination, syphilis was generally associated with its last phases—insanity and paralysis. Grand draws upon the public's fear to dramatize the vulnerability of women to men. The secret at the heart of *The Heavenly Twins* is that patriarchy disciplines women through sexual exploitation and abuse of the female body—structuring physical difference as social hierarchy—whether that body belongs to an upper-class, respectable woman or to a prostitute. When Angelica is goaded into her adolescent experiments with gender disguise, the playful antics of childhood become a daring venture into the "masculine" sphere, after she learns how dangerous the world is to women who have not learned what men see when they look at women.

Edith's mad, melodramatic death of syphilis—precisely at the center of the novel and the heart of all three of the novel's plots—shifts the register from entertainment to imperative. In her article "'Helpless and Unfriended': Nineteenth Century Domestic Melodrama," Martha Vicinus shows that melodrama provided "a psychological touchstone for the powerless" (128), offering "consolation and hope without denying the social reality that makes goodness and justice so fragile" (137). The melodramatic style of Edith's death cruelly forces Angelica's development, but it also provides a fantastic context in which Angelica can protest the social reality of venereal disease in prophetic, mythic terms that would violate the norms of domestic realism.

To Angelica, Edith's death signifies sexual difference and sexual abuse. Angelica witnesses Edith's ravings when she inopportunely arrives for a visit (her absence from home is calculated to punish her family for their threats to separate her from her twin). Confronted with the horrors of Edith's death, Angelica has what Norma Clarke calls "an epic dream" (100). The dream opens with the shadowy form of a lover; Angelica senses that "if their two lights could be added in equal parts to each other and mingled into one, their combined effulgence would make a pathway to heaven" (294). When the phantom materializes into an unnamed figure and kisses her, she knows "love" for the first time. This perfect union—of lovers? of twins?—is prevented by "a chorus of men from earth" who begin to shout, "You're beginning to know too much. You'll want to be paid for your labour next just as well as we are, and that is *unwomanly*" (294). As she watches, her lover turns into a series of legendary heroes, while a group of women begin dividing Solomon among them, "cherishing the little bits in the Woman's Sphere of their day...." Angelica refuses her portion, demanding all or nothing, which infuriates the choric males who evolve into various cardinals and the pope. "Slamm[ing] the doors of the Sphere in his face," Angelica leads the women in revolt as the men are reduced to peering through the keyhole. Together, the women begin "revising the moral laws" as Angelica "arm[s] herself with the vulgar vernacular, which was the best weapon, she understood, to level cant" (295).

In her gender-blending role as twin, Angelica can be the heroine or the hero—whatever she needs to be in order to "save" these women. For support, the women call on their saints, the popular women writers Ouida and Rhoda Broughton. When the men declare the women "UNWOMANLY" and abandon them, Angelica finds that she has only confused the women and realizes she will have to save them in spite of themselves. Rejecting the self-abnegating role of "Esther," she turns, instead, into one heroine after another—Judith, Jael, Vashti, Godiva, "all the heroic women of all the ages rolled into one, not for the shedding of blood, but for the saving of suffering" (297). However, when Angelica turns to address the crowd, she finds "men, women, and children crowding like loathsome maggots together" and wakes crying " 'All this filth will breed a pestilence....and I shouldn't be surprised if that pestilence were ME!' " (296). Perhaps her flexibility in donning and discarding gender roles as part of her play with Diavolo suggests Angelica's shape-shifting powers in her dream. Interestingly, she imagines herself as the actress, Vashti, who had such a hold on the Victorian imagination, as well as Lady Godiva, who was famous for using her revealed body to demand tax relief for the poor. Yet the bodies in this dream—couched in the real nightmare of syphilis—are diseased and disgusting.

Clarke suggests that Edith's death-bed ravings, which awaken Angelica from her dream, and Angelica's violent reaction actually constitute a second part of the dream (100). I would argue that Grand indulges in a fantasy of feminist melodrama by allowing Angelica to act out the implication of her dream at the "literal" level of the plot. To escape Edith's ranting, Angelica ducks into the library, and Edith's husband, who has just arrived at the Beale's but is always on the prowl, follows her. Galvanized by the dream, Angelica takes revenge: "seizing the heavy quarto Bible from the table, she flung it with all her might full in his face. It happened to hit him on the bridge of his nose, which it broke" (301).

The dream is a far more radical attack on Grand's society than the larger novel; it marks Angelica's initiation into the cultural and personal significance of sexual difference. Fragmented images shadow forth the causes of and possible solutions to the oppression of women, as discontinuous pictures associatively reveal how gender oppression works. On the personal level, the dream links Edith's literal disease with the social body of "Woman." To be female is to be pestilent. The public references of the dream hint that church and state collaborate not to protect women, but to prevent their financial independence. More optimistically, Angelica draws courage from the epic catalogue of women writer/warriors, who represent the female literary tradition and the political space of the Women's Movement. Driven by these images, Angelica turns from the intimacy of her relationship with Diavolo to an exploration of masculinity in other guises.

Angelica's unlady-like behavior, along with several mischievous episodes which follow, convince her elders that she and Diavolo should finally be separated. When the Hamilton-Wells announce that Diavolo will attend Sandhurst and Angelica will be "brought out" at Court, she rebels. Unhinged by Edith's death and all it implies about the world's cruelty to women and frightened by the prospect of losing her brother, who is also in a sense her self, she desperately, impulsively grasps at a ritual which promises adult liberties, a ritual which she believes will provide her with another version of her twin relationship and this time one which social custom and the law will support—marriage.

To gain the protection while avoiding the responsibilities of marriage (apparently including sexual duties), she selects Mr. Kilroy, a kindly neighbor twenty years her senior, as her groom. The proposal is strikingly unconventional and violent. Storming through the woods, Angelica encounters Mr. Kilroy:

When he saw her he dismounted, and Angelica snatched the whip from his hand, and clenching her teeth gave the horse a vicious slash with it, which set him off at a gallop into the woods.

Mr. Kilroy let him go, but he was silent for some seconds, and then he asked her in his peculiarly kindly way: 'What is the matter, Angelica?'

'Marry me!' said Angelica, stamping her foot at him— 'Marry me, *and let me do exactly as I like.*' (321)

The narrator repeatedly dramatizes Angelica's futile attempts to find satisfactory freedom within marriage. Mr. Kilroy remains kind in the face of Angelica's moods and romps, partially because they spend most of their time apart. He holds a Parliament post in London, and Angelica insistently remains at home to avoid him.

In some ways Angelica and her husband's relationship reveals a profounder if subtler criticism of marriage than Evadne's clearly disastrous marriage to a libertine. Though Angelica possesses all that should satisfy the ambitions of ideal womanhood—a kind, caring husband, a beautiful home, wealth, position, and family—she feels miserable. Mr. Kilroy is the embodiment of masculinity in its kindest forms, but he is no Diavolo:

She was conscious of some change in herself, conscious of a racking spirit of discontent which tormented her, and of the fact that, in spite of her superabundant vitality, she had lost all zest for anything. Outwardly, and also as a matter of habit, when she was with anybody who might have noticed a change, she maintained the dignity of demeanor which she had begun to cultivate in society upon her marriage; but inwardly she raged— raged at herself, at everybody, at everything. (477-78)

Angelica's struggle replicates Evadne's, but Angelica's determination and commitment to action forestall Evadne's fate. Grand extends the analysis of marriage and womanhood begun in Edith's plot and problematized in Evadne's by suggesting an escape from the limited sphere of action in Angelica's plot. Angelica alone possesses potential for escape or resistance because she has watched the formation of gender and the systematic devaluing of women it enforces at first hand—as an opposite-sex twin.

In a conventional novel marriage marks a progression toward maturity; in a novel protesting marriage we might expect a movement toward regression. In a daring alternative twist of the plot—demarcated as a separate book and designated as an "Interlude"—Grand digresses into implausibility, a world which first escapes, then denounces the simple, hierarchal gender dichotomies that dictate the boundaries of plot and character in life as well as fiction.

As a child, Angelica has learned the delight of cross-dressing by exchanging places with Diavolo. When biological developments and social constraints impose femininity along with a female body on her in adolescence, she turns to masquerade once again, this time in resistance to the life of idleness and domesticity Diavolo escapes when he leaves for Sandhurst. For a brief, dream-like period, Angelica exists not as man or as woman, but as what Shelley called a "sexless thing," as what she calls a "bright particular spirit" (393). When her disguise is discovered, she loses the power of the triangulated third self she feels she's become—as Angelica, Diavolo, and the third "being" in between.

This interlude, which forms Book IV, constitutes the most bizarre and wonderful form of Angelica's resistance to marriage. As Gerd Bjorhovde points out, this book differs significantly in style and tone from the other books that form *The Heavenly Twins*, for Grand weaves mystery, fantasy, comedy, and poetry together in "The Tenor and the Boy." The Interlude had a special status, as indicated by its history. Grand tried to publish the piece as a separate, autonomous novel in 1890, and after the success of *The Heavenly Twins* she wrote a playscript of "The Tenor and the Boy," though it never appeared on stage (Black 318).

Angelica's gender play begins after she packs Mr. Kilroy off to his Parliamentary responsibilities in London. Restless and bored, s/he roams the streets of Morningquest at night in men's clothes and a blonde wig. As Angelica, she hears the Tenor sing in church; that same evening s/he encounters the Tenor in the market square, masquerading as Diavolo. S/he adopts the Tenor as an older brother, pestering him, haranguing him, debating the position of women with him, and delighting in a friendship with a man who treats her as an equal. The oddest feature of their friendship is that the Tenor adores the "real" Angelica from afar—based solely on his vision of her in church—and the "Boy" teases him unmercifully, first fueling the Tenor's infatuation, then puncturing the romance with stories of "Angelica's" temper and eccentricities. The narrator explains, "He saw in the girl an ideal, and had found soul enough in the laughter-loving Boy to make him eager to befriend him" (385). As the Boy, Angelica plies the Tenor with innuendoes and clues to which he remains oblivious, despite the Tenor's remarks about his/her effeminacy, girlishness, unshapely head, and vampirish tendency to appear only at night.

The Tenor attributes the Boy's strangeness as well as his "genius" to "androgyny," quoting from "The Witch of Atlas":

> A sexless thing it was, and in its growth
> It seemed to have developed no defect
> Of either sex, yet all the grace of both. (403)

The Boy's correction—he argues that "genius" is a matter of intellect, "the attributes of both minds, masculine and feminine, perfectly united in one person of either *sex*" (403)—confutes the Tenor's assumption that genius is a sex-characteristic or that sex is a physical defect and so further disengages *gender* from *sex*. Gender ceases to be male and female; instead, it becomes a costume, a set of characteristics, flexible relations, a point of view.

The moment of unmasking exposes not only Angelica, but also the tremendous anxiety provoked when sexual identities are unsettled. The Tenor feels horrified, shocked, repulsed, abused, and deceived, especially when Angelica fights to keep her newfound pleasures even though she has lost her disguise. To his surprise, she blames her dilemma on his lack of imagination and open-mindedness as much as on her own deceitfulness. First, she describes the joyful freedom from "the restraint of our tight uncomfortable clothing"

(456). Next, she defends herself through analogy, arguing that if George Sand and the legendary female doctor, James Barry, could pass as men, so can she. Finally, she throws the Tenor into utter confusion when he unhappily seeks to resolve what he perceives to be their problem—i.e. her fall from respectability—by asking her to marry him. He can only interpret cross-dressing as a strategy to entrap a man rather than a means of escaping male desire:

The charm...has all been in the delight of associating with a man intimately who did not know I was a woman.... Had you known that I was a woman—even you—the pleasure of your companionship would have been spoilt for me, so unwholesomely is the imagination of a man affected by ideas of sex. The fault is in your training; you are all of you educated deliberately to think of women chiefly as the opposite sex. (458)

The equation between sexual desire and immorality, even illness, sounds conservative, perhaps. Grand probably did not think so since she became a supporter of the Social Purity movement a few years later. In any case, juxtaposed with the predictable structures of romance, this turn of the plot is certainly innovative. Here we see a married woman, dressed as a man, rejecting an idealized lover, and finally growing exasperated with his predictable behavior even under such fantastic circumstances. When the Tenor silently reproves her, Angelica flashes back at him,

If you are deceived in me you have deceived yourself.... You go and fall in love with a girl you have never spoken to in your life, you endow her gratuitously with all the virtues you admire without asking if she cares to possess them; and when you find she is not the peerless perfection you require her to be, you blame her! oh! isn't that like a man? (459)

Stunned and uncomprehending, the Tenor escorts her home through the rain, then conveniently dies of pneumonia. Perhaps Grand so feared capitulation to romance (or so dreaded untangling Angelica from this embedded plot) that she had to kill off the potential lover. Refreshingly, Angelica soon recovers from his death. Though his parting words, "you will be a good woman yet" (462), encourage her to live more purposefully, she never succumbs to guilt or self-abnegation. (Perhaps this last detail, above all, marks this segment of the novel as fantasy.)

"The Tenor and the Boy" interlude is motivated by a longing for alternative relationships which would permit honest, unself-conscious, non-hierarchical friendships between men and women that sexual division too often prevents. The relationship Angelica-as-boy forms with a musician (the gender affiliation of artists also being suspect), on the basis of his fantasies about Angelica-as-girl, blurs conventional boundaries between heterosexuality and homosexuality. Grand's audience countered the homoeroticism by calling her men hopelessly effeminate, ineffectual, and lifeless. (For example, see "The Strike of the Sex," as well as recent articles by Showalter, Cunningham, and Clarke.) Yet, we can read this same "confusion" or "weakness" as deliberate undermining of the dichotomous logic that organizes social roles and privileges as the oppositional and hierarchical consequences of neatly dividing people into two sexes: Angelica insists that she has become a third, resistant being.

What does this disruption accomplish? In part, Angelica's disguises enact the drama of femininity—the secret, self-creating self that moves and speaks openly, but only in the dreamlike world of night versus the flattened character who exists in daylight only as a vision. Or, this self-divisiveness may dramatize the alienation of women who can imagine themselves only as objects of the male gaze (as Laura Mulvey's early work in film spectatorship suggested). Most importantly, through her cross-dressing, Angelica appropriates the gaze and shares it with her readers—and with sight comes speech.

Having seen the world with a man and as a man, Angelica finally understands the message of her earlier dream. As she sits in her grandfather's centuries old home, grieving over the tenor, she envisions the series of male inheritors, including her grandfather and her brother, who will share "the horrible monotony" of patriarchal ownership. But now the patriarchy is under siege by women with her vision:

the vulgar outcome of a vulgar era, bred so, I suppose, that I may see through others, which is to me the means of self-defense. I see that in this dispute of 'womanly' or 'unwomanly,' the question to be asked is, not 'What is the pursuit?' but 'What are the proceeds?' No social law-maker ever *said* 'Catch me letting a woman into anything that pays!' It was left for me to translate the principle into the vernacular. (534)

Her childhood struggles with Diavolo over family property, her family's refusal to grant her a career, and everyone's insistence that Diavolo live up to his masculine responsibilities and Angelica subside into her feminine duties suddenly all coalesce into a political vision that gives Angelica's life, even her marriage, purpose. Her dream reveals that women's words have transformative power and offers "the vernacular" as a tool of resistance against the mysteries of the clergy.

Once Angelica sees what men see, she translates the masculinist codes she's discovered into a political strategy. Having learned that clothes make the woman a man, she reconciles herself to marriage by consciously adopting a new disguise as "wife." In reality, she spends the rest of the novel (and of Grand's next novel, *The Beth Book*) writing speeches on behalf of women which her husband delivers as a willing mouthpiece. In effect, Angelica once again disguises herself as a man, but this time she becomes, one removed, a nearly invisible spy—a sober, kindly, elder statesman—in Parliament.

In the late nineteenth century, as independent women took to bicycles, athletics, protest lines, and militant pro-suffrage activities and decadent men embraced ennui, foppish clothing, and sexual experimentation, opposite-sex twins embodied the confusion, the potential liberation, and the dangers of resisting sexual polarities. Grand's novel *The Heavenly Twins* is an important representation of both the promise and the limitations of seeking personal autonomy through the corporeal rather than the political body. Perhaps we can read Angelica as Grand's double since both worked resolvedly and successfully to change their worlds through the medium of language. Just as Grand worked out her political plots in fiction, Angelica pens the speeches for her "character"—in Angelica's case, her husband—trusting her words to inspire the psychological, social, and legal changes still largely located in fantasy at the end of the nineteenth century.

Works Cited

Bjorhovde, Gerd. *Rebellious Structures: Women Writers and the Crisis of the Novel, 1880-1900*. Oslo: Norwegian P, 1987.

Black, Helen. *Notable Women Authors of the Day*. 1893. Reprint. Freeport, N.Y.: Books for Libraries P, 1972.

Butler, Judith. *Gender Trouble: Feminism and the Subversion of Identity*. New York: Routledge, 1990.

Clarke, Norma. "Feminism and the Popular Novel of the 1890's: A Brief Consideration of a Forgotten Novelist." *Feminist Review* 20 (1985): 91-104.

Cruse, Amy. *After the Victorians*. London: Allen and Unwin, 1938.

Cunningham, Gail. *The New Woman and the Victorian Novel*. London: Macmillan, 1978.

Donnison, T.E. "Famous Book-Covers as They Might Have Been." *The Idler* 14 (1899): 703.

Fuss, Diana. *Essentially Speaking: Feminism, Nature, and Difference*. New York: Routledge, 1989.

Goodman, Ellen. "The Lost Brother, The Twin: Women Novelists and the Male-Female *Bildungsroman*." *Novel* 17 (1983): 28-43.

Grand, Sarah [Frances Bellenden Clarke McFall]. *The Heavenly Twins*. Privately printed, 1892. 3 vols. London: Heinemann, 1893.

Rev. of *The Heavenly Twins*. *The Athenaeum*. Mar. 18, 1893: 342.

Heilbrun, Carolyn. *Toward a Recognition of Androgyny*. New York: Alfred A. Knopf, 1973.

Kersley, Gillian. *Darling Madame: Sarah Grand and Devoted Friend*. London: Virago, 1983.

Mulvey, Laura. *Visual and Other Pleasures*. Bloomington: Indiana UP, 1989.

Rowlette, Robert. "Mark Twain, Sarah Grand, and *The Heavenly Twins*." *The Mark Twain Journal* 16 (1972): 17-18.

Showalter, Elaine. "Syphilis, Sexuality, and the Fiction of the Fin de Siecle." *Sex, Politics, and Science in the Nineteenth Century Novel*. Ed. Ruth Yeazell. Baltimore: Johns Hopkins UP, 1986: 95-108.

"Strike of a Sex." *The Quarterly Review* 179 (1894): 289-318.

Vicinus, Martha. " 'Helpless and Unfriended': Nineteenth-Century Melodrama." *New Literary History* 13 (1981): 127-43.

Weintraub, Stanley. "George Bernard Shaw Borrows from Sarah Grand: *The Heavenly Twins* and *You Never Can Tell*." *Modern Drama* 14 (1971): 288-97.

The Circles of Ran and Eugene MacLain: Welty's Twin Plots in *The Golden Apples*

Allison Pingree

"How much might depend on people's being linked together?"

Early in Eudora Welty's *The Golden Apples,* her narrator probes how two characters—Miss Eckhart, the German piano teacher, and Virgie Rainey, her student—become tied together by the surveillance and gossip of the surrounding community:

> Perhaps nobody wanted Virgie Rainey to be anything in Morgana any more than they had wanted Miss Eckhart to be, and they were the two of them still linked together by people's saying that. How much might depend on people's being linked together? Even Miss Snowdie had a little harder time than she had had already with Ran and Scooter, her bad boys, by being linked with roomers and music lessons and Germans. (63)

In Morgana, Mississippi, "links" between people do have large social consequences, and the particular bond between Ran and "Scooter" (Eugene) MacLain, Snowdie's sons, is no exception. But these brothers' connection is fashioned out of more than gossip: as identical[1] twin brothers, they share the same genetic composition, in addition to the other attachments common to all siblings. Identical twins are born at the same time, and, in a sense, with the same body; consequently, they live with a keen sense of simultaneity, and are often forced to share (or compete for) the same cultural space.

Some readers might ascribe Welty's use of identical twins to her larger preoccupation with duality, for patterns of doubling are very common in her work. *The Golden Apples* is no exception, as it abounds with a variety of pairs; for example, Katie Rainey remembers that "the day had a two-way look" (17); " 'opponents doubling' " and " 'two-suited' " hands play into Miss Lizzie's card game (170); and the narrator in "Music From Spain" recounts that "two homemade kites...nodded like gossips" (213) and that "sea gulls...must be two varieties of birdkind, or the birds themselves must have two lives" (218). Duality emerges, too, in Virgie Rainey's life philosophy—her conviction that "all the opposites on earth were close together...unrecognizable one from the other sometimes, making moments double upon themselves, and in the doubling double again, amending but never taking back" (265). Finally, Welty refers to doubles in her description of the narrative act itself: "[the writer] is always seeing double, two pictures at once in his frame, his and the world's..." (*Eye of*

Story 125). As a general category of vision and experience, then, "doubling" is indeed prolific in Welty's writing.

While it is undoubtedly true that literal twins fit loosely into this broad category of "doubling," I believe that Welty's narratives in *The Golden Apples* grant them a status that is distinct—one which stems, paradoxically, from their very indistinguishability. But few Welty scholars have noted this difference. Rather, they group twinship (if they mention it at all) with other brands of duality, instead of probing its peculiarities.

For example, Carey Wall's analysis of liminality, doubling and oppositions makes no mention of the twins; this is partly due to Wall's focus on "June Recital," but her observations could be strengthened by considering twinship's complexities. While the title of another essay, J.A. Bryant's "Seeing Double in *The Golden Apples*" seems promising, Bryant actually does not address twinship at all (and doubleness *per se* very little); he focuses, rather, on the role of wanderers in the stories. Susan Donaldson's study of Welty's strategies for "recovering otherness" includes a survey of how various double figures break down the conformity of Morganan society. But the focal pairs of her analysis—Cassie and Virgie, Mattie and King, Nina and Easter, Eugene and the Spaniard—do not lead her to explore twinship, and she thus ignores a relationship that implicates sameness and difference in ways fruitful to her argument.

Peter Schmidt comes closest to looking at the specific dynamics of the twins' lives when he posits that Ran and Eugene's twinship "makes the evidence for the psychological problems even more intriguing....[T]hey experience many of the same neuroses, implying that the deepest causes of their problems indeed lie in their childhood" (64). But Schmidt's subsequent analysis never gives twinship itself another look, and instead reads Ran and Eugene's traumas as Oedipal struggles with both parents. In short, the uncanny power of Ran and Eugene MacLain's twinship has been essentially overlooked in Welty scholarship. While readers often mention the two characters together, and analyze each on his own, none has used the particularities of twinship as a lens through which to access a fresh perspective on *The Golden Apples*.

One indication that twins occupy an unusual position in the collection is the fact that Ran and Eugene's bond is treated with much more intensity than any other sibling relationship in the text. In fact, the only other sibling tie that receives any significant attention is that between Cassie and Loch Morrison. While as children, this brother and sister share an affection similar to twinship's intimacy (they "loved each other in a different world, a boundless, trustful country all its own" [27]), that early bond is "different altogether" from the "solitary world now" in which each lives (28). Welty makes that separation clear in narrative terms, as Loch and Cassie present radically different points of view in "June Recital," and later, when Loch escapes to New York City (261), to a "life of [his] own" (272), while Cassie stays behind.

In contrast, because of their unique connection, twins can never truly escape to a "life of their own." As we shall see, even the extreme geographical distance that comes between Ran and Eugene does not—and cannot—erase the bonds that they share. The union between these identical twins is potent, and the narrative elements depicting them reflect that extremity. Indeed, these twins—different from the general category of doubles, and from other sibling relationships—offer an alternative reading of many cultural myths. One of the most striking revisions results when twinship is brought to bear on the long-standing trope of romantic love as a search for one's "other half."

This image derives from a section of Plato's *Symposium*, where Aristophanes proposes that "the primeval man was round, his back and sides forming a circle; and he had four hands and four feet..." The two faces on these creatures looked (prescient of identical twins) "precisely alike." These circular, primitive people were mighty and strong, so much so that the gods felt threatened, prompting Zeus to " 'cut them in two' " so they would be " 'diminished in strength and increased in numbers' " (354). Thus, the smaller, weaker beings that resulted were, in actuality, "halves"—and thus began the search:

...so ancient is the desire of one another which is implanted in us, reuniting our original nature, making one of two, and healing the state of man. Each of us when separated, having one side only, like a flat fish, is but the indenture of a man and he is always looking for his other half. (355)

As this ancient myth has been received in later periods, it most often is appropriated as a metaphor of the quest for romantic (and usually heterosexual) love, such as in Shelley's "Epipsychidion." But identical twins, in fact, present a more direct embodiment of the myth, for they are more truly each other's "halves": they are literally split from the same egg, and, in the case of conjoined twins, their physical ligature actually creates the "idealized" state of the two-headed, four-limbed primitive man. Thus, twins more truly complete each others' "circle," two "flat" figures coming together into one round.

Just as twins literalize and also complicate the notion of "finding one's other half," so do they give new meaning to other notions and phrases that appear in Welty's text. In fact, the very roundness of Aristophanes' primitive man emerges in other images of the closeness of twins. In *The Golden Apples*, circles—shapes that have thematic and narrative uses within the stories themselves—come to represent the philosophical puzzle of identity which lies in the surreal and curious closeness of twins.

"A Thing of the Flesh Is [An] Endless Circle"
In the title itself, Welty's book uses circular shapes. Moreover, as Thomas McHaney notes, "it is *cycle*, as subject, as allusion, and as form, that is repeatedly drawn into the reader's presence" (187) by *The Golden Apples*. Indeed, the stories end close to where they begin, in autumn, at the Rainey home, with Katie Rainey as a central figure—around and through whom we observe the other inhabitants of Morgana.

Moreover, circularity marks Morgana's claustrophobic social world of sewing circles, bridge games, and wedding rings—all of which are mediated through circuits of gossip and rumor. As Mrs. Stark comments, the talk of the town is embodied in just such a shape: "Waiting, she heard *circling* her ears like the swallows beginning, talk about lovers. *Circle* by *circle* it twittered, church talk, talk in the store and post office, vulgar man talk possibly in the barbershop" (233, emphasis mine). Similarly, Perdita Mayo uses the word "circle" to describe her friends; indeed, this group seems to have so much power that the figure itself takes on a life of its own, as evidenced in her description of it: "My Circle declares.... I told my Circle, [it] won't last" (165).

Within this context, Perdita asks a question which, while referring specifically to an extramarital affair, actually describes the larger ring of Morganan life: "how could you all get away from each other if you tried? You couldn't.... It's an endless circle. That's what a thing of the flesh is, endless circle. And you won't get away from that in Morgana" (165). Indeed, an illicit affair would be an item enticing enough, in this voyeuristic community, to place the lovers in an "endless circle" of blame and tarnished reputation. More remarkable, though, is how Perdita's claims are even truer for Ran and Eugene. Each detailed use of this phrase takes on new meaning when seen in the light of twinship: twins most obviously share a "thing of the flesh" because of their replicated genes; their bond is "endless" because, unlike living in Morgana, one can never consent to—or completely escape from—being a twin; finally, their relationship is a "circle" in the way that the identity of one twin merges easily into that of the other, creating a cycle in which each occupies the structural space of the other.

Within this slipperiness of individual identity, every notion of reputation or accountability acquires new, more intricate valences. In fact, with identical twins, our most basic assumptions about individual agency are called into question. If twins occupy the same cultural space, both or neither must be blamed or praised. Indeed, in a legal context, *visual* identification becomes vexed where twins are involved, for how can a witness be sure an act was committed by a particular person—and not his or her twin? Bluntly put, if we cannot tell who is who, how can we know who is responsible for what?

The circles which Welty ascribes to the MacLain twins enact these puzzles of confused and interchangeable identity and accountability. The first circle they create, in "Shower of Gold," surrounds their own father, King, who has abandoned his family for a life of wandering and philandering, and who unexpectedly visits one Halloween. Snowdie is inside, and thus doesn't notice her husband's approach. But the boys, clad in roller skates, see him coming and respond: "they sailed out the door and *circled* around their father, flying their arms and making their fingers go scarey, and those little Buster Brown bobs going in a *circle*" (15, emphasis mine). In the middle of such a centripetal onslaught, King, a strong man of "six foot height" who "weighs like a horse" (16), is nonetheless caught. The twins are so tenacious that they are compared to "monkeys" and "cannibals in the jungle" (15):

they got their papa in their ring-around-a-rosy and he couldn't get out...And after they went around high, they crouched down and went around low, about his knees.

...King just couldn't get out quick enough. Only he had a hard time, and took him more than one try.... [H]e was confused. (15-16)

Circularity resonates here at many levels. In this group, both disguise and recognition are confounded, leaving everyone, in a sense, blind: "Skating around and around their papa, and just as ignorant! Poor little fellows" (15). This blurring occurs first, because the twins' physical resemblance makes it so hard to differentiate them. To all observers, they present a dizzying image of the same person, replicated over and over. Even Plez Morgan, who out of "anybody in Morgana" is least "likely to make a mistake in who a person is" (12), isn't certain which twin is which (15), so their father, trapped inside their circle, must feel that confusion profoundly. In fact, although in this particular moment, Ran and Eugene *can* be distinguished by the masks they wear (Ran's is of a "lady, with an almost scary-sweet smile" while Eugene's is of a "Chinaman" [12]), those very masks actually enact the confusions that they, as identical figures, create. That is, twins are *always* "masked" to the public world, their individual identities always hidden behind a screen of replication. But for the artificial differences created here by the toy masks, the MacLain boys are, both figuratively and literally, "dead *ring*ers" of each other. Similarly, to the sons, King is "masked" in the sense that they do not recognize him as their father, and instead call him "Mister Booger" (15).

The circles in "Sir Rabbit," when the little boys have grown into young adolescents, continue to mark the ambiguities of twinship. One day in the woods Ran and Eugene come upon Mattie Will, a country girl, and eagerly prod her into sexual play; using a ring that is reminiscent of the one used on their father, they ensnare her in a configuration that once again manifests a bewildering fluidity of boundaries: "They made a tinkling circle around her. They didn't give her a chance to begin her own commotion, only lifted away her hoe" (99); moreover, after the seduction, all three "sat up in a circle" and ate candy "out of one paper sack for three people" (100). The giddiness of this cyclicality stays with Mattie for years, as she later reminisces: " 'it wasn't fair to tease me. To try to make me dizzy, and run a ring around me, or make me think that first minute I was going to be carried off by their pa' " (100-01).

In this memory, Mattie seems flustered in part by the slippage of identity between King and his boys, for after all, it was their legendary father whom she had expected when she first noticed them:

If it was Mr. King, he was, suddenly, looking around both sides of the tree at once—two eyes here and two eyes there, two little Adam's apples, and all those little brown hands....

Then as she peeped, it was two MacLains that came out from behind the hickory nut tree. Mr. MacLain's twins, his sons of course. (98)

Ran and Eugene are here depicted as freakish, with multiple limbs flailing, two halves of a nut, split on either side of the hickory tree. In Mattie's mind, these imps are forever diminished in size, and seem almost like a sideshow spectacle: "Who would have believed they'd grown up?...People aren't prepared for twins having to grow up like ordinary people but see them always miniature and young somewhere" (98).

In fact, this contrast between grandiose father and his diminutive replications already has been made, subtly, in the earlier story. Fate Rainey tells Katie that on his visit to Jackson to buy her a new bucket, he sees the "spit-image" of Mr. MacLain, marching "right up with the big ones and astride a fine animal" in the Governor's inaugural parade (10). Katie mentions, simultaneously, that Fate brought back a bucket that is the "wrong size" because it is "just like the ones at Holifield's" (10-11). In a sense, Katie dislikes the new bucket because it is too much the same, too much a "twin" to the others she can buy in Morgana. Not surprisingly, Katie scoffs at her husband's claim that places King in the same mundane category of dulling replication: "But he said he saw King or his twin. *What twin!*" (11, emphasis mine). To Katie, King doesn't act like or need a twin, given his magical presence and his powerful solitude. He is not physically or genetically split, and cannot be a replication—like the bucket—of all the other commonplace men in Morgana; rather, his unique essence is *multiplied*, spawning more and more grandiose legends of majesty that run through the county.

Just as Katie's new bucket is the "wrong size" because of its utter similitude with other buckets in town, so are the twins, "halves" of each other, the "wrong size" to be like King, as in the *Symposium* the rounded creatures were kept from rivalling Zeus by being split. Thus, while the twins do bear a resemblance to King—they are called "King all over again" (9) and "the very spit of Mr. King" (98)—they are never presented as his equal. Rather, Mattie's perceptions of them highlight both their smallness, as well as their replicated, interchangeable identity.

The confusion surrounding the twins' identities emerges not only in relation to their father, but in other narrative details of the story. Personal names are never used for either boy, emphasizing Mattie's utter inability to distinguish one from the other. This linguistic blurring is paralleled by Mattie's thoughts as she romps on the grass with them:

...little matching frowns were furring their foreheads....

One of the twins took hold of her by the apron sash and the other one ran under and she was down. One of them pinned her arms and the other one jumped her bare, naked feet. Biting their lips, they sat on her...

...She felt the soft and babylike heads, and the nuzzle of little cool noses. Whose nose was whose? (99)

In this frisky circle, it is again unclear which twin is responsible for what. In fact, this fusion of blame is so acute that instead of being angry, she is distracted: "She might have felt more anger than confusion, except that *to keep twins straight* had fallen her lot" (99-100, emphasis mine). Furthermore, at one point, she sets her teeth in the ear of one, and then "dared the other twin, with her teeth at his ear, since they were all in this together, all in here equally now" (100). By the end, when one twin speaks and breaks the spell that has captivated all three of them, the circularity of identity has become so complete that she thinks: "What did it matter which twin said that word, like a little bark?" (100).

Indeed, throughout the book, Ran and Eugene are presented as comprising a single unit, especially early on, where, as Ruth Vande Kieft describes, they are "almost indistinguishable...mischievous, feebly disciplined little monkeys" (104). For instance, after the piano recital, even though presumably Eugene has just performed and Ran hasn't (since "he and not Ran" took lessons [203]), the emphasis is on their sameness: "The MacLain twins, now crashing restraint, rushed downstairs in identical cowboy suits, pointing and even firing cap pistols" (74). Similarly, when they are older, Loch cannot distinguish them as he watches Cassie's friends visit the house: "Ran MacLain...or was it his brother Eugene, always called to Mrs. Morrison, teasing..." (95).

Thus, the "thing of the flesh" that ties Ran and Eugene together traps them into "endless circles" of fused, miniaturized identity. Moreover, this flux of boundaries transforms traditionally stable categories of individual agency and responsibility into a flowing continuum. In the stories of the twins' adult lives, "The Whole World Knows" and "Music From Spain," this instability continues, particularly (and not surprisingly) within the worlds each man shares with his wife, his *conjugal* (and inadequate) "other half."

"A Fault Of Course Lay All Through the Land"

Late in "Music from Spain," Welty gives a vivid description of the San Francisco shoreline: "Here and there a boulder had lately fallen and lay in [the] path wet within its fissures...it was sandy and grassy and very wild. A fault of course lay all through the land" (219). Like this beach, the city of San Francisco itself, where Eugene lives, is "very wild" and teems with "fissures." First of all, the city is ethnically and demographically diverse; during the day, Eugene encounters Filipino waiters (200), a "Negro" with a "fan of hair" (209), the sounds of a comedian speaking French (211), a "sprawled old winehead" (212), nuns looking "indestructible as smokestacks" (212), an "old Chinese gentleman" with a "wispy white beard" (213), and a "Negro or Polynesian" woman who is "marked as a butterfly" with "scrolls" of birthmarks (197). Moreover, the city's spatial and geographic configurations are fluid and schismatic; San Francisco is known for its hills, its crooked streets, and its fires and earthquakes, all of which counter any sense of stable boundaries.

But Welty's allusion to "faults" describes more than just the city's geological history; this phrase, too, spawns multiple meanings when applied to the twins' plight. Given the ways in which agency is diffused in their circling, their "fault" (blame) is indeed spread out, "all through the land." In fact, in "The Whole World Knows" and "Music From Spain" this shared "fault" paradoxically exists despite another "fault" (fissure)—the twins' physical separation, with one in Mississippi and the other in California.

This geographical distance does not keep them from thinking of each other. For instance, San Francisco awakens in Eugene a "longing" for "the winter swamp where his own twin brother, he supposed, still hunted" (191). Ran, too, muses about his twin: "Eugene's safe in California, that's what we think" (158). Others in Morgana also continue to view the brothers, even when adult, as inextricably connected. Perdita Mayo, for example, conjectures that "Ran will kill somebody," especially with "Eugene gone that could sometimes hold him down" (163). She also ruminates: "Who else in Morgana would there be for Jinny Stark after Ran, with even Eugene MacLain gone?" (162), implying that a woman who fit with one twin might be equally well-matched with the other. Snowdie, too, continues to see her sons as a single unit, telling Ran:

If you were back under my roof...if Eugene hadn't gone away too. He's gone and you won't listen to anybody.... The Lord never meant us all to separate. To go and be cut off. One from the other, off in some little room. (172)

The mutual "fault" or culpability that the men *share*, as twins, as well as the "fault" which *separates* them make it all the more difficult for Ran to establish balanced relationships with his wife Jinny, and others. Indeed, the way he responds to his wife's infidelity only plays out the patterns of replication which twinship embodies. For instance, Ran finds a "twin" of Jinny in Maideen Sumrall, who "looked like Jinny...[and] was a child's copy of Jinny...there was something of Maideen in Jinny's [face], that went back early—to whatever I knew my Jinny would never be now" (163). Ran uses his wife's "twin" to assuage his anger and misery, as well as to avenge: he parades Maideen around in Jinny's house, and then takes the young girl on a wild ride, ending in a cheap country motel, where he eventually pulls a gun on her. It is clear that her close resemblance to Jinny re-surfaces for Ran as he faces Maideen, because when he does, "[f]or a minute I saw her *double*. But I pointed the gun at her the best I could" (180, emphasis mine). Ran eventually turns that gun towards himself, in a suicide attempt which is unsuccessful. His aim at Jinny's "twin" is eventually followed through, though, as Maideen later kills herself (181, 238).

Not only does Ran create and then destroy Jinny's twin, he also fantasizes about hurting Woody Spights, the man Jinny has inserted into *his* place as her lover, and who thus temporarily "twins" *him*: "Then I beat on him. I went over his whole length, and cracked his head apart...beat on him without stopping till every bone, all the way down to the numerous little bones in the foot, was cracked in two" (167). These images of splitting, cracking and division underscore the sense of halfness that Ran has had to live with all his life as a twin.

In "Music From Spain," we see Eugene similarly infected by his twinship. Throughout the story, as he continually chastises himself for slapping his wife Emma at breakfast, he transposes his internal agitation onto the external world—a strategy which again recalls the blurred sense of culpability that his twinship fosters. This haziness is, at times, figured forth in images within Eugene's mind that are sometimes frightening, sometimes alluring. For example, he thinks at one point that

it would be terrifying if walls, even walls of Emma's and his room, the walls of whatever room it was that closed a person in in the evening, would go soft as curtains and begin to tremble. If like the curtains of the aurora borealis the walls of rooms would give even the illusion of lifting—if they would threaten to go up. (202)

Eugene is obsessed with the flow and instability of boundaries; he yearns for bonding, yet also dreads the chaos—akin to the "death of volition" he felt when earlier in his life he "once nearly drowned" (220)—that such fluidity brings.

Within this flux of boundaries, Eugene continually envisions replications of his wife in the cityscape around him. This extended "twinning" recalls Ran's association with Maideen, except that with Eugene, the clones are mass-produced and mechanical—indicative of the urban climate in which he lives. First of all, Eugene fantasizes about "Miss Dimdummie Dumwiddie," a woman whom he only knows from a newspaper photograph:

[A] face from nowhere floated straight into that helpless irony and contemplated the world of his inward gaze, a dark full-face, obscure and obedient-looking as a newsprint face, looking outward from its cap of dark hair and a dark background—all shadow and softness, like a blurred spot on Jones Street. (186)

Eugene then encounters a more harsh—and more direct—substitution of Emma as he passes the shouts of ticketmen crowing " 'Have—you—seen—Em-ma?' " The attraction they are touting is an "enormously fat" woman with "small features bunched like a paper of violets in the center of her face"; this sideshow Emma is a grotesque yet curiously similar version of her namesake in that she, too, gives a certain look in her "crushed, pushed-together countenance"— "accusation, of course" (198), thus reminding Eugene once again of his "fault." A final image that he sees, at a deserted fun house, of a "shouting mechanical dummy of a woman, larger than life" (216), similarly acts as a mocking, mechanical replacement of Emma.

Instead of obscuring blame, *these* "twins" heighten Eugene's keen sense of culpability, as they give physical form to his self-questioning that pervades the story. In fact, he reprimands himself at least five times for the slap during the course of the narrative, so it is not surprising when those very confrontations also materialize in the atmosphere around him:

Why…had he struck Emma? His act—with that, proving it had been a part of him— slipped loose from him, turned around and looked at him in the form of a question. At Sacramento Street it skirted through traffic beside him in sudden dependency, almost like a comedian pretending to be an old man. (184)

In this moment, his "fault" becomes an alter-ego, a twin being which is dependent on him, yet also concrete enough to stand apart and indict him. This evolution of the abstract questioning into a concrete personage continues, Welty suggests, even until the end of Eugene's life, when he still feels pursued: "[he] seemed to hesitate on the street of Morgana, hold averted, *anticipating questions*" (273, emphasis mine).

Eugene's transference of guilt takes its most obvious form when he encounters the Spanish guitarist he and his wife had heard the night before. Eugene recognizes the musician from far away and thinks his detection is "clever": "Eugene had no doubts about that identity.... He could not think of the Spaniard's name, but it was pretty observant the way he recognized the man at this distance and from the back, after seeing him only the one time..." (193). Eugene's pride in having "no doubts about that identity" evokes the instability that has surrounded his own individuality as a twin.

As the two meander through the city, Eugene imposes his guilt on his companion, addressing the Spaniard as if he were Eugene himself: " '[Y]ou didn't know you had it in you—to strike a woman. Did you?' " (212). A while later, Eugene again accuses: " 'You know what you did.... You assaulted your wife. Do you say you didn't know you had it in you?' " (218). Just as images of Emma and of Eugene's acts themselves are external embodiments of his guilt, so does the Spaniard become a mirror for Eugene that he can merge with and also confront—a pattern reminiscent of the floating circle of blame and identity that he shares with Ran.

To be sure, Welty's depictions of Eugene's transference onto the Spaniard are not completely identical to Eugene's relationship with Ran. First and most obvious are the stark physical differences that exist between Eugene and his friend: the Spaniard is dark and large, while Eugene is fair and small; the Spaniard speaks no English and Eugene no Spanish. Such differences make the men so visually distinct that they—unlike Ran and Eugene—could never be "erased" into each other. In fact, on that day Eugene himself "felt sure in some absolute way that no familiar person could do him any good.... In panic—and, it struck him, in exultation—seek a stranger" (192).

Moreover, Eugene and the Spaniard choose and control the nature of their bond, a quality which Welty underscores by the metaphor she uses to describe their disposition together: "some meditative mood between them *bound them like consenting speech*" (208, emphasis mine). The narrative then highlights this affiliation of consent by immediately contrasting it with a pair of literal, and ridiculously identical twins:

At a corner two old fellows, twins, absurdly dressed alike in plaid jackets, the same size and together still, were helping each other onto the crowded step of a streetcar. Eugene and the Spaniard noticed them at the same moment and [cast] each other amused glances.... (208)

Although Eugene and the Spaniard's meeting occurs by complete accident and is lived out with utter spontaneity, this picture highlights how different the pair is from the twins they observe, and from previous images of Ran and Eugene.

Of course, Eugene also has consented to his marriage to Emma, but it seems that she represents *too much* otherness for Eugene's twin sensibilities. Rather, Eugene symbolically substitutes the Spaniard for her, as his lover—a slippage conveyed largely by Welty's language surrounding their physical exchanges: "Eugene clung to the Spaniard now, almost as if he had waited for him a long time with longing, almost as if he loved him, and had found a lasting refuge. He could have caressed the side of the massive face..." (221). Similarly ecstatic language describes Eugene's feelings as he is lifted up in the arms of the Spaniard: "He was without a burden in the world.... He was up-borne, open-armed. He was only thinking, My dear love comes" (224-5). This figurative replacement is repeated when later, in Morgana, people speculate that Eugene's wife " 'could even be a Dago' " (273)—a label used previously by Eugene for the *Spaniard* (215), not Emma.

Not surprisingly, in the homoerotic moment between Eugene and his other "twin," he remembers his literal twin, Ran:

And Eugene felt all at once an emotion that visited him inexplicably at times—*the overwhelming, secret tenderness toward his twin*, Ran MacLain, whom he had not seen for half his life, *that he might have felt toward a lover*. Was all well with Ran? How little we know! For considering that he might have done some reprehensible thing, then he would need the gravest and tenderest handling. (212, emphasis mine)

Assigning to his twin both endearment as well as guilt (Ran needs both "grave" and "tender" treatment), Eugene has blended himself with the Spaniard and with Ran, who figure as both his "lovers" and as his partners in "fault."

Soon after that heady moment of twinning fusion, familiar strains of circles and miniaturization come to Eugene's mind, this time in a more surreal key:

[H]e felt a strange sensation.... Something *round* would be in his mouth. But its *size* was the thing that was strange.

It was as if he were trying to swallow a *cherry* but found he was only the *size* of the stem of the cherry. His mouth received and was explored by some *immensity*. It became more and more immense while he waited. All knowledge of the rest of his body and the feeling in it would leave him...his mouth alone felt and it felt *enormity*.... He seemed to have the *world* on his tongue. And it had no taste—only *size*. (223, emphasis mine)

Eugene's bizarre fantasy fixates on two physical aspects that have pervaded his experience as a twin from the beginning: circularity and size. In his efforts to ingest and contain this gigantic "cherry," Eugene seems to be struggling against the perception, as Mattie Will described it, that twins are as "always miniature and young somewhere." At several points, in fact, he feels constantly dwarfed by the overwhelming and affronting strength of the Spaniard, of Emma, and of the "big-boned" immigrant waitress, who tells him that her husband is also " 'a little man, and sits up as small as you' " (226-7). In all of these moments, the confusions and limitations of Ran and Eugene's bond become so overpowering to Eugene that they literally balloon into a "world"—a world that is, for the infantilized twin, too much to swallow.

Such oral incapacity emerges in other instances where Eugene is unable to use language effectively: "It was a lifelong trouble, he had never been able to express himself at all when it came to the very moment" (221). As a child, Eugene could not articulate his fear of a perverse exhibitionist who haunted his piano lessons: he was "afraid of Mr. Voight's appearances" and felt "nervous," but "he kept mum" (48). This oral paralysis is paralleled in the method that Ran chooses for his attempted suicide: "I put the pistol's mouth to my own" (180).

These indictments of self that the twins experience through an impotence in their mouth are countered by the oral confidence and creativity of other characters. For example, after Eugene returns home to Emma, she "pops" grapes onto "her extended tongue" (228). Earlier, he has seen the Spaniard eat with great vigor, "spitting out the bones of his special dish, breaking the bread and clamping it in his teeth with the sound of firecrackers" (205), as well as peer into seashore caves "like a dentist into alluring mouths" (220). King's impish feasting during Katie Rainey's funeral is depicted as similarly empowered: "Mr. King sucked a little marrow bone and lifted his wobbly head and looked arrogantly at Virgie.... Then he cracked the little bone in his teeth. She felt refreshed..." (257). Virgie, too, contrasts the twins' oral entrapment from the beginning, when, as a baby she mischievously swallows "a button off a shirt" (11).

This final example is telling, because Virgie is the clearest example of one who is not impaired by restrictive circles of language and kinship. Not only does she ingest—and thus control—a button (instead of *losing* one, as Ran does in "The Whole World Knows" [169]), she also refuses other modes that typically circumscribe women. She rejects the "circles" of gossip and marriage, both of which are epitomized, in "The Wanderers," by Jinny Love, who by then has reconciled with Ran. In fact, Jinny flaunts her ring, on a circling hand, at Katie Rainey's funeral: "With her hand out, she showed a ring about the room.... 'I deserved me a diamond,' she went on to say...twisting her hand on its wrist" (243). Not surprisingly, Jinny's identity depends upon everyone around her imitating her, joining her "circle." For instance, Jinny earlier implored Perdita (who calls the girl a "monkey") to " 'do like *me*. Do like *me*...' " (165). This need to be "aped" continues into Jinny's adult life: "It appeared urgent with her to drive everybody, even Virgie for whom she cared nothing, into the state of marriage along with her. Only then could she resume as Jinny Love Stark, her true self" (255).

In contrast, Virgie divests herself of circles—the societal circles of Morgana that ensnare Jinny, and the kinship circles of replicated identity that link Ran and Eugene. Welty concretizes this freedom by having Katie imagine, as she is dying, that Virgie plans to sell her mother's quilts—quilts.... quilts whose very names imply the more restraining connections behind them: "For sale, *Double* Muscadine Hulls, Road to *Dublin*, Starry Sky, Strange Spider *Web*, Hands All *Around*, *Double* Wedding *Ring*" (235-6, emphasis mine). All these names (including "Starry Sky," which subtly suggests the twin figures of Gemini) symbolize a circularity that comes from too much connectedness, a blurring of identity that comes from too much sameness.

Thus, even though Virgie herself has made circles throughout her life (as a child she runs "closer and closer circles around Miss Eckhart" at a concert [52], and as a teen, she darts "in circles around the room" [30] with her boyfriend Kewpie Moffit), these relations contrast the circles of Ran and Eugene because they allow her to maintain clear boundaries of her identity, and because they enact relations of direct control or reciprocity. In these scenes, Virgie is a self-possessed subject, and is never wedged into sharing the same cultural space with another. Juxtaposed to the tangled web of the MacLain twins, Virgie's independence allows her the freedom to connect yet also to disengage.

This singular balance is echoed in a figure that Virgie observes at the book's end, who, although called a "twin," is whole in and of himself:

It was Mr. Nesbitt, she thought at first, but then saw it was another man almost like him.... He was all alone out here. His round face, not pushed out now, away from other faces, looked curiously deep, womanly, dedicated. Mr. Nesbitt's twin passed close to her, and down the street he turned flamboyantly and entered what must have been his own door.... (274)

The energy, confidence and autonomy of this false "twin" does indeed present a different picture from the self-imploding circles of Ran and Eugene. Virgie astutely observes the costs of such bonding when she sees the intensity of the "thing of the flesh" that ties the MacLains together: "Perhaps that confusion among all of them was the great wound in Ran's heart..." (257). She ponders further that such tight kinship is "an indelible thing which may come without friendship or even too early an identity, may come even despisingly, in rudeness, intruding in the middle of sorrow" (257).

By the concluding pages of *The Golden Apples*, this kinship "wound"— most particularly the restraint of twinship—has created varied effects in Ran and Eugene. Ironically, after so many years of miniaturization and physical interchangeability, their bodies end up looking very different. Ran has become "fat" (262) and prosperous, while Eugene is "light" (273) and sickly. In fact, Ran is the mayor of Morgana, while Eugene's last days, before his death from tuberculosis, are filled with loneliness, even though he has returned to Morgana.[2] It might seem, then, that Ran and Eugene have "grown out" of their twinship, and that they are, as Ruth Vande Kieft asserts, "clearly differentiated" (104) by then.

But Welty's choice for Eugene's ailment is significant: tuberculosis, or consumption, offers a metaphor for the interdependence that the twins continue to share, one which Ran, in fact, has capitalized on in his political ventures. Indeed, he has won his mayoral seat because people voted for him "for his glamour and his story, *for being a MacLain and the bad twin*, for marrying a Stark and then for ruining a girl.... They voted for the revelation..." (238, emphasis mine). Ran "consumes" his twinship and thus caters to the community's thirst for scandal; moreover, Ran's corpulence and Eugene's shrivelling seem to recall how, as children, these boys were lightheartedly tagged as "cannibals." While that label is obviously inaccurate in a literal sense, it does aptly underscore how even in their opposite trajectories, the twins' relationship is parasitic and gripping.

Welty's own "twin myth" in *The Golden Apples* begins with a sportive innocence. As youthful creatures, the MacLain boys run playfully, trotting "down and up through the little gully like a pony pair that could keep time to music in the Ringling Brothers', touching shoulders until the last" (99). But seen in the context of twinship, the subtle details in this passage are sobering. These uncannily yoked siblings, these twin "*Ring*ling Brothers," share an indelible bond. Welty's narratives show, in their literalization of the romantic myth of the "other half," how the twins' "thing of the flesh," is the most "endless circle" of all—more penetrating than even the harsh circumscriptions of Morganan society. The brothers' "shoulders" do touch "until the last," in a fusion of identity and "fault"; in the rounds of their lives, their twinship continues again and again to define and confine who they are. For the MacLain twins, very much indeed has "depended" on "being linked together."

Notes

[1]Technically, Welty never specifies whether Ran and Eugene are identical or fraternal twins. I classify them as identical because, although we cannot know for sure that they emerged from a single fertilized egg, they are described—especially in their youth—as extraordinarily similar in appearance and personality.

[2]In fact, Michael Kreyling points out that in an earlier version of "The Wanderers" (published as "The Hummingbirds"), Welty emphasizes Eugene's loneliness with such phrases as " 'He had stayed lonely and quiet, until he wasted away' " (100), which were later deleted. Kreyling further summarizes that in this same early version, Welty accentuates the twins' distance by describing that at the cemetery, "one of the tots sits astride brother Eugene's gravestone. It does not bother Ran" (101).

Works Cited

Bryant, J.A., Jr. "Seeing Double in *The Golden Apples*." *Critical Essays on Eudora Welty*. Eds. W. Craig Turner and Lee Emling Harding. Boston: G.K. Hall, 1989: 142-53.

Donaldson, Susan V. "Recovering Otherness in *The Golden Apples*." *American Literature* 63 (1991): 489-506.

Kreyling, Michael. *Eudora Welty's Achievement of Order*. Baton Rouge: Louisiana State UP, 1980.

McHaney, Thomas L. "Falling Into Cycles: *The Golden Apples*." *Eudora Welty: Eye of the Storyteller*. Ed. Dawn Trouard. Kent, Ohio: Kent State UP, 1989: 173-89.

Plato. *Symposium*. *The Works of Plato*. Trans. Benjamin Jowett. Ed. Irwin Edman. New York: Modern Library, 1928.

Schmidt, Peter. *The Heart of the Story: Eudora Welty's Short Fiction*. Jackson: UP of

Mississippi, 1991.

Shelley, Percy Bysshe. "Epipsychidion." *English Romantic Writers*. Ed. David Perkins. New York: Harcourt Brace Jovanovich, 1967: 1038-46.

Vande Kieft, Ruth M. *Eudora Welty*. Rev. ed. Boston: G.K. Hall & Co., 1987.

Wall, Carey. " 'June Recital': Virgie Rainey Saved." *Eudora Welty: Eye of the Storyteller*. Ed. Dawn Trouard. Kent, Ohio: Kent State UP, 1989: 14-31.

Welty, Eudora. *The Eye of the Story: Selected Essays and Reviews*. New York: Vintage, 1979.

_____. *The Golden Apples*. 1947. San Diego: Harcourt Brace Jovanovich, 1977.

First Sisters in the British Novel:
Charlotte Lennox to Susan Ferrier

Michael Cohen

The presence of plot-significant sisters in novels virtually always means the contestation of feminist issues in those texts. But plot-significant sisters are not there in the British novel from the beginning. Early nineteenth-century novelists are the inheritors of a tradition that makes only limited use of sisters. Defoe, Richardson, Fielding, Sterne and Smollett take virtually no advantage of the opportunities offered by sisterhood for enriching plots, for multiplying formal relations of symmetry and opposition, or for showing the commonality of women's experience in ordinary social situations such as courtship and marriage as well as extraordinary social concerns such as prostitution and sexual deviance. From the work of Charlotte Lennox in the 1760s to that of Susan Ferrier in the teens of the new century, sisters begin to come into their own as plot movers and as representatives for all women's relation to each other. Novels during this 50-year period establish the usefulness of the sisters subject, which is used by the major novelists of the nineteenth century. Critics have begun to attend to these early sisters novels as important for their own sake and for what they point toward. Patricia Meyer Spacks looks at novels by Charlotte Lennox and by Jane West in her 1986 article "Sisters." She thinks that they deserve attention in our reading of Austen, who certainly read them, that their emphasis on "bad" characters must be looked at for what it says about the nature of female power (beauty and being loved = power), and that sexual competition between sisters is inevitable in these books: "Sex provides the arena of conflict in a society which defines a woman's worth by her marriage" (141). Susan Morgan believes that novels by Burney, Edgeworth, and Ferrier are part of a new definition of the heroine which will ultimately allow for the substitution of a more humane "feminine heroic" for the masculine heroic code that had prevailed in British fiction until the nineteenth century (Morgan 11-19, 24). Not enough examination has yet been made, however, of the synecdochic relation of sisters in these novels to the situation of all women. The appeal for solidarity among women always asks for symbolic "sisterhood," but literal sisterhood already depicts in small the relation of all women, and that depiction enables the concerns of all women to be expressed in novels whose scope may never seem to extend beyond the domestic scene.

Lennox, Goldsmith and West

One of the first British novelists to use the sisterhood subject is Charlotte

Lennox, whose *History of Harriot and Sophia* appeared serially in 1760-61 and was published as *Sophia* in 1762. Lennox limits her plot to the two women, opposing her sisters temperamentally and morally. She also makes them rivals for love. When hard times come to the widowed Mrs. Darnley and her two daughters Harriot and Sophia, Sophia goes into service, and her virtue wins the love of the rich Sir Charles Stanley, formerly one of Harriot's suitors. After being kept for a time by a lord, Harriot eventually emigrates to the colonies with the poor captain she has married—a method of getting rid of the "fallen" woman later to be used by Dickens in *David Copperfield* and Collins in *The New Magdalen*. Lennox's sisters have only limited interest for readers because they do not have any dimension beyond their antithesis, and they are incapable of affecting each other.

Goldsmith's Olivia and Sophia Primrose are differentiated, but not opposed morally, though Olivia is more flirtatious and livelier than her sister Sophia. *The Vicar of Wakefield* (1766) makes use of the plot devices of rivalry and false rivalry between the sisters. There is also extended "sisterhood" in the sisters' relation to their eventual sister-in-law Arabella Wilmot, whom George Primrose marries after many harrowing plot turns. All three women are pursued, more or less literally, by Squire Thornhill at various times during the action, another feature that tends to "sister" them. But they are all such puppets in the rapid reversals of fortune and they are so little together that not much can be said about them as individual characters or as sisters.

The novels of Lennox, Goldsmith, and one by Jane West, *A Gossip's Story* (1797)—in which the two sisters are starkly opposed as to temperament and the sensible sister proved unerring—are hampered in introducing significant issues about women's relation to each other because the sisters are not independently realized as characters: in Lennox and West each sister constitutes only one half of a contrast, and in Goldsmith the plot moves so rapidly each sister scarcely knows what is happening to the other, so that their relation is only through reference to the title character—Olivia and Sophia are daughters of the vicar more than they are sisters to each other.

A development in the novel of the nineties brings with it sisters who do affect each other's lives, who are something more than opposed poles of a duality, whose characterization brings other women into their circle and makes figurative sisters of them, and who begin to function not merely in relation to one man but as a small society. The new development is the novel of education that makes up part of what Moira Ferguson calls feminist polemic (27). These novels argue specifically for an enlightened approach to the education of women. Notable examples employing sisters are books by Maria Edgeworth and Fanny Burney. Susan Ferrier caps this development in the teens of the new century with a novel whose title is *Marriage* (1818) but whose real topic is education. And before the teens are over Jane Austen will have written her books, perhaps partly inspired by the novel of education, but taking the subject of sisters through new virtuoso turns of social comedy. At the same time Scott will graft a true account of sisterly heroism onto a historical background at times in contest with his main story, and, despite himself, enable female rescue plots for the next century.

The Novel of Education as Feminist Polemic

The plots of the novels of education tend to multiply sisters. Where there are sisters there are likely to be sisters-in-law or the relation created when one woman wishes her friend and her brother to marry, though one or the other has romantic interests elsewhere. Around sisters there tend to be formed figurative sisterhoods out of shared experience or romantic rivalry. "Extended" sisterhoods, half-sisters, stepsisters, sisters-in-law, can also be a way of distancing women with moral or sexual differences. Sisters and "sisters" tend to be involved in romantic rivalries or in false rivalries where one sister imagines the attentions of a man are directed toward her sister when he is really wooing her. And in Maria Edgeworth's novels there is at least a hint of the rescue plot that will become an important feature of so many sisters plots from the teens of the new century on. Edgeworth writes stories in which a sisterly confidence binds two women, and where there may be an anticipated further relationship of sisters-in-law. She also has plots in which one woman attempts or accomplishes what might be called an armchair rescue of another—on the analogy of the armchair detective who solves the crime from a distance. Edgeworth's plots, as Susan Morgan points out, place "the favored heroine, Belinda Portman in *Belinda*, Helen Stanley in *Helen*, at a distance from the center of the action. That center offers a traditional sexual ingénue caught in her traditional plot. The lead heroine stands to the side, as visitor, as observer, and finally as repairer of other people's lives" (Morgan 24). This "lead heroine" attempts to rescue the ingénue by establishing a closer relation as her sister-in-law, but she usually fails.

In the first of such Edgeworth stories, for example, the *Letters of Julia and Caroline* in *Letters for Literary Ladies* (1795), Caroline Percy is the adviser and confidante of Julia, who does not profess to think, but "only to feel" (Edgeworth 3), and who fears apathy more than anything else (5). The two, friends since infancy, are shortly to be even more closely related when Julia marries Caroline's brother. But instead she enters a loveless marriage with a Lord V—, and subsequent letters detail Julia's leaving her husband and Caroline's fears that she is morally disintegrating. In Letter V, Caroline writes that at recently seeing Julia she had observed "that from whatever cause the powers of your reason had been declining, and those of your imagination rapidly increasing," and "the boundaries of right and wrong seemed to be no longer marked in your mind" (57). Caroline attempts a rescue of Julia: "I no longer *advise*, I *command* you, quit your present abode; come to me; fly from danger and be safe" (60-61). But Julia disregards the advice and the command. She goes to France, apparently an encoding here for committing adultery, and when Caroline next sees her in England Julia is dying. Caroline takes her home, where Julia in her last words pleads with her own daughter, now apparently adopted by Caroline, to "*be good and happy*" (78).

This account would suggest that Edgeworth's main point here was an attack on Julia's exaggerated sensibility, her passion for feeling at the expense of thought, and her horror of apathy. Certainly that strain of end-of-century feminism, represented best by Mary Wollstonecraft's attacks on Rousseau in *A Vindication of the Rights of Woman* (1792), is important not only as background to Edgeworth but also to Fanny Burney and to Susan Ferrier. But I believe it may be exaggerated, for example by Margaret Kirkham, who identifies the condemnation of sensibility as the most important strain of what she calls "Enlightenment feminism" in her book *Jane Austen, Feminism and Fiction* (xi-xiii). Feminists in the Mary Astell—Catherine Macaulay—Mary Wollstonecraft tradition indeed begin from the argument that human nature—male *and* female—is rational and therefore should be governed by one rule of conduct. But "sensibility"—sensitivity to affect and feeling—made up *less* of an exclusive part of the gender construct for women at the end of the eighteenth century than at any time before or since, simply because the influence of people like Rousseau had made the *man of feeling* so fashionable.

In any case there is more to the *Letters for Literary Ladies* than the *Letters of Julia and Caroline*. The book begins with the Letter from a Gentleman to his Friend upon the Birth of a Daughter, with the Answer. The first gentleman is a kind of straw man who knows his friend to be "a champion for the rights of woman" (2) who "insist[s] upon the equality of the sexes" (3), and he baits the new father by warning him from too much education for his new daughter. The discussion moves with startling rapidity to the question of power. The first correspondent leaps from the self-directed dangers of female power—"their power over themselves has regularly been found to diminish, in proportion as their power over others has been encreased" (10-11)—to the threat to national security female empowerment poses: "tell me whether you can hesitate to acknowledge, that the influence, the liberty, and the *power* of women have been constant concomitants of the moral and political decline of empires" (12). The answer argues that power rightly understood "is an evil in most cases" (53), and will be seen to be such by women taught properly. "If, my dear sir, it be your object to monopolize power for our sex, you cannot possibly better secure it from the wishes of the other, than by enlightening their minds, and enlarging their view of human affairs" (53). In this section Edgeworth gives variety to the play of ideas by having two men debate the issues that involve her heroines, but it is still a feminist debate, making a dialogue of the points made by Wollstonecraft and also by Catherine Macaulay.

The idealism expressed by the second male correspondent, for example, bears most resemblance to the tone of Macaulay rather than to that of Mary Wollstonecraft, and arguments from Macaulay's *Letters on Education* (1790) are frequently behind Edgeworth, Burney and Ferrier in the works discussed here. Wollstonecraft was much influenced by Macaulay, as her moving eulogy to Macaulay in Chapter 5 of the *Vindication* attests, and some of their arguments would of necessity be similar even had they been ignorant of each other's existence. But the two women are writing in historical circumstances that have given them hearing and that call out for particular arguments. The argument for women's rights from the basis of a common rational human nature, formulated so tellingly by Mary Astell in *A Serious Proposal to the*

Ladies in 1694, just four years after Locke's *Essay Concerning Human Understanding*, seized *its* historical moment and made up a part of the feminist platform ever after. A century later when Wollstonecraft and Macaulay were writing, the revolutionary spirit of the time called out for arguments based on liberty, and there were always minor circumstances such as the temporary triumph of the Whigs that could inspire constitutional debate points in a Whig polemicist such as Macaulay. For Astell, Macaulay and Wollstonecraft the general arguments always began from common rational nature and from the moral conviction that virtue is genderless and requires the same instruction whether it is being nurtured in men or in women. Sometimes Macaulay's turn of phrase and sometimes Wollstonecraft's particular juxtaposition of ideas is identifiable behind a passage in Edgeworth, Burney or Ferrier.

Edgeworth's feminist, new-father correspondent has asserted that power is an evil and that enlightenment can be relied on to make its attractiveness seen to be meretricious; Macaulay had written "I know of no learning, worth having, that does not tend to free the mind from error" (Ferguson 402). Then Edgeworth's writer argues that predispositions and tempers are not natural to one sex, but a consequence of education (54). A half dozen lines below her comment on learning and error Macaulay had written, "all those vices and imperfections which have been generally regarded as inseparable from the female character...are entirely the effects of situation and education" (402). On the other hand, when Julia and Caroline are corresponding, and Caroline attempts to talk Julia out of her conviction that "the sole object of a woman's life" is "to *please*" (12), her pleading sounds more like Wollstonecraft's ninth chapter: "Men are not aware of the misery they cause and the vicious weakness they cherish by only inciting women to render themselves pleasing" (Wollstonecraft 214). But whether she is relying on Macaulay or on Wollstonecraft, Edgeworth most effectively uses feminist polemic when it is a dialogue between those whom it most concerns—the women. For this purpose the relation of the would-be sisters-in-law works most dramatically for her.

The moral supporter and confidante is an actual sister in Fanny Burney's *Camilla* (1796), another novel of education. Burney uses three sisters and a cousin to tell her complex and strangely lifeless story about the importance of moral education very early in life and the dangers attendant upon bad advice. Lavinia Tyrold is Camilla's beautiful sister, two years older; Eugenia is two years younger, intelligent, with features scarred by smallpox, and lame as a result of an accident that occurred at the time she caught the disease. Eugenia is educated in the classics and rich because her indulgent uncle, Sir Hugh Tyrold, who feels himself responsible for her illness and her accident, spares nothing in the way of tutors and legacies. Eugenia provides subplot incidents throughout the book but Lavinia is so like Camilla that she virtually drops out of the action. Burney needs a cousin more beautiful than Camilla or Lavinia, Indiana Lynmere, to oppose Camilla, to be a rival for the love of the man Camilla will eventually marry, and to be her foil in illustrating certain thematic principles concerning instruction. Indiana's complete self-absorption is a result of her neglected education. She eventually breaks an engagement to run off with a "wild and eccentric" Irishman named Macdersey (821). Both Eugenia and Camilla are led into perilous situations by bad advice, but their moral foundation—based on parental instruction—is sound, and they come through.

Camilla moves rapidly and with sudden changes of fortune, very much like *The Vicar of Wakefield*, which it also resembles in the basic family situation—a vicar with several daughters and a hapless son—and some incidents—Eugenia is abducted, Dr. Tyrold is thrown into prison for debt. But the book also remorselessly presses home its themes of early moral education. The sisters and the cousin illustrate these themes for the most part, but a passage late in the book applies them to the men as well, and makes clear that moral indoctrination and instruction at a very early age is what instills "radical worth" and is more important than formal education later. Lavinia has married Henry Westwyn, the college friend of her dissipated cousin Clermont Lynmere, Indiana's brother. Lord O'Lerney is an Irish nobleman related to the Macdersey with whom Indiana has eloped, and he has pledged himself to help support his kinsman. Lavinia goes to her new home among the Westwyns:

Like all characters of radical worth, she grew daily upon the esteem and affection of her new family, and found in her husband as marked a contrast with Clermont Lynmere, to annul all Hypothesis of Education, as Lord O'Lerney, cool, rational, and penetrating, opposed to Macdersey, wild, eccentric, and vehement, offered against all that is National. Brought up under the same tutor, the same masters, and at the same university, with equal care, equal expence, equal opportunities of every kind, Clermont turned out conceited, voluptuous, and shallow; Henry modest, full of feeling, and stored with intelligence. (909)

Early moral education creates "radical worth" in Burney's system, for men or women. Its effects surpass any imagined predispositions that come from ethnicity, and cannot be made up by formal instruction later. Once those roots are established, further "education" does not touch them. It is a point reiterated by Astell, Macaulay, and Wollstonecraft that genuine moral education, even at the beginning, is not mere indoctrination. Pitying the condition of the young lady "taught the Principles and Duties of Religion, but not Acquainted with the Reasons and Grounds of them," Astell writes that "her Piety may be tall and spreading, yet because it wants Foundation and Root, the first rude Temptation overthrows and blasts it" (Ferguson 183).

To be one of Camilla's sisters is to be morally safe, regardless of how much time one spends later in households like Sir Hugh's. The book asserts that just being a sister is enough. Burney scorns the Hypothesis of Education and the National Hypothesis, but does not address the Blood Hypothesis. What would happen if two sisters differed in this early radical training? Is it possible to imagine two sisters as different as the cousins Camilla and Indiana? To the question whether the child was predisposed from the womb for either good or evil, Astell, Macaulay, and Wollstonecraft say no, that the child is predisposed neither by the family into which it is born nor by its sex. But these ideas wait for narrative illustration until after the turn of the century and Susan Ferrier's *Marriage* (1818).

Marriage and Education

In *Marriage* (1818), Susan Ferrier puts twin sisters at the center of a novel. What results is an unsubtle moral tale but nonetheless a subtle narrative demonstration of how the binary of likeness and unlikeness can work, as the identical sisters recapitulate different parts of their mother's experience. Ferrier's narrative denies the "identity" of the sisters, or rather denies any importance to their genetic identity while it assigns everything of importance to their early education. Lady Juliana, the pampered daughter of the Earl of Courtland, having refused a match with the 53-year-old Duke of L—because she can't love him, marries the penniless Henry Douglas and ends up in his family's remote Highlands seat, Glenfern Castle. There she meets her husband's brother, Archibald Douglas, and his wife Alicia Malcolm Douglas, a sensible, well-bred woman.

The contrast between Alicia and Lady Juliana sets up the first antithetical "sisters" pairing of the book. The two women have had very different upbringings and marriages. Rather than having been petted by her parents, Alicia was orphaned at two years of age, and taken in by her aunt, Lady Audley, in London. When Alicia and Sir Edmund, Lady Audley's son, fell in love and he wished to marry her, she would not agree because of Lady Audley's disapproval. Alicia left to visit other relations in Scotland, and when, after two years, Edmund made clear he would not marry anyone else but her, in order to free him she accepted the proposal of Archibald Douglas, the oldest son of Mr. Douglas of Glenfern. She refused a love match for the sake of honor, but now lives with her husband in faithfulness and affection. These very different women will be the formative influences on the twin daughters of Lady Juliana.

Alicia Douglas tries to amuse and occupy Lady Juliana, but her "attempts to teach her to play at chess and read Shakespeare, were as unsuccessful as the endeavours of the good aunts to persuade her to study Fordyce's Sermons, and make baby linen (59-60). Alicia takes Lady Juliana to her home at Lochmarlie Cottage, not far from Glenfern Castle. It is all that nature and art can make it, and even in its upkeep Alicia is busy improving the neighborhood children, whom she enlists to be gardeners. But even there Lady Juliana suffers from *ennui*, "the sad fruits of a fashionable education" (98). Where Alicia's tuition is vain in Lady Juliana's case, though, it will be wonderfully effective on her daughter Mary.

After the birth of her twin daughters, Lady Juliana refuses to nurse either child, and the Laird will hire only one nurse. Alicia offers to take the other girl. When Henry manages to get himself reinstated in the army and given an allowance by a general he knows, he and Juliana and one girl go to London. There Adelaide Julia is christened—significantly, at a ceremony scheduled to conflict with a soirée of one of her mother's rivals in the London social scene. Meanwhile her twin sister Mary has been quietly baptized in Scotland. For 18 years the book allows the education of the twins to go on separately. Lady Juliana's other sister-in-law, Lady Lindore, leaves her husband to go off with a lover. Henry's expectations from his benefactor General Cameron are frustrated by Cameron's marriage, and when the Earl of Courtland dies he leaves nothing to Juliana. Penniless, Lady Juliana is received by her brother, who pays Henry's debts and secures him a regiment in India, to which Juliana refuses to accompany him.

When she is 18, Mary becomes ill, and Alicia Douglas sends the girl to her mother, now in Bath, to get well. It will be her first meeting with her mother and with her sister Adelaide, whom the narrator finds "as heartless and ambitious as she was beautiful and accomplished" (187). Ferrier, not content with contrasting the twin sisters Adelaide and Mary, sets up yet another contrast with Lord Lindore's daughter, Lady Emily Lindore, whose character "had undergone exactly the same process in its formation as that of her cousin; yet in all things they differed" (187). Unfortunately, the introduction of Lady Emily tends to confuse all the points Ferrier has been making about the importance of education and the insignificance of one's genetic makeup. The generalization the narrator derives from Lady Emily's difference is, "It sometimes happens, that the very means used, with success, in the formation of one character, produce a totally opposite effect upon another" (187). The expected result, the narrator ironically implies, of "the sophistry of her governesses, and the solecisms of her aunt," would have been a character like that of Adelaide. But Lady Emily is neither heartless nor immoral like her cousin. At this point in the book we seem to have an optimistic theory of education developed—*Marriage* is far more concerned with education than with marriage—which asserts that there is no natural depravity, that Adelaide's spoiled character owes everything to her education and nothing to her birth. On the other hand, Lady Emily has been able partially to withstand the effects of the identical education, and what could have enabled it except some strength of character derived from birth?

The sisters finally meet, exactly halfway through the book. Adelaide, the spoiled, sophisticated twin, is controlled where Mary is warm, emotional and affectionate. Adelaide's "usual sweetness and placidity" (229) accompanies reserve and coolness. But more interesting than the temperamental differences ascribable to the distinct upbringings of the twins is the apparent need to differentiate them even in physical ways. Adelaide is not only taller than Mary—not surprising considering the lamentable starving of Mary during her first few weeks, before Alicia Douglas took over her care—but even her eye color is different from her twin sister's! This careful differentiation seems to be intended to insulate the virtuous Mary from too much connection with her morally lax sister and to emphasize just what education can do.

One scene in the middle of the book is emblematic of the reunion of the cast-off child with her mother and sister:

> Lady Juliana looked in upon her [Mary] as she passed to dinner. She was in a better humour, for she had received a new dress which was particularly becoming, as both her maid and her glass had attested.
> Again Mary's heart bounded toward the being to whom she owed her birth; yet afraid to give utterance to her feelings, she could only regard her with silent admiration, till a moment's consideration converted that into a less pleasing feeling, as she observed for the first time, that her mother wore no mourning [Lady Juliana's father-in-law, Mary's grandfather, has recently died].

> Lady Juliana saw her astonishment, and, little guessing the cause, was flattered by it. "Your style of dress is very obsolete, my dear,' said she, as she contrasted the effect of her own figure and her daughter's in a large mirror; 'and there's no occasion for you to wear black here." (230)

The "obsolete" style of dress is that her mother would have worn twenty years before in Scotland, when she was the age of her daughter now, before the twins were born. The narrator makes use of the peculiar way in which the twin daughters each recapitulate part of the mother's experience: Mary representing her mother's brief Scotland period, but making good use, unlike her mother, of Alicia Douglas's friendship and tutelage. Mary, for example, sincerely mourns the passing of the old laird her mother had found insufferable, and she finds affectionate friends instead of monstrous strangers in Henry's three aunts and five sisters. Adelaide's experience, restricted to the urban, the sophisticated, and the trivial part of Lady Juliana's existence, has made her so like her mother that they can represent each other, as in the passage above, which might as easily be a meeting of the twins as of Juliana and Mary.

The two most significant features of the story, as both formative and representative of the way sisters can be used in British fiction, are the differentiation of the sisters (twins, but so different in their young adulthood Ferrier even feels constrained to give Adelaide eyes colored differently from Mary's) and the apparent necessity to *construct* additional sisterly relations. Alicia Douglas, a sister-in-law, befriends and tries to educate Lady Juliana; failing that, she becomes a sister nurse-and-mother of Juliana's child Mary. Lady Emily, who has grown up in the same household with Adelaide, the child of Juliana's brother Lord Courtland and his bolted wife, becomes—not the "sister" of her cousin Adelaide, whose education she has shared, but the sister of Mary. Emily is attracted to Mary because the latter has a settled and educated virtue which Emily has been unable to reach merely by reaction against the vapidity of her own education: "her notions of right and wrong were too crude to influence the general tenor of her life, or operate as restraints upon a naturally high spirit, and impetuous temper...Lady Emily remained as insupportably natural and sincere, as she was beautiful and *piquante*" (187). Part of their mutual attraction is the ironic humor both women share, and the fact that their liveliness, though as compassionate on Mary's side as it is satirical on Emily's, contrasts with the coldness and lack of feeling of their "sister" Adelaide.

Much is made of Adelaide's "indifference" (277). In one episode her intervention would persuade her mother to allow Mary to attend a masked ball, but she impassively refuses to help:

> With a few words, Adelaide might have obtained the desired permission for her sister; but she chose to remain neuter, coldly declaring she never interfered in quarrels.
>
> Mary beheld the splendid dresses and gay countenances of the party for the ball with feelings free from envy, though perhaps not wholly unmixed with regret. She gazed with the purest admiration on the extreme beauty of her sister, heightened as it was by the fantastic elegance of her dress, and contrasted with her own pale visage, and mourning habiliments.

"Indeed," thought she, as she turned from the mirror, with rather a mournful smile, "my aunt Nicky was in the right: I certainly am a poor *shilpit* [feeble] thing." (260-61)

In these passages one sister is the mirror of comparison for the other sister, and the fashionable mother and the fashionable sister are interchangeable in the glass, which shows the heroine, smaller and paler, in her dark garments, against the fairer, taller, and more elegantly fitted out other.

In mirroring a part of her mother's potential life, each twin makes it actual and extends it. Mary profits from the instruction of Alicia Douglas and the experience of coping with her eccentric great aunts, where Juliana was consumed by *ennui* and the desire to get out of Scotland. Though Juliana began by loving Henry Douglas, eventually she was only too happy to be separated from him. Tutored by Scots women, Mary sees their merit as well as the merit of the country and the men—eventually marrying a man with ties to Scotland. Adelaide marries a Duke twice her age, as Juliana came near doing, and the resulting loveless marriage does not even give Adelaide the freedom that money and a title seemed to promise. Her husband, though not clever, is stubborn, and his old-fashioned ideas of propriety restrict Adelaide at every turn. When she elopes with her former admirer Lord Lindore, the man she jilted to marry the duke, she enacts a possibility from which her mother was apparently only saved by a torpor that extends to sex as well as to all her other behavior. For Adelaide, whose dispassionate if willful nature has been insisted on throughout the latter half of the book, the elopement is somewhat less believable than it is for Lindore, whose mother was a bolter.

As for Mary, her "grief and horror at her sister's misconduct, was proportioned to the nature of the offence":

> She considered it not as how it might affect herself, or would be viewed by the world, but as a crime committed against the law of God; yet, while she the more deeply deplored it on that account, no bitter words of condemnation passed her lips. She thought with humility, of the superior advantages she had enjoyed, in having principles of religion early and deeply engrafted in her soul; and that, but for these, such as her sister's fate was, hers might have been. (433-34)

Difficult as it may be to disregard the sanctimonious tone of this passage, we have to admire the downright admission in Mary's last observation. The writers of the teens have a straightforward approach that says two women of the same parents can differ in sexuality and defiance of convention to the extent that one is an Adelaide and one a Mary, one a Lydia Bennet and one an Elizabeth, or one an Effie Deans and the other a Jeanie—though Scott is so squeamish about this issue as to change his source and make the two women who show such a sexual difference only *half*-sisters. Except for Meredith (who offers as excuse the *class* of his sisters), no one among the Victorians quite wants to admit such different women could have the same father *and* the same mother; frequently the connection between the unconventionally sexually active woman and the story's other important woman is attenuated to that of cousins (*Adam Bede*'s Hetty

Sorrel and Dinah Morris) or that of niece and aunt (*Mary Barton* and her aunt Esther), or the blood relation is removed entirely.

Ferrier uses sisters to show us the development of moral difference, demystifying sexuality by making it a matter of education. In the first hundred years of British novelists' use of the sisters subject, only Austen is able to do more with the plot potentialities offered by the sisters' relationship.

Sisters and Difference

Differences of height and coloring have always been used by authors and painters to reflect temperamental variations among women. Shakespeare's use of the device demonstrated its efficacy in helping gender identification: it could even be employed in transvestite theater when the repertory company had two teenage boys of markedly different height. The taller became Helena, Portia, or Rosalind; the shorter, Hermia, Nerissa, or Celia. The only other difference was a wig color. The difference somehow made each boy actor more convincingly gendered as a woman character. In nineteenth-century novels, the differences of appearance tended to enact or to encode ethical or sexual difference or more subtle differences of temperament that could include or transcend ethical and sexual difference. In *Marriage*, a difference in appearance conveys one of ethical education—conscious morality versus amoral laxity or ignorance. Eventually, with the bolting of Adelaide from her marriage to Duke Altamont, the educational difference becomes ostensive as sexual difference. In *The Heart of Midlothian*, contemporaneous with *Marriage*, and in *Rhoda Fleming* decades later, the taller, fairer sister is sexually active while the darker sister is chaste, but it would be a mistake to generalize about the way these differences dispose themselves, because frequently the darker of a pair of sisters or women closely related in a plot—Rebecca and Rowena in *Ivanhoe*, for example—is the more sexually *attractive* or the one, like Mary here or Elizabeth in *Pride and Prejudice*, with whom almost all of the eligible men are in love and to whom two or more propose. Smaller can also mean more acceptably passive, in the manner of Little Dorrit and of Fanny Price in *Mansfield Park*. In books such as *Cranford*, *Wives and Daughters*, and *Middlemarch*, activity is once again presented as praiseworthy—as it had been for Elizabeth Bennet, for example, in *Pride and Prejudice*. Dorothea itches to improve the lot of those about her and that of the larger world—but her activity also implies a measure of discontent. The apparent passivity of Celia and of Rosamond, on the other hand, reveals a complacency that approaches ethical anaesthesia or conceals an active and discontented manipulation through gender.

Difference is always exploited in sister plots, and it is a force always striving to blow the plots apart and destroy the advantages to be gained from the sister relationship. In *Marriage* the plot manages to so distance the heroine from both sister and mother that the relation is effectively lessened to a kind of step-relation. In fact, the archetype behind this story is the tale of Cinderella. Lady Emily brings up the Cinderella comparison—in this case it is real mother and real sister both playing wicked stepsisters (328), and it is also Lady Emily who points out that Mary's relation with her sister and mother is characterized on their side by "prejudice, narrow-mindedness, envy, hatred, and malice" (318). These are strong words—more so, perhaps, as applied to the woman conceived and born with Mary than to the woman who conceived and bore them both. The book's point about the importance of education requires the close relationship of the two women so disparately educated, but it is significant that no novelist of any reputation twins women at the center of a story again in the century. Dickens's tentative use of twins in *Little Dorrit* comes near to destroying sympathy for the characters in his subplot. Any suggestion of a resemblance near twinning is enough to infuse a plot with danger, as is the case with the Eliza/Marianne resemblance in *Sense and Sensibility* and the Anne Catherick/Laura Fairlie near identity in *The Woman in White*.

Works Cited

Austen, Jane. *The Novels of Jane Austen*. Ed. R.W. Chapman. 3rd edition with revisions. Oxford: Oxford UP, 1965.

Burney, Fanny. *Camilla, or A Picture of Youth*. Ed. Edward A. and Lillian D. Bloom. London: Oxford UP, 1972.

Collins, Wilkie. *The Works of Wilkie Collins*. 30 vols. New York: Peter Fenelon Collier, n.d. Rpt. New York: AMS P, 1970.

Dickens, Charles. *The Works of Charles Dickens*. The Gadshill Edition. 34 vols. London: Chapman and Hall, n.d.

[Edgeworth, Maria.] *Letters for Literary Ladies. Includes Letter from a Gentleman to his Friend upon the Birth of a Daughter, with the Answer and Letters of Julia and Caroline*. London: J. Johnson, 1795.

Eliot, George. *Middlemarch*. Ed. Bert G. Hornback. A Norton Critical Edition. New York: W.W. Norton, 1977.

Ferguson, Moira, ed. *First Feminists: British Women Writers 1578-1799*. Bloomington: Indiana UP, 1985.

Ferrier, Susan. *Marriage*. Ed. Herbert Foltinek. Oxford: Oxford UP, 1986.

Gaskell, Elizabeth Cleghorn. *The Works of Mrs. Gaskell*. The Knutsford Edition. 8 vols. 1906. Rpt. New York: AMS P, 1972.

Goldsmith, Oliver. *The Vicar of Wakefield*. London, 1766.

Kirkham, Margaret. *Jane Austen, Feminism and Fiction*. Sussex: Harvester P, 1983.

Lennox, Charlotte. *Sophia*. London, 1762.

Meredith, George. *The Works of George Meredith*. Memorial Edition. 27 vols. New York: Charles Scribner's Sons, 1909-11.

Morgan, Susan. *Sisters in Time: Imagining Gender in Nineteenth-Century British Fiction*. New York: Oxford UP, 1989.

Scott, Sir Walter. *The Heart of Midlothian*. Ed. Claire Lamont. New York: Oxford UP, 1982.

Spacks, Patricia Meyer. "Sisters." *Fetter'd or Free? British Women Novelists, 1670-1815*. Ed. Mary Anne Schofield and Cecilia Machelski. Athens: Ohio UP, 1986.

West, Jane. *A Gossip's Story*. London, 1797.

Wollstonecraft, Mary. *A Vindication of the Rights of Woman, with Strictures on Moral and Political Subjects*. 1792. Ed. Charles W. Hagelman, Jr. New York: Norton, 1967.

Sisters in Collusion:
Safety and Revolt in Shirley Jackson's
We Have Always Lived in the Castle

Karen J. Hall

> She understood that telling what you remembered, and writing down what had happened to you when you were young were radical acts of personal history that would force the rewriting of social history.
>
> Louise DeSalvo, *Virginia Woolf*

> And for a minute we stood very still, pressed together by the feeling of people all around us.
>
> Shirley Jackson, *We Have Always Lived in the Castle*

In the first paragraph of Shirley Jackson's *We Have Always Lived in the Castle*, the narrator introduces herself as Mary Katherine Blackwood, known affectionately as Merricat, an 18-year-old who lives with her sister, Constance. With any luck, she says, she would have been a werewolf "because the two middle fingers on both [her] hands are the same length" (1). She dislikes washing herself, dogs and noise; she likes her sister Constance, Richard Plantagenet, and *Amanita phalloides*, the death-cup mushroom. Everyone else in her family is dead.*

As the plot unfolds we learn that Merricat and Constance live with their invalid uncle, Julian, that the rest of the family died of arsenic poisoning, that Constance stood trial for the murders but was acquitted for lack of evidence, and that there is a change in the air. Cousin Charles Blackwood embodies this change and will appear on the scene and attempt to transmogrify himself into the dead patriarch John Blackwood until Merricat frightens him away by setting fire to the Blackwood ancestral home. We also learn that Merricat, not Constance, killed her family by putting arsenic in the sugar bowl, and that Constance knew what her sister had done but remained silent for six years.

Castle is a complex and violent novel which has been relegated to the realm of juvenile fiction where its core of physical and psychic pain and its transgressive forces have been reinscribed, silenced and made safe for

*My thanks to my colleague Rosaria M. Champagne whose own work helped me formulate the theoretical framework for this essay and who, along with Audrey Jaffe and Debra Moddelmog, read the many drafts this work has gone through.

adolescent female readers. My goal as a reader is to untangle the psychological horror story told in *Castle* by borrowing the assumptions of theorists who are contesting the categorical boundaries and definitions of evidence and experience, and the discourse of the current recovery movement.[1] To this end, I read Merricat's and Constance's behaviors and actions in the novel as symptoms of the aftereffects of sexual abuse. I then theorize their behaviors as feminist interventions against the patriarchy which violates and oppresses them.

Uncle Julian has the most recognizable symptoms of trauma—on the night of the family murders, he consumed enough arsenic to leave him crippled and confined to a wheelchair. Julian is the only character in the novel who has a discourse available to him which allows him to say, "I am a survivor" (45). Julian is also the only character who has symptoms which a doctor can diagnose and treat. The way Julian copes with his trauma, however, suggests that rather than acting as a point of closure, the trauma which occurred on the night of the poisoning acts as a point of departure which explains the anxieties, rituals and behaviors the surviving Blackwoods manifest.

Despite Julian's ability to name and classify his victimhood, he is unable to reassure himself that the family murders really did take place. When Helen Clarke tells Julian at tea that he must forget about that night and put his morbid thoughts away, Julian turns to Constance to ask, " 'Didn't it really happen?' " and when Charles refuses to discuss the murders with him, he again asks Constance, " 'It *did* happen?' "—both times touching his fingers to his mouth as if searching for a trace of the arsenic (46, 95). Julian is obsessed with the murders and makes their study his life's work (43). His life is a ritualized, compulsive pattern of days in which he rises from sleep to eat, nap and study his notes of the events of the family's final day. Julian's obsessive compulsive behavior and his inability to believe in or even to remember his own victimization suggests that the Blackwood house was a dangerous place even before the murders.

To say that the family lacked closeness is an understatement. Mrs. Blackwood refused to cook or to garden or to nurture any living thing, jobs which all Blackwood women had traditionally made a show of fulfilling. She was intent on keeping a private home where the only visitors were people of the proper class. She trained her daughters to clean the house thoroughly, especially her drawing room which she could not bear to see untidy; for this reason she never allowed her daughters to come in the room, except of course to clean (34).

The only descriptions we get of John Blackwood come from Merricat, who says that her father kept a small notebook where he listed the people who owed him money or whom he felt owed him favors, and from Julian who remembers that he was inconsiderate on the last morning, whistling and waking his wife, Dorothy, who was still sleeping (67), that he was stingy, and that he was dishonest (121). Julian also remembers that John Blackwood was very fond of his person, "given to adorning himself, and not overly clean" (113). Julian's most descriptive recollection of his brother labels the most likely perpetrator of violence in the Blackwood home narcissistic and dirty.

This description of the Blackwood family corresponds to the portrait Louise DeSalvo paints of an incestuous family. Relying on Judith Herman and Lisa Hirschman's work, *Father-daughter Incest*, DeSalvo claims that incest is not a deviance from the ethics of family care, but is "a logical outgrowth of how the patriarchal family is organized" (8). One of the key players in such a family is a father who maintains despotic paternal rule (DeSalvo 9). This is a reasonable description of John Blackwood, a vain man who readers are told asserts power over his brother and sister-in-law by always making Julian and Dorothy aware that they are guests in his home, who meddles in and mediates family arguments which do not immediately concern him, who keeps thorough accounts of his finances, including debts of social obligation, and who maintains his status as much through his accumulation of personal possessions as through the power he asserts over his family and within his class.

Before the murders, Constance was in charge of all the family's cooking. Julian tells the inquisitive visitor Lucille Wright that the family "relied upon Constance for various small delicacies which only she could provide" (48). Mrs. Wright comments that Constance should not have been doing all the cooking. Julian replies, "Well, of course, there is the root of our trouble" (50). Mrs. Wright feels Constance was an unfit family cook because of her vast knowledge of poisons, but Julian knows that Constance's cooking is quite safe; what is not safe is the fact that, following the pattern of many incestuous homes, Mrs. Blackwood was a disinterested, absent mother, which left Constance to stand in for Mrs. Blackwood in the kitchen.

Many incest survivors develop eating disorders in an attempt to regain control over their bodies—control of the shape of their bodies, control of what can and cannot enter their bodies, and, by mediating a fine line between starvation and nourishment, survivors control who will punish their bodies. Although Merricat does not manifest what we may recognize as an eating disorder, food is a mystified, powerful substance for her. She has an extremely complex set of rules for what food she can and cannot touch, and she refuses to eat in front of people. Constance enables these behaviors. She feeds Merricat alone in the kitchen after meals are over or guests have left, she does not force Merricat to touch foods or kitchenware she does not want to touch, and she takes special car in the preparation of Merricat's meals. Most of all, Constance does not challenge Merricat's systems; she doesn't punish Merricat, make fun of her, or expect her to behave differently.

E. Sue Blume suggests in her work *Secret Survivors* that more women than men manifest eating disorders because women have "primary responsibility for providing food for those around them" (151). Food has long been an overdetermined signifier of power for Blackwood women. Generations of Blackwood women leave traces of their lives and nurturing abilities by filling the basement of the Blackwood ancestral home with their preserved foodstuffs. The script which stipulates that Blackwood women are responsible for maintaining the family through food production pre-exists Constance, and she is forced to assume this responsibility before she reaches adulthood, much, I suspect, as she is forced to assume responsibility for her father's sexual desires before she is an adult. Thus, it is no wonder that the majority of rules Merricat creates involve the preparation and eating of food or that the weapon she uses against her family is food. Merricat transforms the substance they force Constance to nurture them with into a poison, and she chooses to poison the sugar specifically—a food witches believed was unhealthy (Carpenter 34), a food Constance refuses to allow into her body, and, perhaps most importantly, a food their younger brother Thomas, the heir to the Blackwood fortune and a privileged son who "possessed many of his father's more forceful traits of character" (48), eats in excessive amounts.

Unlike Constance who assumes the role of the responsible child, the little parent of the dysfunctional family, Merricat is the child who manifests her symptoms by abreacting a number of psychosomatic symptoms when she feels threatened or frightened.[2] She claims that she cannot see color in the village, that everything is a dull gray, and when Constance begins to be converted into "one of them" by Cousin Charles, even Constance looks gray (88). Merricat feels chilled and shivers when she is approached by villagers, when she first sees Charles outside the house, and when Constance whistles the tune John Blackwood whistled on the morning of the last day of his life. Whenever Merricat panics, she feels as though she cannot breathe. When she fears Constance will leave her, she feels tied with wire and cannot breathe (39); when she first sees Charles, she cannot breathe (79); when Charles first stands in their kitchen, Merricat "was held tight, wound round with wire, [she] couldn't breathe, and [she] had to run" (82); and the thought of her father's ring around her finger made her feel tied tight (111). Each time Merricat's surroundings trigger her fears and she panics, she feels the sensation that she is bound and cannot breathe. Merricat is describing what sounds like a body memory, a physical sensation the body remembers but the mind has no narrative for. Ellen Bass and Laura Davis state that such memories are stored in survivors' bodies "and it is possible to physically re-experience the terror of the abuse" (74-75). The sensation of being strangled or being unable to catch one's breath is common among survivors of abuse, and I feel it is significant that one of Merricat's memories is linked directly to her father his ring, and a possession which symbolizes union with him.

A further symptom of Merricat's earlier abuse is her ability to split when she feels threatened. Splitting is a coping mechanism common among survivors of sexual abuse:

In its milder form, you live exclusively on the mental level, in your thoughts, and aren't fully present. At its most extreme, you literally leave your body. This feat, which some yogis work for decades to achieve, comes naturally to children during severe trauma. They cannot physically run away, so they leave their bodies. (Bass and Davis 209-10)

At the grocery store Merricat stops in the doorway "feeling around inside myself for some thought to make me safe" (13). Moments later during her confrontation with Jim Donell in Stella's diner, Merricat distances herself by watching her hands rip her napkin into tiny pieces and making a rule for herself that whenever she sees tiny scraps of paper she will be kinder to Julian (17). As Merricat leaves the diner and Donell's cruel laughter, she thinks to herself, "I liked my house on the moon, and I put a fireplace in it and a garden outside" (21). The moon is Merricat's safe place, a world a winged horse carries her to when she is threatened, punished or afraid. As Merricat passes the Harris' house and the Harris boys taunt her, she pretends she does not speak their language, "on the moon we spoke a soft, liquid tongue and sang in the starlight, looking down on the dead dried world," and she thinks to herself that it is strange to be inside herself, "hiding very far inside but [still able] to hear them and see them from the corner of my eye" (23).

Merricat thinks and talks about the moon a great deal more once Cousin Charles arrives. Charles threatens her safety by transgressing the boundaries of his role as guest and as cousin by desiring to marry Constance. Merricat is well practiced at thinking herself out of her body and into a place of safety, so well practiced that as her burned out house is invaded by violent villagers she thinks, "I am on the moon...please let me be on the moon" (154). Merricat is able to dissociate during all of this violence yet still be present enough to protect herself and Constance from the villagers and escape to the safety of the woods. And it is to Merricat's safe place that Constance and Merricat retreat after the fire, "We are on the moon at last," and Constance replies, "I'm glad to be here...Thank you for bringing me" (165).

Critics who claim Merricat is crazy refer most frequently to her violent desires to act out rather than to her frequent breaks with reality. Even before readers find out Merricat poisoned her family, we see her imagine all the customers in the grocery store falling over, writhing in pain and dying while she steps over them to help herself to the groceries she needs. Merricat asserts that she was never sorry when she had thoughts like this; she only wished they would come true (12). She wishes she could see the Harris boys lying dead on the ground (23), and even the thought of Charles' big white face, a face which looks very much like John Blackwood's, makes her want "to beat at him until he went away...to stamp on him after he was dead, and see him lying on the grass" (116).

Even more disturbing than Merricat's desires are the scenes where she carries them out. Worried that Constance may venture outside their home, Merricat goes into the kitchen and smashes their best milk pitcher (39). Furious that Charles will not leave the house even after she has politely asked him to, Merricat carries all the furnishings out of his bedroom, pulls down the curtains, and dumps twigs and dirt and water in his bed. These acts are symbolic, indeed; in a more contemporary novel Merricat would no doubt have defecated in Charles' bed.[3] What provokes her most violent and confrontational rages, however, is the threat of punishment. On the night of the murders, Merricat had been sent to her room without dinner for bad behavior, and on the night when she sets fire to the house, Charles has threatened to punish her for making his room filthy.

As Charles rants about the filth in his room, he completely collapses into the identity of John Blackwood. Even Julian confuses him with the dead patriarch and says to Charles, "You are a very selfish man, John, perhaps even a scoundrel, and overly fond of the world's goods; I sometimes wonder, John, if you are every bit the gentleman" (134). Merricat calls Charles an evil ghost and Julian, once he recognizes him as his nephew, not his brother, calls him a bastard. Charles says the house is a crazy house. Readers have a perspective which allows them to see the "craziness" of the present scene and its striking, and for Merricat and Julian, confusing, resemblance to the crazy house of the past in which John Blackwood often stood in the kitchen and yelled just as Charles yells now.

Merricat's reaction to Charles' insistence that she be punished is intense. She stands in the kitchen doorway shivering, shrieks at him, "Punish me? You mean send me to bed without my dinner?" and then flees the house in search of safety. She then goes to the summerhouse, a wild, abandoned ugly place the family never used because it was damp and mold grew on everything. Here she sits and fantasizes that she is at the dinner table surrounded by a loving family. Everyone is extending themselves to her, offering her presents, saying they love her, vowing never to punish her, and even ordering her brother to give her his dinner (139). This wish fulfilling fantasy suggests that at least a part of Merricat's trauma involved neglect and fear of abandonment. Merricat is not the only character who recognizes these fears; Julian believes that Merricat literally died of neglect six years ago in an orphanage (135), and, on the morning after the fire while their house stands in ruins, Constance's primary concern is that Merricat has missed her dinner (165).

Charles calls up a wealth of Merricat's childhood memories. She can run away to a safe place and create a fantasy script where her memories are rewritten, but she must return to the house for her dinner, and Charles is unwilling to forget the mess this wild child has made in his room. When Merricat enters the house, she can hear Charles' voice in the dining room droning on about his need to punish her. Past and present again conflate for Merricat. She climbs the stairs, goes into Charles' room, and, in an act of erasure, throws his lit pipe and smoldering ashes into the garbage. Lynette Carpenter argues that this is the only point in the novel where readers are asked to believe that Merricat's perceptions are "limited" and "inadequate" (35). Merricat's perceptions are not limited, I would argue, but because she feels threatened by Charles, her altered ability to perceive colors is a return of the psychosomatic symptom we have seen her exhibit before. I would also argue Merricat is splitting when she goes into Charles' room. Because she is confusing the present with the past, it is not the 18-year-old Merricat who throws a burning pipe onto newspapers without understanding the consequences. Merricat is acting out rage against John Blackwood and Charles Blackwood simultaneously, and though the narrative may offer scant material evidence for why her rage is so intense, there is more than enough symptomatic evidence to suggest that Merricat has reason to be angry. Alice Miller points out in her book, *Thou Shalt Not Be Aware*, that rage is "an appropriate reaction to cruelty" (qtd. in DeSalvo 6) despite its frequent misinterpretation as a sign of mental imbalance, and Merricat's aftereffects extensively document her experience of cruelty.

Merricat's and Constance's behaviors are reasonable. Before the fire Constance fulfilled a maternal role. She was the sibling who accepted full responsibility for her father's abuse, for her own victimization, and for the results of Merricat's rages. Constance represses her father's abuse and Merricat acts out. She is the container of the sisters' unspoken rage, the signifier of a violent household. Their characters are distinct, but they collude in their silence and the boundaries between them blur. When Julian tells Mrs. Wright the stories of the poisoning, Constance admits that she bought the arsenic to kill rats, and as she says this she turns to Merricat and smiles (52). Merricat and Constance also share a glance during a conversation about their family's murder which suggests to Merricat that Constance was as full of merriment as she was (44). Constance cleans the sugar bowl before the police arrive, waits to call the doctor, and confesses to Merricat's crime, telling the police "those people deserved to die" (53). In quiet but revealing ways, Constance is able to collude with her sister and to share Merricat's rage.

Merricat and Constance strive to erase the abusive patriarchal power structure they live under. For six years that power structure is weakened enough to allow the sisters to live in safety. But there were Blackwood men who lived outside their house whom the arsenic-poisoned sugar could not reach, and Charles' penetration of their space makes action necessary. Charles' power to convert Constance into a phallic mother is as dangerous as living with his big white face is disturbing. Constance is easily swayed by Charles and the familiar order he represents. Shortly after Charles has established himself in the castle, Constance takes up the refrain that she hasn't been doing her duty (114), that she and Merricat and Julian should be living "normal lives" (118), and that the situation they are now living in is all her fault; this "was her new way of thinking" (131) and it demonstrates how quickly Constance is re-absorbed into the phallic patriarchal structure where Charles' prerogatives (which are always on the brink of collapsing into John Blackwood's) rule the house and her obligations and responsibilities enable him. Before Constance is irretrievably lost, Merricat must erase Charles.

Neither of Merricat's acts of erasure are simple inversions of the patriarchal order. In the first instance, she and Constance collude to turn Constance's obligation to nourish the family against them and they kill all of the dangerous participants of the phallic order. Constance and Merricat manipulate feminine obligations rather than usurp masculine power. James Egan argues in his essay, "Sanctuary: Shirley Jackson's Domestic and Fantastic Parables," that Constance and Merricat are unable to create a better world. He claims that they create a nihilistic, inescapable Gothic maze, an endless procession of destructive illusions and that a "'family' more bizarre and monstrous than the one Merricat poisoned [has] risen to take its place, a mutated family, without parents, which cannot rise above distorted emotional relationships" (23). Egan's interpretation of the family Constance and Merricat establish is not entirely inaccurate, though his definition of family sounds frighteningly similar to current ultra-conservative definitions of the family unit. Erasing the dangerous presence of

John Blackwood, the perpetrator of violence sanctioned by the patriarchal family, provides no guarantee that Constance and Merricat will be able to establish healthy emotional relationships. Their obsessive compulsive behaviors will not magically disappear. And though they are free of John Blackwood's violence, they realize that they are unable to control all forces which may harm them. Merricat checks the locks on the doors approximately 30 times in this short novel, checks the fence line enclosing their property every Wednesday, buries magical safeguards on the property which she checks every Sunday, and realizes Charles' presence must be erased immediately upon his arrival.

Merricat's second act of erasure like her first is instinctive. Only a week after his arrival, Merricat intuits that this erasure of the patriarchal order must be more complete than the first, and just as she and Constance manipulated their feminine obligations rather than attempting to usurp masculine power the first time, Merricat again attempts to rid the house of the patriarchal order by turning it against itself. Merricat claims that the fire belongs to Charles; it is not her rage or wrongdoing but his own carelessness and evil which is responsible for the fire which burns the Blackwood home, and also gets rid of Charles and enables the sisters to sever all ties with the outside world.

When Julian dies in the panic caused by the fire, the sisters no longer need to invite Dr. Levy into their home. Though he returns once to threaten and coerce these two errant daughters, Merricat and Constance will never again have to admit this powerful enforcer of the patriarchy into their castle. The dining room which stood as a memorial to the family who died in it, the stately living room in which Mrs. Blackwood held court, the attic where trunks of their clothes were stored (clothes which Merricat dressed up in every Thursday), and the bedrooms where Merricat and Constance slept are all gone, either burned away by the fire or closed off for all time. Also changed forever is the pattern of Merricat's and Constance's days. They no longer clean the house on Fridays as Mrs. Blackwood taught them to, they do not admit their parents' friends into the house for tea, and they no longer have reason to go to their father's safe in his study for money. Life on the moon truly is a new life for the sisters.

But even after an apocalyptic fire, all traces of the patriarchal order are not gone. The sisters use the remnants of wedding china and silver, and though Constance has never seen it used and does not know what Blackwood woman brought the china and silver into the house, both sisters know patriarchal enforcement of heterosexuality and laws of inheritance are responsible for its presence in their castle (178). Merricat continues to assert control by creating food rules: "[u]sually I ate fruit and vegetables still moist from the ground and the air, but I disliked eating anything while it was still dirty with the ash from our burned house." All the food from the garden now must be washed first and even then Merricat thought the smoke from the fire would always be in the ground where their food grew, that the Blackwood ancestral home would always penetrate what she relied on for sustenance (196). And locks are still a necessity in this new world because the sisters are aware that people are still watching them.

Despite their attempts to erase the patriarchal order, Constance and

Merricat can never be completely free of its abusive structure. Traces of John Blackwood's world exist inside their secure locks, and outside on their lawn villagers come and stare at the burned out house. The castle and the sisters have been reinscribed into the patriarchal structure as haunted, monstrous beings. Strangers frighten each other with stories and discipline their children with frightening lies about Constance and Merricat:

"They'd hold you down and make you eat candy full of poison; I heard that dozens of bad little boys have gone too near that house and never been seen again. They catch little boys and they—"
"Shh. *Honestly*, Ethel."
"Do they like little girls?" The other child drew near.
"They hate little boys and little girls. The difference is, they *eat* little girls." (206-07 Jackson's italics)

Women cannot live self-sufficiently under the law of the father, nor are they supposed to transgress his law. Constance and Merricat must be represented in a way which will serve a function in the patriarchal system; they become witches, monsters used to frighten children by day and adults by night back into the boundaries of acceptable, obedient behavior.

Merricat tells Constance that life on the moon " 'is not quite as [she] supposed it would be.' " Constance replies, " 'It is a very happy place, though' " (195), and Merricat echoes this sentiment in the final line of the novel, " 'Oh, Constance,' I said, 'we are so happy' " (214). Merricat desires a safe home. This in itself is a transgression against patriarchal structures, but because Merricat's resistance is motivated by her personal experience of trauma, her actions are not necessarily transformative. Safety means containment in the castle and containment means watching without being heard. When Helen Clarke and her husband come back to the castle to bring Merricat and Constance back to the world outside, Merricat wants to laugh out loud but does not (189). When Charles returns to their castle to try to talk to the sisters or at least get a picture of them that he can sell to a newspaper, Constance finally sees Charles as Merricat has seen him all along: as "a ghost and a demon, one of the strangers" (209). Constance smiles unpleasantly, and both sisters restrain their laughter until Charles finally leaves, which is not soon enough for Merricat. She "did not know whether Constance was going to be able to contain herself until he got down the steps and safely into the car" (211). Merricat is afraid Constance will not be able to hold back her laughter and her rage until Charles is gone. If Merricat and Constance felt free enough to laugh or if they could leave their home as Ruthie and Sylvie do in Marilynne Robinson's novel, *Housekeeping*, perhaps my reading of the novel would feel more satisfying and liberating, but because Merricat and Constance accept safety in containment, their resistance against the patriarchal order is readily contained. Collusive sisterhood is only truly powerful when sisters remain in motion and allow each other to laugh out loud, and when sisterhood extends beyond the boundaries of our families or origin, uniting us in politically transgressive struggle.

Notes

[1]See Joan W. Scott, "The Evidence of Experience," *Critical Inquiry* 17 (1991): 773-797, and the two special issues of *Critical Inquiry* entitled, "Questions of Evidence," 17.4 and 18.1 (1991).

[2]A number of works on adult children of dysfunctional families include descriptions of the roles children assume. I have relied on Claudia Black's book, *Double Duty: Help for the Adult Child who is also Gay or Lesbian* (New York: Ballantine, 1990) 15-23 for my description here of the responsible child and the child who acts out.

[3]For more on the way anthropologists have explained the politics of dirt for contemporary literary critics, see Mary Douglas *Purity and Danger* (London: Ark Paperbacks, 1966).

Works Cited

Bass, Ellen and Laura Davis. *The Courage to Heal: A Guide for Women Survivors of Child Sexual Abuse.* New York: Harper and Row, 1988.

Black, Claudia. *Double Duty: Help for the Adult Child who is also Gay or Lesbian.* New York: Ballantine, 1990.

Blume, E. Sue. *Secret Survivors: Uncovering Incest and its Aftereffects in Women.* New York: Ballantine, 1990.

Carpenter, Lynette. "The Establishment and Preservation of Female Power in Shirley Jackson's *We Have Always Lived in the Castle.*" *Frontiers* 8.1 (1984): 32-38.

DeSalvo, Louise. *Virginia Woolf: The Impact of Childhood Sexual Abuse on Her Life and Work.* New York: Ballantine, 1989.

Egan, James. "Sanctuary: Shirley Jackson's Domestic and Fantastic Parables." *Studies in Weird Fiction* 6 (1989): 15-24.

Hoffman, Steven K. "Individuation and Character Development in the Fiction of Shirley Jackson." *Hartford Studies in Literature* 8.3 (1976): 190-208.

Jackson Shirley. *We Have Always Lived in the Castle.* New York: Penguin, 1962.

Parks, John G. "Chambers of Yearning: Shirley Jackson's Use of the Gothic." *Twentieth Century Literature.* 30.1 (1984): 15-29.

_____. " 'The Possibility of Evil': A Key to Shirley Jackson's Fiction." *Studies in Short Fiction* 15.3 (1978): 320-23.

Scott, Joan W. "The Evidence of Experience." *Critical Inquiry* 17 (1991): 773-97.

Woodruff, Stuart C. "The Real Horror Elsewhere: Shirley Jackson's Last Novel." *Southwest Review* 52.2 (1967): 152-62.

Sister Bonds:
Intersections of Family and Race
in Jessie Redmon Fauset's *Plum Bun*
and Dorothy West's *The Living Is Easy*

Eva Rueschmann

It is the interactions among sisters that instigate the heroine's journey toward self, toward psyche....Our sisterly relationships challenge and nurture us, even as we sometimes disappoint and betray one another.

Christine Downing, *Psyche's Sisters* (3-4).

While the conflicted mother-daughter bond has garnered much attention by feminist critics and theorists in the last decade, an analysis of biological sisterhood is noticably absent from feminist theory, narrative interpretations, and psychological views of female relationships. Toni McNaron's *The Sister Bond* and Christine Downing's *Psyche's Sisters* are rare examples of studies on the roles that sisters play in literature and women's lives. Downing claims that "[a]lthough feminists have written often enough about the power and beauty of 'sisterhood,' they have rarely acknowledged those actualities of kinship experience that underlie the metaphor" (154).

Even less scholarship has appeared on the influence of race, culture, class, and ethnicity on the representation of sisters in literature. In her collection of stories about family relationships by black writers, *Memory of Kin*, Mary Helen Washington contends that there are few stories in the black American tradition which focus on sisters, and she dismisses them for emphasizing conflict and rivalry (304, note 3). While conflicts between opposite sisters is a recurring feature in literary representations of the sibling bond, I suggest that this turbulent relationship invites a more detailed discussion. I argue that the sister relationship has a more complex role to play in the larger context of female identity formation, which has been revised by feminist psychoanalytical views of women's psychosexual development, notably by Chodorow, Dinnerstein and Benjamin. Jessie Fauset's *Plum Bun* (1929) and Dorothy West's *The Living Is Easy* (1948) are two novels by black women writers of the Harlem Renaissance that portray the particular narrative and psychological significance of sisters in the development of a sense of self in black women and that use the sister bond to problematize the individual's relationship to the black community.

For African-American women, the problem of self-definition and self-fulfillment has been doubly difficult because they have had to struggle with the shackles of societal sexism and racism. According to Barbara Christian, "most

120

novels [by African-American women writers] published before the 1950s embodied the tension between the writers' apparent acceptance of an ideal of woman derived from white upper-class society and the reality with which their protagonists had to contend" (237). Both Fauset and West wrote their novels with an awareness that the values of the dominant culture have wielded a decisive impact on the problems of female self-definition within black American culture. The particular struggle between a desire for individual freedom and the need to identify with the larger black community is a dilemma that permeates much of pre-1950s African-American women's fiction. Susan Willis calls the return to the black community "the single most common feature in fiction by black women writers" (116). This conflict between individual and group identity is particularly difficult for the protagonists of *Plum Bun* and *The Living Is Easy* because of their color- and class-consciousness and their desire for social advancement and economic security.

Fauset and West were writing about the emerging black middle-class after World War I in the urban areas of the North, New York and Boston, and the particular problems of black self-definition which resulted from the black bourgeoisie's dream of upward mobility in a racially segregated society. According to such black sociologists as Franklin Frazier and Nathan Hare, the black middle-class began to imitate the values, standards and life style of the white middle-class in an attempt to assimilate. This form of assimilationism, which Robert Bone calls "a kind of psychological 'passing' at the fantasy level" (4), and the actual "passing" of light-skinned middle-class mulattas featured in many novels of the Harlem Renaissance, also inform the plots of *Plum Bun* and *The Living Is Easy*.

While Fauset's novels have been dismissed in the past as superficial romances, more recent feminist re-evaluations of Jessie Fauset's writing, primarily by Deborah McDowell, Carol Sylvander, and Cheryl Wall, emphasize that her novels need to be re-examined for their sensitive portrayal of the impact of racial and gender stereotypes on black female development in 1920s America. In her book on gender and ethnicity in American culture, Mary Dearborn writes that "[t]he characters in her [Fauset's] novels are motivated by the search for familial identification and lost inheritance, and her treatment of the passing black and the mulatto is informed by the same ambivalence and confusion that characterizes other female-authored mulatto novels" (145).[1]

The lines of an old nursery rhyme (To market, to market,/To buy a plum bun:/Home again, home again,/ Market is done) that structure *Plum Bun* comment ironically on the life of its black heroine, Angela Murray. The hopeful lines about a successful trip to the market contrast with the difficult realities that an African-American girl encounters on her way to adulthood. Angela Murray can take advantage of the "American market" in the 1920s only at a high cost, namely through 'passing,' which entails a denial of her entire past and her African-American heritage. The overdetermined "plum bun"—the product to be purchased at the market—turns out to be a miserable, degrading affair with a prejudiced, sexist white man. She can only achieve a certain degree of happiness after she acknowledges her past and has shed her fairy-tale illusions about life and her own fate.

Plum Bun's dual focus on a fairy tale structure and the subversion of the fairy tale as a literary vehicle of female socialization intersect with the theme of sisterhood in important ways. Christine Downing has identified the sibling bond—and the sister relationship in particular—as a central theme in fairy tales "because of the role that sisters and brothers play in helping one another separate from their parents and grow up" (23). It is not surprising, then, that the sister relationship plays such a crucial role in Plum Bun, a novel that relies so overtly on fairy tale conventions and traces the identity crisis of the main character Angela Murray (signified by her attempt at 'passing'), her search for familial identification and lost heritage.[2]

Plum Bun uses the sister complementarity in a critical way to undermine Angela's romantic assumptions about life and love and to expose her 'passing' as a form of denial of her self and her African-American history. Angela's sister Virginia, who represents a more race-conscious black woman, plays a significant role in her identity formation. All the key events in Angela's psychological development—her separation from home, her denial of her heritage and rejection of her sister, her guilt, her growing appreciation of black culture and its beauty, her longing for meaningful relationships, and her final refusal to 'pass'—are connected to her younger sister Virginia and their evolving relationship. Virginia becomes, in the words of Christine Downing, an unconscious guide to Angela's journey toward self, toward psyche, that is, to an increased consciousness of her roots and true identity.

Female identity formation is compounded by the difficulty of self-definition for black children whose relationship to the larger society will be more conflicted because of internalized racism. Drawing on Carol Gilligan's emphasis on the importance of attachment and connection for female children, Janie Victoria Ward describes the central developmental tasks for black female adolescents in her article "Racial Identity Formation and Transformation" and emphasizes that "[t]he effort to understand identity formation in black adolescents is incomplete without an appreciation of the concept of racial identity. Psychologists argue that a stable concept of self both as an individual as well as a group member (black) is essential to the healthy growth and development of the black self" (218). During the specific psychosocial crisis of adolescence, the black adolescent needs to construct and affirm an identity that includes a positive identification with her black culture in the face of negative social perceptions of race. "For blacks, identity formation is a necessary rebirth in one's own terms" (Ward 219).

The conflict over separation from and attachment to the black community intersects with Angela Murray's confusion about her racial identity, which reaches back to her childhood. For instance, in contrast to her condescending dismissal of her black neighborhood in Philadelphia, Angela's first impressions of Manhattan betray her unbridled enthusiasm and a naive belief in equal opportunity, personal freedom and a "phantasm of total individuality, which she locates as the privilege of whites" (Kubitschek 106):

[S]he was young; she was temporarily independent, she was intelligent, she was white. She remembered an expression "free, white and twenty-one,"—this was what it meant then, this sense of owning the world, this realization that other things being equal, all things were possible. (88)

Angela's longing for a life of adventure and pleasure, which she sees just within her reach because of an "accident of heredity" (136), contrasts with her sister Virginia's idealization of their parents' marriage and way of life. Although Angela and Virginia have different expectations for life, they have both been nurtured on a steady diet of fairy tales in childhood; their mother Mattie ends each story with "And so they lived happily ever after, just like your father and me" (33). Angela and Virginia await their own "princes"; Virginia hopes for a man "who would be just like her father," and Angela fantasizes about a white prince who would rescue her from a life of poverty and mediocrity. When their parents die, Angela sees a life of freedom ahead of her—"almost as though by magic her affairs were arranging themselves" (81). Handsome Roger Fielding, a fabulously wealthy American "blue blood" seems to hold the "golden keys which could open the doors to beauty and ease and—decency" (142). Roger pursues her, and she envisions their marriage and sees "her life rounding out like a fairy tale" (131). In order to live this fairy tale life, however, she needs to sacrifice her sister, the last member of her family who connects her to her past. This decision to completely "pass" is psychologically well-prepared for by several incidents in Angela's childhood.

As a young girl, Angela's weekly excursions in Philadelphia involved a game of deception in which her mother would "pass" for white. This experience instilled in her a belief that passing is the only way for some light-skinned blacks to enjoy the pleasures denied to African-Americans in the years of racial segregation. "It was from her mother that Angela learned the possibilities for joy and freedom which seemed to her inherent in mere whiteness" (14). When, on one occasion, Mattie makes no effort to greet her husband and Virginia in the street, her behavior—confusing to an impressionable young girl whose identity is so intertwined with her mother's—lays the psychological foundations for Angela's identity confusion and for her later refusal to recognize her sister in public.

A childhood game of mistaken identity that Angela and Virginia play repeatedly as a joke in the first part of the novel plays a more sinister role in Angela's rejection of her sister and ultimately reveals Angela's troubled self. When Angela meets her sister at the train station in New York and she happens to run into her lover Roger Fielding at the same time, the old childhood game saves Angela from disclosing her true self but it also marks the estrangement between the sisters and Angela's decision to cut her ties to the past. Angela's public denial of her sister forces her to rethink her inner conflict between her social ambitions and her attachment to her sister, and by extension her heritage. "For the first time in the pursuit of her chosen ends she began to waver. Surely no ambition, no pinnacle of safety was supposed to call for the sacrifice of a sister" (159).

Virginia recognizes the self-deception involved in Angela's attempt to sever her ties to the African-American experience and places Angela's decision in historical perspective. In their discussion of Angela's refusal to acknowledge Virginia, the latter remembers "that it had been possible in slavery times for white men and women to mistreat their mulatto relations, their own flesh and blood, selling them into deeper slavery in the far South or standing by watching them beaten, almost, if not completely, to death. Perhaps there was something fundamentally different between white and coloured after all..." (167-68). As Kubitschek notes, Virginia remembers what the decision to be white entailed and permitted; her harsh statement here justifiably calls her sister to account for the contemporary manifestations of that choice (109). Angela, for whom the romantic couple is all, refuses to acknowledge the historical implications of her action and believes she can fashion a new life and self. Indeed, in order to fulfill her romantic visions, Angela splits off her identity as a black woman and projects it onto her sister. " 'Oh Jinny, you don't know, I don't think you can understand the things I want to see and know. You're not like me—' " (78). Virginia, who is visibly shocked by her sister's deception, accepts their separation and claims "you and I are two separate people and we've got to live our lives apart, not like the Siamese twins" (171).

However, Angela's denial of her family and past comes back to haunt her when she breaks off the demeaning love affair with Roger Fielding and experiences loneliness and isolation. "[L]ife which had seemed so promising, so golden, had failed to supply her with a single friend to whom she could turn in an hour of extremity" (234). Angela realizes that the Cinderella fairy tale where love and material gain mesh so felicitously is just a dream and, in the process of her disillusionment, she comes to appreciate the emotional bonds with her sister and rediscovers her ties to her own culture.

Angela's rejection of her sister weighs heavily on her as all her ambitions seem to lead nowhere. Her false identity ("stolen waters are the sweetest") leaves her unable to secure attachments in either white or black communities. Angela longs for the former intimacy with her sister but is not yet able to give up the social advantages of 'passing.' Angela's renewed attachment to her sister is accompanied by her growing appreciation for the black community and her changing attitude towards Harlem. While Angela had first observed Harlem as an outsider, she later feels a secret kinship with the African-American audience at a lecture by Van Meier (a thinly-disguised W.E.B. DuBois) in Harlem and notices her inner distance from her white friends. "[L]ittle waves of feeling played out from groups within the audience and beat against her consciousness and against that of her friends, only the latter were without her secret powers of interpretation" (216). This realization is an example of what black writers and critics have termed "a complex double-consciousness, socialized ambivalence or double vision" (Bell 6), that is, an acculturative process whereby black Americans remain rooted in an African-American tradition within a white Western culture.

On her visits to her sister in Harlem, Angela is startled to recognize Virginia's beauty and radiance and she envies her sister her "utterly open life, no secrets, no subterfuges, no goals to be reached by devious ways" (243). Whereas she once scorned her sister for her concern for racial uplift, Angela now recognizes the possibility for a more authentic identity in Virginia's choice to live among "a happy, intelligent, rather independent group of young coloured men and women" (209) in Harlem. Angela has always relied on Virginia's generosity and expects to overcome their differences quickly after their reconciliation and to understand her decision to 'pass.' But Virginia, injured by Angela's rejection, keeps her sister at an emotional distance. It is only through a series of painful experiences that Angela can recapture her former intimacy with her sister, which is inextricably intertwined with the development of her race-consciousness.

When Angela finally realizes that she loves Anthony Cross, that a woman can be her "true self" with him, she discovers that he too is black and that he is engaged to Virginia. Virginia had met Anthony on the evening that Angela disavowed her in public and after Angela had rejected Anthony as a suitor. The coincidence seems contrived by standards of the realistic novel, but the love triangle between Angela, Virginia and Anthony creates a powerful entanglement that forces Angela to make a choice; she atones for "the really cruel and unjust action of her whole life" and refuses to take Anthony away from her sister. More than once she thinks of dying, then considers "the race of her parents and...all the odds against living which a cruel, relentless fate had called on them to endure. And she saw them as a people powerfully, almost overwhelmingly endowed with the essence of life. They had to persist, had to survive because they did not know how to die" (309). Angela's identification with her heritage and her people marks a significant development in her acceptance of herself, or to use Ward's expression, in her "rebirth in her own terms." Angela reclaims her racial heritage not through marriage to a black man (Anthony Cross) but rather, she develops a positive sense of herself as a black woman through identification with her biological and a spiritual sister.

Angela is given an opportunity to reconnect with her African-American heritage when she and her black fellow student Ms. Powell both win a competition and prize money to study art in Paris. The two young women have become friends and when the judges withdraw Ms. Powell's prize because of race, Angela can no longer distance herself and pretend to be an innocent bystander. During her affair with Roger Fielding, Angela had observed the plight of other black women with pity and had described them as "different, like Jinny" and "from the other world of her childhood and adolescence." Now, for the first time, Angela completely identifies with another black woman and with her intense anger and frustration at the blatant racism that destroys her lifetime's ambition. Angela's recognition of Ms. Powell's beauty and her identification with her are connected to her understanding of her sister. Angela makes this link herself when she contemplates:

After all, this girl [Ms. Powell] was one of her own. A whim of fate had set their paths far apart but just the same they were more than "sisters under the skin." They were really closely connected in blood, in racial condition, in common suffering. Once again she thought of herself as she had years ago when she had seen the coloured girl refused service in the restaurant: "It might easily have been Virginia." (340-41)

Angela then reveals her secret heritage to the press, and when she later discusses the consequences of her revelation with her sister, she acknowleges that "if it hadn't been for her [Ms. Powell], you and I probably never would have really found each other again" (353-54). Psychologically, Angela's act of identification implies a reparation of her severed relationship with her sister and a return to the black community. Before she leaves for Europe, Angela even returns to her childhood home in Philadelphia in an attempt to recapture the connection with her family. In the end, the sister relationship endures: "[Angela] thanked God in her heart for the stability implied in sisterhood" (349). "Wise" Virginia, who has saved her share of their parents' inheritance (and has preserved their memory), enables Angela to go to France to perfect her artistic talents and develop her career as a portrait painter. Unlike Cinderella, Angela repairs her relationship with her family before she marries her "prince"—a union that is not an escape from but rather an affirmation of her familial and racial bonds—a "plum on the bun," that is, an extra treat beyond the nourishing and vital ties to the black community (Sylvander 175).

The enduring internal bonds between sisters also play an important, if more ambivalent role in Dorothy West's *The Living Is Easy*, a novel that has been ignored or read in reductive ways by critics, among them black feminists who disagree on an evaluation of the novel's main character, Cleo Jericho Judson. Washington has written the most sympathetic analysis of West's novel and its controversial heroine, drawing largely on its autobiographical content and locating the emergence of Dorothy West's voice in her identification with her mother Rachel, who is the model for Cleo Judson. But like other critics she neglects to dissect the complexity of the sister bond in the novel, focusing instead almost exclusively on the mother-daughter relationship ("My Mother's Name" 143-63). Before Cleo became a wife and a mother, she was a sister and a daughter—a dimension of the novel that is highlighted in the chapters on Cleo's childhood in the South, a time when "the living was easy."

Washington sees the novel as split into two parts, one that describes Cleo's childhood when she was an active, talented, artistic child and another part that focuses on her as an adult woman who finds no creative outlet for her abundant energies and becomes a status-seeking, controlling and, finally, powerless woman. Washington claims in *Invented Lives*:

Since she clearly feels the impossibility of narrating the story of woman as artist, West creates a novel that is in contradiction with itself: Cleo the girl artist becomes Cleo the woman monster. (350)

Rather than read Cleo in Washington's terms as a failed artist, I suggest that there is a psychological continuity between the childhood scenes and Cleo's adult life. To this end, it is necessary to analyze the role of her sisters in both sections in shaping Cleo's self-image.

As in *Plum Bun*, the sisters in this novel represent the past and heritage that Cleo denies for the sake of her social ambitions, yet to which she is inescapably drawn. The psychological portrait of Cleo Judson intersects with the problems of racial identity formation in much the same way as it does for Angela Murray in *Plum Bun*. The very title of West's novel, *The Living Is Easy*, suggests Cleo's nostalgic view of her childhood days while reflecting West's ironic comment on the middle-class aspirations of the black Brahmins in Boston.[3]

Cleo Judson is a complex character, a woman who rebels against the narrow definitions of women's roles in the early part of the twentieth century, and who has a compelling sense of humor, what Dorothy West describes as the "Rabelaisian half of her mind" (245). Yet she is also relentless in her pursuit of her social ambitions and merciless in her treatment of her husband and all people whom she sees as inferior to herself. She wants to raise strong women, yet she will not tolerate any opposition or independence in her sisters or her daughter and nieces. Novelist Paule Marshall was one of the first critics to acknowledge Cleo's character as an early modern example of the psychological complexities of the black women's psyche. Marshall sees a sense of self-division at the root of Cleo's conflict:

Ruthless and despotic in her quest for acceptance, in constant terror that her lowly origins in the South will be found out, she is, at the same time, nostalgic for that past. She lives in perpetual conflict with the self she has assumed and the person she is. (qtd. in Washington, *Invented Lives* 352)

I contend that the split between her attachment to her Southern roots and her desire to recreate herself as a black Brahmin socialite is expressed in Cleo's conflicted enmeshment with her sisters and her mother, an attachment that needs to be viewed in light of her narcissistic personality and her position as the oldest child.

Even as a young girl, Cleo alternates between craving for affection and adulation and withdrawing into self-absorption and self-indulgence. Cleo is a bright child with tremendous vitality who is constantly driven to perform for her sisters and her white friend, Josie Beauchamp, whether she dares to ride a dangerous wild horse, does cartwheels or hangs upside down from a tree. Her younger sisters, Charity, Lily and Serena, are her main audience and as long as they focus their attention and admiration on her, Cleo feels happy and complete as a person: "[Cleo] was their oldest sister, their protector. She wasn't afraid of the biggest boy or the fiercest dog, or the meanest teacher...They accepted her teasing and tormenting as they accepted the terrors of the night" (16).

When she tells her sisters about riding Beauchamps' wild horse, embroidering her story to turn herself into a daring heroine, her sisters are "bewitched by her fanciful telling" (17) and are only released from her "spell" when she is finished with her outrageous tale. Cleo's performances continue to enchant her sisters in adulthood and bring them together as a female community. As Cleo's voice is silenced in a man's world, her sisters remain her primary adoring audience throughout her life: "Was it because [Cleo] was so full of life that she made things move inside you, tears or laughter or anger, and when she went out of a room something like something alive left with her?" (202). However, Cleo's storytelling is also a means of controlling her sisters, who have been dependent on her protection since childhood. Feeling threatened by all those who possess power, Cleo feels tenderness and affection only for those who show themselves to be weaker than herself.

Longing to be her mother's favorite, young Cleo imagines herself dead in a coffin at one point, "dressed up fine as [her white friend] Josie Beauchamp" (19), with her sisters and mother sobbing over her dead body. Her fantasy of being dead combines wish-fulfillment and displaced aggression: envious of her rich white friend and angry at her mother for not choosing her as a favorite daughter, Cleo both "punishes" and identifies with Josie and garners all the attention she craves from her mother and sisters. Cleo's split identity, expressed by her early ambivalence towards Josie, is later transferred onto her daughter Judy: "I want her to be a Bostonian, but I want her to be me deep down. Judy, her frightened heart cried, be me as my sisters are Mama" (141). Cleo's sisters remain her only sense of psychological continuity—a link to her childhood past that makes Cleo feel complete and powerful.

Another crucial scene in her childhood highlights Cleo's fierce attachment to her sisters and illustrates her sense of powerlessness, but this time it is not based on her class and race but on her gender. Cleo fights a black boy after he has dared to laugh at her split drawers while she was dangling from a tree. When she hits him in the groin and expects her sisters to cheer her victory over him, they comfort him instead:

She watched them with wonder. What was there to being a boy? What was there to being a man? Men just worked. That was easier than what women did. It was women who did the lying awake, the planning, the sorrowing, the scheming to stretch a dollar. That was the hard part, the head part. A woman had to think all the time. A woman had to be smart. (21)

Unlike her sisters who dream of being swept away by a shining prince on a white horse, tomboyish Cleo would rather ride the horse herself. In this scene, Cleo is overcome with grief as she suddenly understands what happens to girls when they grow up: "sisters turn into wives...men take their women and ride away...childhood is no longer than a summer day" (22).

Cleo is so attached to her mother and sisters that a separation from them means the loss of a preoedipal sense of plenitude and happiness. Seeing her sisters care more for the injured boy than for herself, Cleo realizes that she will not always be the center of her sisters' lives:

Now, seeing her sisters, with their tender faces turned toward the boy, a terrible sorrow assailed her. Some day they would all grow up. They would all get married and go away. They would never live together again, nor share the long bright busy days. Mama, too, would go. Mama would die. (22)

Here, for the first time, Cleo is dimly aware of the social effect of sexual difference and at the same time is confronted with the transience of her childhood. Cleo is unable to treat her sisters as individuals, for they are a reflection of her mother and her own sense of completeness and invincibility. In each one of her sisters she sees some likeness of her mother "—in Charity the softness and roundness, the flush just under the thin skin, the silver laughter; in Lily the doe eyes, liquid and vulnerable, the plaited hair that kept escaping in curls; in small Serena the cherry-red mouth, the dimpled cheeks" (21). During this moment of intense pain over the imagined loss of her sisters, she understands her desire for their constant presence. Conflating the boundaries between her mother and her sisters, Cleo suppresses the realities of loss and separation: "So long as her sisters were within sight and sound, they were the mirrors in which she could see Mama. They would be her remembering of her happy, happy childhood" (22).

Cleo's intense libidinal attachment to her mother and prolonged enmeshment with her sisters coincides with her fierce resentment of men. When her mother dies in childbirth, she pronounces her father guilty of murder. The intrusion of men into her mother's and sisters' lives means the end of a "charmed life" for Cleo. Later Cleo describes her sisters' husbands as madmen who are out to kill their wives. For Cleo, the presence and absence of her sisters sharply separates her childhood, which she associates with summertime, fun, complete control over her life, from her adult life, which she identifies with loss, separation, death and loneliness. However, Cleo's sisters not only bring back childhood memories but represent a repressed part of herself, her own vulnerability, her fears, her sense of social deprivation. Her memory of "easy living" is a defense against the very real experiences of racism and loss, and her grandiosity represents a mask for her feelings of inferiority and powerlessness.

As an adult mother, Cleo has for a time an audience in her small daughter; but as Judy grows more independent and critical of her mother, Cleo loses one of her adoring "mirrors." Cleo's narcissistic view of her daughter as an extension of her self is necessarily frustrated, and she returns to an earlier time—her memory of her own childhood—to heal her sense of alienation and to recapture a sense of completeness. "The more her child grew alien to all that had made her own childhood an enchanted summer, so in like degree did her secret heart yearn for her sisters" (44). When Charity, Lily and Serena finally come to visit her in Boston and bring back memories of her mother, Cleo "knew that some part of her interrupted childhood was restored" (165).

It is significant that Cleo's sisters are absent at the high point of her social climb—her Christmas party, which represents a showpiece for herself and her most public attempt to deny her Southern roots. To her great disappointment, her sisters cannot be integrated in her new, "upscale" lifestyle. She works for days to make the party "perfect" and is deeply wounded when the discussion turns to poverty and racism in the South (revealing the gulf between middle-class blacks in the North and poverty-stricken people in the South) and to Serena's husband Robert, who has "passed" for white and been involved in the murder of a klansman. Cleo's denial of her roots is literally enacted by Robert's attempt to pass; her father's death during Robert's escape brings home to Cleo her past from which she had dissociated herself.

The party is the turning point in the novel because Cleo no longer completely controls her family, and her facade of invulnerability begins to crumble. It marks the beginning of a trajectory that ends in the realization of Cleo's secret fear, the loss of her sisters who represent a part of herself, her connection to an earlier, more authentic self. As Cleo's symbiotic attachment to her sisters wanes, it is entirely consistent with her narcissistic character that she would replace this void with another intense bond, that between mother and son (her nephew Tim).

While Washington sees Cleo in conflict with the narrow social roles for black women in the early twentieth century and argues against "psychologizing" her character, I suggest that Dorothy West's complex portrait of Cleo Judson illustrates the dialectic of psychological and social forces that shape individual character. Although Cleo's intrapsychic conflicts are personal—her grandiosity and unresolved preoedipal attachment to her mother and sisters—, they are connected to a larger social context where a cultural construction of race based on skin color creates a bicultural schism in African-Americans who "pass" or imitate white-middle class values. Unlike Angela Murray, Cleo is never able to grow psychologically and move beyond the cultural split that is reflected in her own internal division. She "steals" an identity as a black Brahmin in order to gain power and influence, which she can neither fully embrace nor abandon. Her constant scheming, stealing from and lying to her husband and sisters are a manifestation of her desperate attempt to sustain an identity that is not her own.

If connections between *Plum Bun* and *The Living Is Easy* seem tenuous at first sight, both novels nevertheless illustrate the difficult trajectory of black female identity formation in the context of the early modern black middle-class and they emphasize the influence of the sister relationship in developing race-consciousness and identity. Angela Murray and Cleo Judson are seduced by white cultural fantasies about women's development, standards of physical beauty and idealized relationships. Intertextual references to traditional fairy tales in *Plum Bun*, and to Louisa May Alcott's *Little Women* in *The Living Is Easy*, comment ironically on women's pre-scripted fantasies about their own development and underline how standards for white women have shaped black women's self-perceptions and expectations. As a romance, *Plum Bun* reunites the estranged Murray sisters in the end to underline their common heritage and struggle; Angela's return to the black community, initiated by her enduring bond with her sister, heals her bicultural split. As a satire and novel of psychological realism, *The Living Is Easy* promises no didactic happy-end. Cleo's distorted ego boundaries and her constant need for an ideal mirroring other to validate her self prevent her from developing a less conflicted identity and relationship with the black community.

Angela's literal "passing" and Cleo's mimicking of the white middle-class create a particular strain on their relations with sisters who are more firmly rooted in African-American culture. The sister relationships in these two novels throw into relief how the characters cast their racial identities and the consequences of disowning their cultural heritage. At the same time, Angela and Cleo remain deeply attached to their sisters even in the face of their split identifications. The blood tie which reaches back into childhood forces Angela and Cleo to acknowledge their racial and class heritage, a past that has shaped their sense of self and that is vital to their emotional stability. Thus the sister bond—whose complexity merits attention in any (con)text—assumes a particular power for black women whose culture and identity have been denied by the larger cultural milieu.

Notes

[1] Critics have generally confused author/narrator Jessie Fauset's perspective with the heroine Angela Murray's point of view in the novel, that is, the latter's uncritical acceptance of white middle-class values which she conceives of romantically and melodramatically. However, Angela undergoes a development in the *Bildungsroman* tradition, from naiveté to an awareness of her black cultural heritage, a trajectory that is reflected in her gradually changing relationship to her surroundings, friends and family. Fauset uses ironic distancing devices like elements of white fairytales and nursery rhymes to create her "double vision" of a young black woman living in a white culture, who is caught in social constructions of femininity and race. (See Feeney for a discussion of Fauset's "double vision" in her fiction.)

[2] *Plum Bun* chronicles the development of Angela and Virginia Murray from their childhood days in suburban Philadelphia to their conflicted adult lives in New York City. Angela, who is light-skinned like her mother, "passes" for white in Greenwich Village where she lives as an art student. An affair with a bigotted rich playboy leads her to dissociate herself from her darker sister. The sisters reunite after the affair ends and Angela publicly reveals her black heritage, thus forfeiting her art scholarship to Paris. In the end, Angela goes to Paris with her sister's support, and on Christmas Day, she is joined by her true love Anthony Cross, who has secretly passed as well, while Virgina marries her childhood sweetheart.

[3] *The Living Is Easy* focuses on light-skinned Cleo Jericho Judson, who is married to the "Black Banana King" of Boston and aspires to becoming part of the black Brahmin class. After she persuades her husband to rent a large house in Brookline, she invites her three sisters and their children to live with them, sans husbands. Alternately charming and bullying them with her stories and promises, like she did during their childhood in the South, Cleo tries to mold her sisters according to her own middle-class aspirations. Cleo's need for control ultimately destroys the family as her husband's financial support of her sisters and their children drains his business during World War I and her sister's marriages fall apart.

Works Cited

Bell, Bernard. *The Afro-American Novel and Its Tradition*. Amherst: U of Massachusetts P, 1987.

Benjamin, Jessica. *The Bonds of Love: Psychoanalysis, Feminism, and the Problem of Domination*. New York: Pantheon, 1988.

Bone, Robert. *The Negro Novel in America*. New Haven: Yale UP, 1958.

Chodorow, Nancy. *The Reproduction of Mothering: Psychoanalysis and the Sociology of Gender*. Berkeley: U of California P, 1978.

Christian, Barbara. "Trajectories of Self-Definition: Placing Contemporary Afro-American Women's Fiction." *Conjuring: Black Women, Fiction and Literary Tradition*. Ed. Marjorie Pryse and Hortense Spillers. Bloomington: Indiana UP, 1985: 233-48.

Dearborn, Mary V. *Pocahontas's Daughters: Gender and Ethnicity in American Culture*. New York: Oxford UP, 1986.

Dinnerstein, Dorothy. *The Mermaid and the Minotaur: Sexual Arrangements and Human Malaise*. New York and San Francisco: Harper & Row, 1976.

Downing, Christine. *Psyche's Sisters: Re-Imagining the Meaning of Sisterhood*. San Francisco: Harper and Row, 1988.

Fauset, Jessie Redmon. *Plum Bun: A Novel Without a Moral*. 1929. Reprint Boston: Beacon P, 1990.

Feeney, Joseph J.S.J. "A Sardonic Unconventional Jessie Fauset: The Double Structure and Double Vision of Her Novels." *CLA Journal* (1979): 365-82.

Frazier, Franklin E. *Black Bourgeoisie*. New York: The Free P, 1969.

Hare, Nathan. *The Black Anglo-Saxons*. New York: Marzani & Munsell, 1965.

Kubitschek, Missy Dehn. *Claiming the Heritage: African-American Women Novelists and History*. Jackson and London: UP of Mississippi, 1991.

McDowell, Deborah E. "The Neglected Dimension of Jessie Redmon Fauset." *Conjuring: Black Women, Fiction and Literary Tradition*. Ed. Marjorie Pryse and Hortense Spillers. Bloomington: Indiana UP, 1985: 86-104.

McNaron, Toni A. *The Sister Bond: A Feminist View of a Timeless Connection*. New York: Pergamon P, 1985.

Sylvander, Carolyn Wedin. *Jessie Fauset, Black American Writer*. Troy, New York: The Whitston Publishing Co., 1981.

Wall, Cheryl A. "Jessie Redmon Fauset." *The Gender of Modernism: A Critical Anthology*. Ed. Bonnie Kime Scott. Bloomington: Indiana UP, 1990: 155-59.

Ward, Janie Victoria. "Racial Identity Formation and Transformation." *Making Connections: The Relational Worlds of Adolescent Girls at Emma Willard School*. Ed. Carol Gilligan, Nona P. Lyons, Trudy J. Manmer. Troy, New York, 1989: 215-32.

Washington, Mary Helen. *Invented Lives: Narratives of Black Women 1860-1960*. Garden City: Doubleday, 1987.

_____. "I Sign My Mother's Name: Alice Walker, Dorothy West, Paule Marshall." *Mothering the Mind: Twelve Studies of Writers and Their Silent Partners*. Ed. Ruth Perry and Martine Watson Brownley. New York: Holmes and Meier, 1984: 143-63.

_____. ed. *Memory of Kin: Stories About Family By Black Writers*. New York: Anchor/Doubleday, 1991.

West, Dorothy. *The Living Is Easy*. 1948. New York: The Feminist P, 1982.

Willis, Susan. *Specifying: Black Women Writing the American Experience*. Madison: U of Wisconsin P, 1987.

"Eat me, drink me, love me":
Orality, Sexuality, and the Fruits of Sororal Desire in "Gob(b)lin(g) Market" and *Beloved*

Leila Silvana May

In the nineteenth century the home was a walled reserve of Apollonian permanence protecting the individual from the Dionysian flux of the external world. This "individual" who sought sanctuary there was clearly a male—the Husband and Father, the paterfamilias, or his proxy, the Son. Yet the ever-present force which guaranteed the stability and purity of that serene site was female—the Wife and Mother, or her apprentice, the Daughter. Indeed, the daughter represented the purest element in the architectonics of the family, she whose desire, unlike that of her mother, was wholly uncontaminated and uncompromised, and whose dedication to the family was ungrudging—a dedication which, though ultimately directed to the father, was often learned and practiced through service to her brother, that son who himself was apprenticing to become a husband and father. Yet behind the dense facade of the nineteenth-century familial structure was a hidden locus of repressed feminine desire. Christina Rossetti's "Goblin Market" cuts a fantastic passage through the stone walls of the Victorian home and reveals its inner chamber; in so doing it exposes the forces which lead to the subversion, and eventual dissolution, of the mechanisms of personal identity within that same edifice which had been constructed to protect and maintain them. "Goblin Market" gives us a vision of sisterhood which, though indirectly derived from the edicts of nineteenth-century family life, is so revolutionary and surreal as to challenge the authority of those edicts and to adumbrate a radically alternative figuration of sisterhood and of feminine desire—one which strangely comes to fruition in a twentieth-century novel, *Beloved,* whose action takes place in the same time-frame as Rossetti's writing of "Goblin Market," but whose concerns are in most respects apparently very different from those of Christina Rossetti.

Although two texts such as "Goblin Market" and *Beloved* might initially appear to be incongruously paired (distinguished as they are by genre, race, historical period, geography, and class), they are in fact united—united thematically by the general dialectics of sororal desire, and united structurally by the indirect intervention into that desire by alien forces (male and economical in "Goblin Market," male and racial in *Beloved*). In both cases sororal desire is mediated by this intervention and yet resists it, and in each work we see a form of triangulated feminine desire and a consequential

133

conflation of identities revealing suspicions about and protestations against the family. Desire confounds itself as its evanescing object becomes its own subject. In each text, the protest against the disciplining of sororal relations is expressed as a subversive form of orality which stokes passions that are capable of consuming the structures which attempt to suppress, contain, and deny feminine desire. The texts are also linked in part by the operations of fantasy, wherein sister-sister representations operate on a level of primal imagination and are hence perhaps less historically shaped and culturally inflected than those which appear in more "realistic" literature. The fantastic traces "the unsaid and the unseen of culture: that which has been silenced, made invisible, covered over and made 'absent' " (Jackson 4). It is these silences, these absences, which I hope to render at least partially visible.

The family is both the foundation of civilization (Freud) and the foundation of the division of labor (Marx); it claims the power to legislate the nature of sameness and difference; it represents the transition between nature and culture, but it is already on the side of culture, hence it "naturally" contains within it its own principle of resistance—a resistance most readily available to and expressed by those from whom culture demands the most: women.[1] The literature of the nineteenth and twentieth centuries reveals a tendency (manifested somewhat differently in the two centuries) for the family constellation to collapse in upon itself across the axis of sibling relationships, and for the very definitions that that structure has created—of identity, difference, and desire—to disintegrate under their own weight. This tendency, and the dread of it, are increased in proportion to the intensity of the structuring. If familial relations are what structure and hence hold the world together, and if those very relationships are subject to a continual flux, blurring, distortion and collapse, then with what are we left? Much of the literature of the nineteenth and twentieth centuries represents family relationships, and specifically sibling relationships, in such a way as to reveal them as being seditious—seditious of subjectivities, families, hierarchies of power and gender, and of societies which need as their cornerstone the notion of an overcharged individualism. This process of disintegration represents a revelation that the naturalness and untainted neutrality attributed in the modern period to the family, and particularly to the sibling bond, was a socio-political construct whose historical function was, among other things, the amassing of patriarchal power in a uniquely unsullied receptacle—the sister.

The fascination with the daughter/sister which permeates much of the fiction by both men and women authors of the nineteenth century and a good deal of the twentieth reveals itself as a cultural desire for what is dreaded and a dread of what is desired—"a sympathetic antipathy and an antipathetic sympathy" (Kierkegaard's definition of anxiety). Behind the loving interest in the sister and the loud praise for the family which is her home lurks a suspicion concerning the passion which fuels family dynamics. Both the exaltation of the family and the poorly suppressed anxiety over it are revealed not so much in the representations of the vertical crosscut, parent to child, but in the horizontal relationship, sibling to sibling. This is because the latter relationship was meant to manifest the virtues of love and duty in their purest and highest form; yet those virtues themselves, or at least one of them, was understood to be the most dangerously corruptible. That safe haven toward which the Victorians steered (the family, and particularly sibling relations) was also feared as a sphere of danger. There was something about sibling relations which was troubling, and it was not simply the scarcely mentioned (though very real) fear of incest which provoked this worry; even (or perhaps mostly) the relation between sisters was to be feared and strictly disciplined at the same moment that it was eulogized and monumentalized. The sister is, in a curious way, the true linchpin of the system—she who is to exhibit the highest virtue that the family can produce, she who is an ironic repository of patriarchal power, she whose desire in its unsullied state is perceived as closest to nature (which, in the Victorian period, was viewed as being closely connected to the Rousseauean/Romantic notion of childhood and innocence [see Davidoff and Hall 28]). But in many cases the representations of sibling love particular to the nineteenth century reveal themselves as duplicitous and self-indicting, and hint at another kind of passion and another kind of "sister" than those they seem to believe themselves to be eulogizing—one who is not the creation of the patriarchal organization of desire.

Helena Michie has attempted to expose Victorian culture's "mechanisms for coping with the specter of female difference" ("Friend" 401). The novels of the period find "a safe, familiar, and familial space" to perform this act of disciplining in sisterhood. Sisterhood is seen as a relationship where female difference is worked out within a framework of sameness. "Difference between sisters is often visually and dramatically rendered; dark and light, blind and seeing, healthy and sick sister compose themselves for the audience in a tableaux of physical contrast." Sisterhood also allows the containment of *sexual* difference among women, which is seen in the Victorian mind as the difference between fallen and unfallen, "the sexual and the pure woman." In this way, "female sexuality can be explored and reabsorbed within the teleology of the family" (Michie 404). In Rossetti and Morrison these very differences so vital to this ideology of sisterhood and feminine desire themselves collapse.

"Goblin Market" anticipates, and *Beloved* manifests, a denunciation of the patriarchal intervention into feminine desire, and as such they can be seen as allied with Luce Irigaray's attempt in *Ce sexe qui n'en est pas un* to posit a different notion of difference—one which replaces the hierarchical heterosexual model with two peer women between whom the self/other distinction is undone. By extending Irigaray's sexual metaphor of the "neither one nor two" of a single female subject to the "strange kind of two, which isn't one" of the two female speakers in "When Our Lips Speak Together," we can describe precisely the problematic of (non)difference which is developed in the depiction of sororal bonds in "Goblin Market" and *Beloved*. Furthermore, the focus on the subversive nature of orality in these two texts might be read as an expression and intensification of Irigarayan "lips."

In "Goblin Market" there appear to be no mothers and no brothers, only sisters and daughters. No mothers, except for the sisters, Laura and Lizzie, who at the end of the poem—"Days, weeks, months, years / Afterwards" (543-4)— have become mothers (they have become mothers perhaps inevitably, but distinctly anticlimactically and with resistance); no brothers, except the goblins—"Brother with queer brother; / ...Brother with sly brother" (94; 96).[2] Nevertheless, the poem is saturated with the desire of the mother and of the brother, and the fusion of those desires. (The Sartrean-Lacanian conception of desire here encompasses sexual desire but is also larger than sexual desire— propelled by the *incompleteness* of human subjectivity, an emptiness seeking fulfillment. My reading of the way in which desire functions is also informed in part by René Girard's concept of mediated desire, and Toril Moi's critique and correction of Girard.) It is true that the dominance of the desire of the mother is concealed throughout the poem, to be revealed perhaps quite casually at the end. When Laura and Lizzie have become "wives / With children of their own" (544-5), they call their daughters together—clearly daughters, though this fact is never explicitly stated. (It is interesting to note that no one reading "Goblin Market"—whether for the first time or the hundredth—ever seems to question that the children at the end of the poem are daughters.) "Their mother-hearts beset with fears" (545), Lizzie and Laura instruct these daughters (the next generation of sisters) with warnings of deep dangers—deep but apparently alluring dangers which they themselves experienced in "pleasant days long gone" (550). We know, then, whence the daughters of Lizzie and Laura received their ambiguous instruction: the warning conveyed to them is identical to the warning which the young sisters Laura and Lizzie already possessed at the beginning of the poem. The warning is imbued with the desire of the mother. What is that desire? Because desire itself is learned, the mother's desire inevitably (if circularly) derives from the nursery. There it is mediated by the desire of *her* mother. An account of the mother who desires presupposes an account of her before she was a mother—an account of her as daughter. Thus, the desire of the mother is, in the diachronic sense, that of the daughter, and, in the case of "Goblin Market" and of Christina Rossetti, that means the desire of the sister.

Feminine desire, then, is the main circuit in the system. But even where the father is excluded from the circuit of feminine desire, there will still be interruptions to be considered whenever there are male siblings present in the nursery. On the one hand, young girls are taught that their only passion should be to serve. Through their submission, sisters and daughters become the locus of tenderness and spirituality in the family.[3] The sister is taught that she must defer to and serve her brother, and learns to accept the fact that eventually she might have to reject a beloved suitor if her brother disapproves of him. According to Johanna Smith in *Incest, Ideology and Narrative*, the sister discovers her submission "might be rewarded with affection, but that any rebellion will certainly be punished" (Smith 56). She begins to learn her role as wife and mother by serving her brother, and thereby becomes an idealized (future) wife. As Smith points out, in one sense this ideal moves toward generating new families, but in another, being ideally asexual, it cannot be such a model. On the other hand, in sacrificing herself to her brother, the sister is imitating her mother's desire, both for her husband and for her son. The desire of the sister, then, is triangulated with the desire of her mother and sibling. Yet in many nineteenth-century middle- and upper-middle-class homes this circuit works itself out in strange and unexpected ways, for the distance between the nursery and the mother in a certain sense alienates the former from the latter— and from the adult world at large. Yet the presence of the brother who is, after all, in training, provides a mysterious connection to a future patriarchy, and to commercial battles still to come.

What is the brother's desire in "Goblin Market"? It is, of course, decidedly oral—we might say pre-genital; it is the desire of boys and not of men. The goblins, the "sly brothers," are different from men, and their wares are different from those of men ("Men sell not such in any town" [101]). The brothers, in trying to become the object of the sister's desire ("come buy, come buy"), tell her that if she waited until a *man* offered her these fruits (the very thing she ought to do according to Victorian standards) they would have dried up: "Such fruits as these / No man can carry; / Half their bloom would fly, / Half their dew would dry, / Half their flavor would pass by" (376-80). The fruits must be accepted, consumed, directly; they cannot be mediated by coinage. Laura has no coin with which to pay (at least, she has none presently), and thinks that instead she must give a lock of her hair. But the brothers do not want a coin, neither of copper, silver, nor gold. They certainly do not want Lizzie's silver penny, which they fling back at her. Coins represent legal transactions, legitimate exchanges of value. But what the brothers offer can never be legitimate or legal; their fruits *must* be forbidden. Furthermore, the use of coins in the poem always represents deferral. (Laura would have to go back to her cottage to get her coin; Lizzie will pay for the fruit with a coin and take them away for consumption later.) But these fruits must be enjoyed immediately. What these brothers offer can only be accepted now (and "now" happens to be only "morning and evening" [1], "night and morning" [302]— perhaps the very time when the siblings would be alone in the nursery).

In "Goblin Market" it is Lizzie who breaks, or tries to break, the sisterly circle of desire determined by the desire of the brother, but she is able to do this only by choosing her sister's desire as her own. Lizzie wants to share in Laura's misery—she "could not bear / To watch her sister's cankerous care, / yet not to share" (299-301)—and, despite still being able to hear and be attracted to the siren-like song of the brother goblins, she chooses her sister's desire over that of the brothers. "Thank you, said Lizzie: "But one waits / At home alone for me" (383-4). However, she is able to choose her sister's desire only by choosing to become a mediary between Laura and the goblins.

What is Laura's desire, which Lizzie chooses? It is to be desired by the goblin brothers: it is the desire of/for the brothers.

Then sat up in a passionate yearning.
And gnashed her teeth for balked desire...
Day after day, night after night,

Laura kept watch in vain
In sullen silence of exceeding pain.
She never caught again the goblin cry,
'Come buy, come buy'—(266-72)

Thus, to choose her sister's desire, Lizzie must choose that of the brothers—that is, she must want to be desired by them. If the brothers desire Lizzie—if she becomes their desire—then Laura will desire her as the desire of the brothers. And indeed, the most erotic and passionate moments of the poem are those expressing Lizzie's act of mediation in which Laura must receive the fruits of the brothers' desire through Lizzie:

'Did you miss me?
Come and kiss me.
Never mind my bruises,
Hug me, kiss me, suck my juices
Squeezed from goblin fruits for you,
Goblin pulp and goblin dew.
Eat me, drink me, love me;
Laura, make much of me;
For your sake I have braved the glen
And had to do with goblin merchant men'. (465-74)

This description of Laura's sucking the goblin juices indirectly—that is, from her sister's body—receives much more attention from Rossetti than does the description of Laura's consuming them directly from the goblin brothers. This act demonizes Laura, but also exorcizes her. Her desire is no longer that of the brother but the reinstated desire of the sister.

Laura awoke as if from a dream,
Laughed in the innocent old way,
Hugged Lizzie but not twice or thrice (537-9)

Laura and Lizzie have returned to "lying close" (40), from which position the call of the brothers had caused Laura to "rear her glossy head" (52).

All of this has an apparently quite conventional moral and ending (by resisting the desire of the brother one saves oneself for marriage and motherhood), and one which is meant to represent the desire of the mother; yet, this very conventionality disguises a much more unconventional moral and terminus to the poem. We catch sight of it not only in the obvious nostalgia for the dangerous times past expressed in the poem's final stanza, but also through a careful scrutiny of what actually transpires when Lizzie and Laura displace the desire of the brother. There we find hints of a protest against the very institution the moral is meant to celebrate—the family, and particularly the feminine role within it.

In many respects, "Goblin Market" fits Michie's formula for the containment of female difference within sameness. Both are of "golden head"

(184), both hear the goblins cry, both possess the same warning ("Laura said, /…'We must not look at goblin men' " [40-1], " 'Oh', cried Lizzie, 'Laura, Laura, / You should not peep at goblin men' " [48-9]). But each initially responds to the prohibition differently. "Curious Laura" (69) both "bowed" (34) and "reared her glossy head" (52) to listen to the goblins, while stalwart Lizzie "covered up her eyes, / Covered close lest they should look" (50-1), plugged her ears with her fingers, and ran. Both sisters feel the excitement of the temptation ("with tingling cheeks and fingertips" [39]), but Laura succumbs, Lizzie does not. Although it is quite correct to read the poem as a Christian fantasy or allegory wherein the one Christ-like sister retrieves the fallen sister from guilt and thereby rescues her from otherness (see for instance Gilbert and Gubar 565-66; Barr 271-82), one of the most ironic features of the poem is that the sisters are made identical only *after* the Fall—thus in effect undermining that very emphasis on difference, on the distinction between fallen/unfallen which the Victorians so strenuously attempted to uphold through their depictions of sororal difference. It is through Laura's sexual sin, through her transgression of the law, that the sisters in fact lose their separate identities. The stanza most clearly indicating the dissolution of individual identities occurs immediately after Laura's fall:

> Golden head by golden head
> Like two pigeons in one nest
> Folded in each other's wings,
> They lay down in their curtained bed:
> Like two blossoms on one stem,
> Like two flakes of new-fallen snow,
> Like two wands of ivory
> Tipped with gold for awful kings…
> Cheek to cheek and breast to breast
> Locked together in one nest. (184-98)

While it is true that after this merging of identities, differences do recur—

> One content, one sick in part;
> One warbling for the mere bright day's delight,
> One longing for the night (212-14)

—Rossetti's imagery depicting the difference caused by Laura's fall again hints at a hidden sameness. Laura, when enticed by the goblin brothers, "stretched her gleaming neck /…Like a lily from the beck" (81-3); Lizzie, when refusing the goblins' seduction, stands "Like a lily in a flood" (409). Lizzie, in her resistance, is "Like a royal virgin town / Topped with gilded dome and spire" (418-19); Laura, in succumbing to the goblin juices brought to her by her sister, is "Like the watch-tower of a town / Which an earthquake shatters down" (514-15). Laura, staggering home after submitting to the goblins "knew not was it night or day" (139); Lizzie, coming home after resisting the goblins "knew not was it night or day" (449). And in the much-discussed stanza beginning, "Hug me, kiss me, suck my juices..." (468), the final extraordinary merging of identities takes place when Lizzie substitutes the goblin juices with herself as the object of her sister's desire as Laura quite literally consumes her. "Eat me, drink me, love me" (471), says Lizzie. Laura "kissed and kissed her with a hungry mouth" (492) and, though the goblin juices are now "wormwood to her tongue" (494), Laura "gorged on bitterness without name" (510). She swoons from this orgy of orally incestuous consummation and cannibalism, and awakens to a renewed innocence and life.

The events which transpire in "Gob[b]lin[g] Market" would most likely have been those most memorable in the lives of the sisters. The description of those events is one of inchoate frenzy, of suffering, of ecstasy, and of madness. Their depiction does not lead logically to the moralistic conclusion which Rossetti felt obliged to give it (namely, one should resist temptation and save oneself for marriage and motherhood, and in this endeavor "there is no friend like a sister"). In fact, it is not altogether obvious that the narrative and its moral are even logically compatible. What is described is not at all advocacy of the patriarchally-organized family and of the traditional role assigned to sisterhood within that system; it must rather be seen as a challenge to it, and as hinting at the possibility of a very different kind of sisterhood than the one Victorian literature was meant to contain.

The desire constituting the key relationship in "Goblin Market" is mediated and perverted by external forces of danger—alien, male, and sexual, but also economic, depicted in terms of the imagery of food, hunger, eating, and satiety. In Toni Morrison's twentieth-century novel about the nineteenth century, desire and the relationships it establishes are structured and mediated by violence, murder and cannibalism (as in Freud's myth of the origin of culture)—but in this case the ultimate agency is racism and slavery. And, as in "Goblin Market," the action is metaphorized in terms of the imagery of the consumption of food. In Morrison's novel, as often in nineteenth-century literature, the family is constructed as a bulwark against an alien external world, yet is contaminated by that same world.

In contrast to "Goblin Market," mothers, and their relationships with their daughters, are directly represented in *Beloved*—though as in "Goblin Market," desire here too is mediated. Mother Sethe's own murderous desire is created in reaction to that of the slaveholding white man, which is manifested in his sexual prerogatives and his power to dis-member the slave family. The mutilated and totally insulated family at 124 is also created by the intervention of the white man's desire into Sethe's. Denver, the daughter spared from the murderously protective desire of her mother, experiences a desire trapped within the familial walls created by her mother as a barricade against the world and against the past. There are too many absences between those walls. She dreams her absent father's return (207), yet even his absence belongs not to her but to others (to Grandma Baby Suggs, to Sethe, to Paul D). Her brothers too are gone, and filling their absence is only a memory of pleasure as she sat between their knees on the stairs listening to their stories. She fears and loves her mother—loves her so that her mother won't kill her (207). She does not tell her mother that she is waiting for her daddy to take her away (207). The ghost of her sister replaces the absence of, and *I*, her desire for, her father and becomes her true companion. Although the ghost's "spiteful antics" fatigue her, she desires its presence to interrupt the disturbing new relation between her mother and Paul D. But Paul D chases off the baby ghost, and Denver is left—for the time being—with nothing.

All of this is altered with the arrival of Beloved, whom Denver, unlike Sethe, recognizes immediately as her dead sister. (Ironically, it is a male's—Paul D's—incursion into the all-female household which prompts Beloved's incarnate return.) It is Denver far more than Sethe who feels the gap left by the baby ghost's absence, just as it is Denver, not Sethe, who immediately feels the full force and significance of Beloved's presence. ("Paul D wondered at the newness of her shoes. Sethe was deeply touched by her sweet name;...Denver, however, was shaking" [53]).[4] Beloved becomes Denver's desire. She provides everything missing in Denver's life—"a racing heart, dreaminess, society, danger, beauty" (76)—and Denver creates a net to hold her. She "worries herself sick trying to think of a way to get Beloved to share her room" (67). She desires that Beloved desire her, and is hurt and slighted that she is not the primary reason for her sister's return (75). She wants the secret knowledge of Beloved's identity to remain with her, and begs Beloved not to reveal it to Sethe (76). Throughout the bulk of the novel, Denver tries to protect Beloved from Sethe. She has to warn Beloved, "Don't love her too much. Don't. Maybe it's still in her the thing that makes it all right to kill her children" (296). However, at the end of the novel, in a dramatic reversal of desire, Denver must protect Sethe against Beloved's desire; she is no longer sure whose love is capable of killing whom.

The least complicated desire in the novel is Beloved's. She desires Sethe's desire. She wishes to drain off every one of Sethe's desires and replace them with herself. She wants revenge. Her desire, too, therefore, is mediated by the desire of the other—directly, by that of Sethe, and indirectly by that of the slaveowning white man. "[Sethe] felt Beloved touch her. A touch no heavier than a feather but loaded, nevertheless, with desire" (58). "She is the one. She is the one I need" (76). "[I]t was Beloved who made demands. Anything she wanted she got, and when Sethe ran out of things to give her, Beloved invented desire" (240). "When once or twice Sethe tried to assert herself—be the unquestioned mother whose word was law and who knew what was best—Beloved slammed things, wiped the table clean of plates, threw salt on the floor, broke a windowpane" (242).

If desire is not original but always derivative, if it is not the desire of the individual self but mediated by the desire of the other, then it will be accompanied by the dissolution of individual boundaries and the confounding of identities of those subjects who desire. And if the mediation of desire has its source in an act of violence, then that violence will leave its trace in the fusion of identities. In *Beloved*, as in "Goblin Market," it is feminine desire which establishes the relationships that constitute the family. This signifies that the desire in question is that of the mother and of the sisters, organized against an external, peculiarly male, danger. But such an organization risks the identities of the very individuals whom it means to protect.

The relationship between Denver and Sethe is characterized by indolence and dread. But when Sethe's dead child arrives incarnate as Beloved and falls into a kind of stupor, it is Denver and not Sethe who begins to play the role of mother. In a description strikingly reminiscent of Rossetti's poem, "Denver tended [Beloved], watched her sound sleep, listened to her labored breathing.... So intent was she on her nursing, she forgot to eat" (54). And when Denver hears the story of her birth told to Beloved, she is only then able to identify with her mother. "Denver was seeing it now and feeling it—through Beloved. Feeling how it must have felt to her mother" (78). That is, she feels herself giving birth to herself through Beloved. It is as though she has become both her own mother and her sister. When Denver is observed by Beloved, "Denver's skin dissolved under that gaze and become soft and bright like the lisle dress that had its arm around her mother's waist" (118); that is, when Beloved gazes at Denver, in her own mind Denver *becomes* Beloved, for "she was certain that Beloved was the white dress that had knelt with her mother" (119). When Beloved leaves, Denver weeps because now she feels "she has no self" (123). In fact, Denver had always known that after her mother had killed the baby sister, "Denver took her mother's milk right along with the blood of her sister" (152). "Beloved is my sister. I swallowed her blood right along with my mother's milk" (205). "I tasted its blood when Ma'am nursed me....She's mine. Beloved. She's mine" (209).

But if Denver consumes Beloved's blood, and if Denver's identity merges with her sister's, Beloved consumes Sethe and merges with her—though in manner fraught with tension. "Beloved could not take her eyes off Sethe....Sethe was licked, tasted, eaten by Beloved's eyes....In the lamplight their two shadows clashed and crossed on the ceiling like black swords" (57). As Beloved's desire empties Sethe's, mother and daughter become indistinguishable. "Dressed in Sethe's dresses.... She imitated Sethe, talked the way she did, laughed her laugh and used her body the same way down to the walk, the way Sethe moved her hands, sighed through her nose, held her head...it was difficult for Denver to tell who was who" (241). In a dreamy surreal soliloquy, Beloved identifies her own being with that of her mother: "I am Beloved and she is mine...I am not separate from her there is no place where I stop her face is my own" (210).

Sethe allows Beloved to become her, and she in turn becomes her own daughter. "Beloved bending over Sethe looked the mother, Sethe the teething child...She sat in the chair licking her lips like a chastised child while Beloved ate up her life" (250). Beloved then takes on the characteristics of a pregnant woman, "her belly protruding like a watermelon" (250), about to give birth to herself or to her mother. But it is ultimately Denver who must play the role of mother to both Sethe and Beloved. "Washing, cooking, forcing, cajoling her mother to eat a little now and then, providing sweet things for Beloved as often as she could to calm her down" (250).

Earlier in the novel, Sethe's confusion had not been between herself and her daughter; rather, she conflates the ghost of Grandma Baby (Suggs) and baby ghost (Beloved) as she has her neck stroked first by one and then by the other. (Indeed, Grandma Baby's name itself brings the identification between generations full circle.) The conflation of Grandma Baby Suggs and baby ghost is intensified by the fact that, incarnate as Beloved, baby ghost perpetually craves sugar. Denver too is brought into this circle when she is called "baby" by Lady Jones. It was that word, "'baby', said softly and with such kindness, that inaugurated [Denver's] life in the world as a woman" (248). And at the dramatic moment "when the click came"—that is, when Sethe suddenly recognizes Beloved as her dead daughter returned to life—her thought immediately flies, not to Beloved's childhood, but to her own childhood and the recognition of *her* mother and the way her mother had told her to recognize her corpse if she ever came upon it. "Here. Look here. This is your ma'am. If you can't tell me by my face, look here" (176). That is, the recognition of the murdered daughter living is the recognition of the living mother murdered.

If we put all of these equations together, we might say that Denver = Beloved = Sethe = Baby Suggs = Sethe's mother. Any of these components (A=B=C=D=E) can be exchanged with any other without disturbing the mathematical balance. Or we can simply say, A=A. Within the house at 124 (which, with its "spiteful antics," etc., has itself taken on human characteristics—"a person that wept, sighed, trembled and fell into fits" [29]), everybody is everybody and nobody is anybody. (Even the address of the house doubles itself with each successive number.) Reindividuation in the novel comes about at last from the outside, provoked by Denver's decision to reach beyond the walls of the home that has become a madhouse, no longer simply an asylum.

What is to be made of the fact that the dialectics of desire, and especially maternal and sororal desire, leads to an erasure of identity in *Beloved* and, less self-consciously but equally dramatically, in "Goblin Market"? Their depictions of sororal desire and its consequences are offered to us paradoxically as both dangerous and ideal goals—dangerous, in that much is provoked by mysterious but ever-present threats, and expresses itself as familial pathology, but also ideal in many tantalizing ways (again, more self-consciously by Morrison than by Rossetti). The external male danger which intrudes into Rossetti's Victorian nursery fantasy is ultimately structured by the social organizations of burgeoning nineteenth-century capitalism, and the violence which is thereby threatened is itself ultimately derived from the systematic violence of the new imperialistic industrialism. On the other hand, the external male desire which intrudes into Morrison's African-American novel is directly derived from the structures of slavery and racism. Of course, the images of genocide and infanticide in *Beloved* are far more shocking than are those of lesbian incest in "Goblin Market." The direct effects of slavery and racism on African-American families and individuals were surely more catastrophic than were the more indirect effects of capitalism and imperialism on the inmates of the nurseries in the homes of the perpetrators of those programs of more distant economic and racial violence. Yet in the fantasies of Victorian childhood, those derivative horrors too were magnified to the level of the catastrophic. And in both Rossetti and Morrison, the organization of feminine desire which results from the external masculine intervention creates forces which, if unleashed, could undermine the very social structures which promoted the intrusion. In *Beloved*, most of the truly joyous Nietzschean moments involve the confounding of identities: the mystical unity created by Baby Suggs' voice in the clearing, the blurring of the identities of Sethe, Denver and Beloved on the iced pond, and the merging of Sethe's, Denver's and Paul D's shadows on the road (the latter of whose shadow is subsequently identified as Beloved's). And in both texts, despite their curiously conventional endings, the relationships established among the female figures, and their convergences, produce something not only unique and provocative, but truly subversive of the sociohistorical structures of power which enclose them. Moreover, in these works the language of subversion consists of the vocabulary of oral desire and aggression.

The imagery associated with food and hunger in "Goblin Market" has been commented upon by some critics (see, for example Alan Barr, "Sensuality Survived"), yet the equally pervasive theme of consumption in *Beloved* remains thus far virtually unexamined. In both texts, one sister saves, nurses, and "nourishes" the other, with orality playing a central role in each work. As in Rossetti's poem, in which the original insatiable hunger is provoked by a masculine incursion, Paul D's arrival in *Beloved* occasions Denver's unquenchable desire for her sister. This longing is repeatedly rendered in terms uncannily reminiscent of "Goblin Market's" imagery of hunger, feeding, and sisterly sacrifice. Yet neither sister in *Beloved* plays exclusively the role of either a Lizzie or a Laura; *both* sisters "feed" off one another. Helena Michie, commenting on "Goblin Market," describes Lizzie's desire "for incorporation and introjection" as being akin to Melanie Klein's discoveries in the latter's "attempt to reproduce the fantasies of children." "For Klein, and for Lizzie, the fantasy of incorporating or being incorporated by the other is simultaneously hostile and loving, destructive and recuperative" (418). This, I would argue, is precisely the dynamic also being played out in Morrison's novel.

Before Beloved's arrival, "Denver's imagination produced its own hunger and its own food" (28). When Beloved appears, Denver immediately "look[s] at this sleeping beauty and want[s] more" (53). However, it is Beloved who, like Lizzie, craves sweets. "It was as though sweet things were what she was born for.... It was a need that went on and on" (55). Steven Connor, in discussing "Goblin Market," claims that "[t]he temptation to sin which the goblin men represent is as much to indulge oneself in language, in a kind of verbal promiscuity, as in sexual or sensual abandon. (At one point, Laura is said to be unable to hear the 'iterated jingle / Of sugar-baited words', which seems to me make the identification explicit)" (444). The identification which seems to *me* to be made explicit here is at least as much that between words and *food* as between textuality and sexuality. Of course, the common denominator is that all three can be viewed as forms of oral desire. (It is significant that, in contexts describing either the desire for sex or for food, one can use the words "appetite," "desire," "craving," and "hunger," interchangably, with no substantial alteration in meaning.) The sensual satisfaction derived from language or from food is often described in precisely the same terms. In Morrison's text, Beloved's "lips open wide with the pleasure of sugar or some piece of news Denver gave her" (74); in "Goblin Market," the sensual (over)indulgence in descriptions of fruit and feeding incorporates the themes of orality, sexuality and textuality. As Steven Connor aptly describes it, "[W]hen Lizzie endures the assault of the goblin men, she must keep her lips shut tight together, lest they should cram in a mouthful of fruit. But to keep one's lips together is a refusal not only of food but of language: 'Lizzie uttered not a word; / Would not open lip from lip' " (444). In Beloved, too, sisterly sacrifice is intimately connected with one sister going hungry—"So intent was [Denver's] nursing, she forgot to eat" (54)—while fixated on feeding (either literally or literarily) the other: "Denver nursing Beloved's interest like a lover whose pleasure was to overfeed the loved" (78).

In Rossetti's poem, Lizzie carries a penny with which to pay the goblin men. As she returns to her sister, her "virtue" still intact, she hears "her penny jingle / Bouncing in her purse,— / Its bounce was music to her ear" (452-54). The penny reappears twice in Beloved, again in the context of hunger, appetite, feasting, yet now as an ambiguous medium of exchange between the sisters themselves. "Deep down in [Beloved's] black eyes, back behind the expressionlessness, was a palm held out for a penny which Denver would gladly give her, if only she knew how...if she pressed too hard, she might lose the penny that the held-out palm wanted, and lose, therefore the place beyond appetite. It was better to feast, to have permission to be the looker, because the old hunger—the before-Beloved hunger...was out of the question. Looking kept it at bay" (118-20). Denver repeatedly claims to fear above all a return of the "original," "before-Beloved," hunger. Yet, it is clearly Beloved's *presence* which provokes Denver's fear of her absence, and hence the accompanying insatiable longing. In a description which could easily have been lifted straight out of "Goblin Market," Denver finds that "[n]o chore was enough to put out the licking fire that seemed always to burn in her" (120). In "Goblin Market," Laura's "consumption" results from her succumbing to the goblin men; yet, the goblin men's absence causes Laura to "burn her fire away" (279-80). As in Beloved, it is the exchange between the *sisters* which causes "swift fire [to] spread through her veins, knock...at her heart, / Me[e]t the fire smoldering there / And overb[ear] its lesser flame" (507-10). Feeding off her sister, then, initially ignites an even more powerful desire in Laura, but, paradoxically, her craving is therewith appeased; Denver, on the other hand, yearns ever more fiercely for Beloved. Perhaps, as with Laura's pining for the goblin men, Denver simply *thinks* that "her Beloved" can extinguish the flame, when in fact she only kindles it further.

Denver, shortly after Beloved's return, is certain that "Beloved was *hers*" (103; emphasis original). She desires Beloved's desire ("to be looked at by her, however briefly, kept her grateful for the rest of the time when she was merely the looker" [119]). In fact, so deeply compelling are Denver's feelings for her sister that, despite the possibility of Beloved's being a mortal threat to their mother, "the choice between Sethe and Beloved was without conflict" (103). Yet, Beloved's desire is clear, and it is clearly not Denver. Beloved has a consuming desire only for her mother's desire. "When her mother is anywhere around, Beloved has eyes only for Sethe" (121). Even her consummated desire for her mother's lover is merely calculated to remove him as an object of her mother's desire. When Beloved at last succeeds in making herself the sole object of her mother's desire ("She's mine, Beloved, She's mine" [209]), Denver is "cut out completely" (240). Having her Beloved wrested from her, Denver's desire is transformed. "The job she started with, protecting Beloved from Sethe, changed to protecting her mother from Beloved.... Whatever was happening, it only worked with three—not two—since neither Beloved nor Sethe seemed to care what the next day might bring.... Denver knew it was on her" (243). Denver has recognized Beloved's desire as an imitation of Sethe's, and hence must protect her mother from what she suspects is her sister's murderous impulse ("little by little it dawned on Denver that if Sethe didn't wake up one morning and pick up a knife, Beloved might" [242]). In the process, Denver becomes "her father's daughter after all," looking "more like Halle than ever" (252; 266). It was Paul D who, immediately after his arrival, recognized that Denver "[g]ot her daddy's sweet face" (12). His initial sojourn was possible only as long as Beloved and the spiteful baby ghost were kept at bay. Only after Denver is no longer identified with/as either sister or mother can Paul D reenter the household.

At the end of both *Beloved* and "Goblin Market" the family and its members' identities have restabilized into more apparently conventional forms—forms more compatible with, and even complicit in, the forces which the works had earlier threatened to subvert. It is almost as though the new unspeakable spectre of sisterhood and sororal desire which has been unleashed must be brought under control by their authors before it sweeps away not only the mechanism of ordering and disciplining against which it protests, but the principle of individuation itself. In "Goblin Market," the world we are left with has at the end been "domesticated." Nevertheless, it is still an all-female one (notwithstanding the implication that there are a couple of husbands out there *somewhere*). In *Beloved*, it is true that in the end the sister is ejected altogether, and the male force which had earlier been disruptive is integrated into the familial enclosure. But is *Beloved*'s ending truly conventional? One senses not; indeed, if one takes into consideration that, unlike in the bourgeois Victorian household, in the African-American family, from slavery to the present, the father has consistently been denied a place, Morrison's conclusion could in fact be viewed as radical rather than conventional. By writing in a father—a "father," moreover, created not from biology but by choice—and by giving Denver the role of autonomous breadwinner, Morrison is presenting us with a re-envisioned, re-claimed, and re-formed African-American family.

Regardless of the endings, the fictional female families which are engendered in "Goblin Market" and *Beloved* become the site of a certain kind of dangerous yet ecstatic self—or rather, of a concatenation of merging and dividing selves whose boundaries are never stable and predictable but are determined by the vagaries of jouissance itself. These "families" are subversive of the conditions that produced them in that they create kinds of identities which, from the perspective of the dominant cultural values, are logically impossible—identities (to use the words of Judith Butler in describing a special threat to the very logic of dominance) "in which gender does not follow from sex and in which the practice of desire does not 'follow' from sex or gender." (17). In "Goblin Market" and *Beloved*, the most powerful images left with the reader are of these destabilized and destabilizing selves which resist the structures of power that threaten them.

Notes

[1] "Women represent the interests of family and of sexual life," maintains Freud, and thus become hostile toward civilizaton even though, ironically, the family is the foundation of civilization. "The family will not give the individual up. The more closely the members of a family are attached to one another, the more often do they tend to cut themselves off from others, and the more difficult it is for them to enter into the wider circle of life" (*Civilization and it Discontents* 50).

[2] Although the goblin "brothers" are not brothers in the literal sense, the striking resemblance between the goblins' taunting, teasing ways and the behavior of male siblings in the nursery has been remarked upon by a number of critics (cf., for example, Ellen Moers' *Literary Women* 159).

[3] By the nineteenth century, "[t]he salvation that Christianity had effected through the father was now to be found through the sister who, as well, took on attributes of a pagan earth-mother. The romantic orphan, looking for a parent, found a sister" (Twitchell 120). This description of the sister's new-found role could serve as the prototype for novels as diverse as *Wuthering Heights* and *Dombey and Son*.

[4] As far as I have been able to determine, no critic as yet has taken seriously the centrality of the relationship between Denver and Beloved—e.g., that it is Denver, not Sethe, who longs for the return of the baby ghost, and who immediately recognizes her sister for who she is, caring for her accordingly.

Works Cited

Barr, Alan. "Sensuality Survived: Christina Rossetti's 'Goblin Market'." Ed. Praz, Mario. *English Miscellany: A Symposium of History, Literature, and the Arts.* Vols. 28-29. Rome: Edizioni di Storia e Letteratura (1979-80): 271-282.

Butler, Judith. *Gender Trouble.* New York and London: Routledge, Chapman & Hall, 1990.

Connor, Steven. " 'Speaking Likenesses': Language and Repetition in Christina Rossetti's 'Goblin Market'." *Victorian Poetry* 22.4 (1984): 440-48.

Davidoff, Leonore and Catherine Hall. *Family Fortunes: Men and Women of the English Middle Class, 1780-1850.* London: Hutchinson, 1987.

Freud, Sigmund. *Civilization and its Discontents.* Ed. and trans. James Strachey. New York: Norton, 1962.

Gilbert, Sandra M. and Susan Gubar. *The Madwoman in the Attic: The Woman Writer and the Nineteenth-Century Literary Imagination.* New Haven: Yale UP, 1979.

Girard, Rene. *Deceit, Desire and the Novel: Self and Other in Literary Structure.* Trans. Yvonne Freccero. Baltimore: Johns Hopkins UP, 1965.

Irigaray, Luce. *Speculum of the Other Woman.* Trans. Gillian C. Gill. Ithaca: Cornell UP, 1985.

_____. *This Sex Which Is Not One.* Trans. Catherine Porter and Carolyn Burke. Ithaca: Cornell UP, 1985.

_____. "When Our Lips Speak Together." Trans. Carolyn Burke. *Signs* 6.1 (1980): 69-79.

Jackson, Rosemary. *Fantasy: The Literature of Subversion.* London and New York: Methuen, 1981.

Kierkegaard, Soren. *The Concept of Anxiety.* Princeton: Princeton UP, 1980.

Michie, Helena, "The Battle of Sisterhood: Christina Rossetti's Strategies for Control in Her Sister Poems." *Journal of Pre-Raphaelite Studies* 3.2 (May 1983): 38-55.

_____. " 'There Is No Friend Like A Sister': Sisterhood as Sexual Difference." *ELH* (Summer 1989): 401-18.

Moers, Ellen. *Literary Women.* Garden City, New York: Anchor Books, 1977.

Moi, Toril. "The Missing Mother: The Oedipal Rivalries of Rene Girard." *Diacritics* 12 (1982): 21-31.

Morrison, Toni. *Beloved.* New York: New American Library, 1987.

Rossetti, Christina. "Goblin Market." *The Pre-Raphaelites and Their Circle.* Chicago and London: U of Chicago P, 1975.

Smith, Johanna. *Incest, Ideology and Narrative: Siblings in the Nineteenth-Century Novel.* Unpublished manuscript.

Twitchell, James. *Forbidden Partners: The Incest Taboo in Modern Culture.* New York: Columbia UP, 1982.

To Survive Whole, To Save the Self:
The Role of Sisterhood
in the Novels of Toni Morrison

Connie R. Schomburg

...I knew my mother as a Church woman, and a Club woman—and there was something special about when she said "Sister," and when all those women said "Sister." They meant that in a very, very fundamental way. (Stepto 474)

Although several critics have addressed the importance of the community in the lives of the numerous black women one encounters in the novels of Toni Morrison—the community she alludes to above—to date there has been no study focusing on the role of sibling relationships in her works. As indicated in her interview with Sandi Russell, however, the term "sister" has "a deep old meaning—it was valid, never secondary. Black women had to be real and genuine to each other, there was no one else" (45).

For Morrison, "sisterhood" unquestionably has a "deep old meaning," one which encompasses not only the biological bonds between women, but the emotional and spiritual ones that are possible as well. In the body of Morrison's work one can see the full range of these possibilities, from the biological sisters Claudia and Frieda MacTeer in *The Bluest Eye*, who draw strength and stability from their relationship, to Sula Peace and Nel Wright in *Sula*, who, although not sisters by blood, nonetheless achieve a relationship so intimate that for a time they are "two throats and one eye" and have "no price" (147). In *Song of Solomon* and *Tar Baby*, the central focus is on what happens to one—and specifically to one who is an only child—in the absence of such sustaining relationships, and by her fifth novel Morrison has come full circle. For it is in *Beloved* that Morrison brings to fruition in her character Denver all the possibilities she sees for fulfilling relationships among siblings, the strength of which Denver uses to enter into another more important and lasting "sisterhood" with the women of her community. Indeed, through a close examination of sibling relationships in Morrison's first five novels, one comes to understand that strong sibling relationships among black girls are not only empowering, but a prerequisite for acceptance into the sisterhood of black women.

Variously described by Morrison as a book "about a victim who is a child," "about beauty, miracles, and self images" (Parker 252; Bakerman 60), her first novel, *The Bluest Eye*, is also a portrait of the close nurturing relationship between the sisters Claudia and Frieda MacTeer. That this sibling relationship is a central focus of the novel is revealed from the very first pages, where Morrison has her narrator Claudia address the reader in the plural voice: "so deeply concerned were we with the health and safe delivery of Pecola's baby we could think of nothing but our own magic: if we planted the seeds, and said the right words over them, they would blossom, and everything would be all right" (9). In this short passage, Morrison displays not only the sisters' belief in themselves, in their ability to perform magic, but their concern for their friend Pecola as well, the importance of which becomes even more striking when one learns it will be the only concern Pecola receives. Although there are passages in the remainder of the book in which Claudia speaks in the singular voice, relates her experiences as an individual, these passages are often marked by uncertainty and insecurity, as seen when she is unable to answer Pecola's question "how do you get somebody to love you?" because "Frieda was asleep and I didn't know" (29).

By contrast, it is the "we" voice, the voice Claudia uses to speak for both herself and her sister, which describes many of the most important events and feelings of the young narrator, suggesting that it is in this relationship that she feels strongest and most self-assured. When she is given the gift of a white baby doll, for example, Claudia says that "I had only one desire: to dismember it. To see of what it was made, to discover the dearness, to find the beauty, the desirability that had escaped me, but apparently only me" (20). When she relates this same experience as a shared one,—when she joins with her sister to contemplate this attraction of adults to the "blue-eyed Baby Dolls" and Maureen Peals of the world—her conclusions are quite different:

What was the secret? What did we lack? Why was it important? And so what? Guileless and without vanity, we were still in love with ourselves then. We felt comfortable in our skins, enjoyed the news that our senses released to us, admired our dirt, cultivated our scars, and could not comprehend this unworthiness. (62)

The strength Claudia derives from her relationship to Frieda is again displayed when the sisters rush to defend Pecola in the school yard, an action one assumes neither would have taken on her own. This attempt to rescue her from the chants of the boys foreshadows their later effort to literally save the life of Pecola's baby. In this scene, too, Claudia uses the "we" voice to describe the kind of power and assurance their relationship provides which would allow them to undertake an action of such magnitude:

We had defended ourselves since memory against everything and everybody, considered all speech a code to be broken by us, and all gestures subject to careful analysis; we had become headstrong, devious and arrogant. Nobody paid us any attention, so we paid very good attention to ourselves. Our limitations were not known to us—not then.... So it was with confidence, strengthened by pity and pride, that we decided to change the course of events and alter a human life. (149)

Armed with the confidence, pride, and love of self provided by their strong sibling relationship, Claudia and Frieda will undoubtedly later join, as adults, the larger sisterhood enjoyed by such women as their mother and Cholly's Aunt Jimmy. There is the hope and the possibility that, like their mother, they will experience "ease and satisfaction" in conversing with their women friends who, in turn, will "not hide their curiosity" (14) about the important events in their lives. Like Aunt Jimmy and her friends, Claudia and Frieda have already begun to understand that even though "[e]verybody in the world was in a position to give them orders," they need not take them from each other, and further, that they can indeed take what the world gives them and recreate it "in their own image" (109).

The fact that the MacTeer sisters have such a strong, sustaining relationship is even more remarkable when one realizes that it is the only such sibling relationship in the book. The absence of other such ties is nowhere more noticeable than in the lives of the Breedloves, whose stories provide a sharp contrast to those of the MacTeer girls. As noted by Barbara Christian, Pecola Breedlove's story "is also Claudia's story," for though she is "not seen as the ugliest of the ugly," she "does know that blue eyes and blond hair are admired by all and that she does not possess them" (*Novelists* 140). While Christian acknowledges that "Claudia fights back" and in so doing "becomes the girl-woman in the book with whom we can identify" (140-41), she does not account for *why* Claudia is able to fight back: because of the strength and confidence that her strong sibling relationship provides.

Elsewhere, Christian links Pecola's tragedy to the lack of coherence in the life of her mother Pauline, who, "[s]eparated from the rural South which allowed her privacy and freedom of imagination, and cut off from the tradition of her maternal ancestors," "falls prey to the destructive ideas of physical beauty and romantic love as the measures of self-worth" ("Community" 66). A closer examination reveals, however, that Pauline has never been connected to the tradition of her maternal ancestors, for although she is the ninth of eleven children, "she alone of all the children had no nickname." Alienated from her parents and siblings for reasons she can only attribute to her deformed foot, Pauline "never felt at home anywhere, or that she belonged anyplace" (88).

Later, when she marries, moves North, and tries to join the community of women she finds there, her efforts are met with derision and rejection. Believing that better clothes will ensure their approval, Pauline quarrels with Cholly "about the money she wanted," even though she "did not really care for clothes and makeup. She merely wanted other women to cast favorable glances her way" (94). Failing at this, Pauline finally "came into her own with the women who had despised her, by being more moral than they" (100). Denied as a child a close relationship to her siblings or to her parents, Pauline cannot forge a sustaining relationship as a woman, cannot gain entrance into the larger sisterhood of women she so desperately needs.

Together with her husband Cholly—himself an only child, "alone in the world since he was thirteen" and "knowing only a dying old woman who felt responsible for him" (127)—Pauline is unable to provide their two children with a place in the community either. Instead, "[i]nto her son she beat a loud desire to run away, and into her daughter she beat a fear of growing up, fear of other people, fear of life" (102). Inheriting the disconnectedness that their parents feel about their individual past experiences as well as about their marriage, Pecola and her brother Sammy are unable to form a supportive bond, a fact Morrison underscores by never depicting them sharing an action, let alone a conversation. Instead, Sammy literally runs away at every opportunity, while Pecola tries her hardest to disappear, to imagine herself into nonexistence. And although the MacTeer girls try to save her, attempt to "adopt" her as a sister by showing care and concern for her, for Pecola, like Pauline, it is "much, much too late" (160).

Morrison does not end the book with this bleak pronouncement, however. By closing the novel with a return to the sisters' shared reflections on the waste of Pecola's life, Morrison suggests that Claudia and Frieda—because of the strength each receives from her sibling—have the potential to be something more. This potential is explored more fully in Morrison's second novel, *Sula*, a book she has described as an exploration of what "the Claudias and Friedas, those feisty little girls, grow up to be" (Stepto 481).

Although not sisters by birth, Nel Wright and Sula Peace become sisters in every other sense of the word, sharing as girls the security and comfort seen earlier in Claudia and Frieda's relationship. Both only children, the "daughters of distant mothers and incomprehensible fathers," Sula and Nel "found in each other's eyes the intimacy they were looking for" (52). Moreover, they "never quarreled, those two, the way some girlfriends did over boys, or competed against each other for them. In those days, a compliment to one was a compliment to the other, and cruelty to one was a challenge to the other" (84).

Later, of course, Nel and Sula will "quarrel" over Nel's husband Jude, but before this happens Morrison provides still another reflection on this relationship, this one from the view of a grown-up Nel:

Her old friend had come home. Sula. Who made her laugh, who made her see old things with new eyes, in whose presence she felt clever, gentle and a little raunchy. Sula, whose past she had lived through and with whom the present was a constant sharing of perceptions. Talking to Sula had always been a conversation with herself.... Sula never competed; she simply helped others define themselves. (95)

As the reader comes to understand by the novel's end, this relationship is the most significant one either woman will ever experience. Although Nel seeks fulfillment first through Jude and later through her children—and Sula captures but cannot keep an intimacy with Ajax similar to that which she shared with Nel—it is only with each other that they are complete. Morrison reflects on the importance of this relationship in her interview with Kay Bonetti, in which she explains that

the real element in [Nel's] life that had made it narrow and dry was not the fact that her husband was gone, but that this woman, this live-wire, this magic lady, who made her see herself in this extraordinary way, and that that friendship was as valuable a relationship as there could be—it's not the only relationship, but it certainly is extremely valuable—and if you ever find a friend like that sometimes it just can't matter what they do...the best thing I can do, if I think I know something important, is to warn people, and she's lucky she found out at 67...I think one of the huge mistakes that we all make and just because we're young—when we're young—is that if you have some good fortune you really think it's common, and you don't know at that moment that it may not be like that ever, ever again.

Morrison depicts no such relationship in either of her next two novels. Instead, she warns in both about the dangers of not having close, sustaining sibling relationship by gradually bringing the predicament of the only child into central focus. Having already suggested the limits of such a position through characters such as Cholly and Junior in *The Bluest Eye* and Nel, Sula and Helene in *Sula*, she uses Hagar in *Song of Solomon* and Jadine in *Tar Baby* as her clearest examples of the devastating effects of being an only child.

Initially introduced to the reader as seemingly self-assured, independent young women–an image which Jadine tries to project to Son when she finds herself alone with him in her bedroom (97-104) and which Hagar likewise attempts to convey to Milkman in the scene leading up to their first sexual encounter (95-6)—both Hagar and Jadine are later revealed to have serious weaknesses, flaws which Morrison addresses both in her interviews and through other characters in the two novels. In her interview with Nellie McKay, for example, Morrison says that

Hagar does not have what Pilate had, which was a dozen years of a nurturing, good relationship with men. Pilate had a father, and she had a brother, who loved her very much, and she could use that knowledge of that love for her life. Her daughter Reba had less of that...Hagar has even less because of the absence of any relationships with men in her life. She is weaker. Her grandmother senses it. (419)

As Morrison makes clear through her character Guitar, though, Hagar's weakness is caused by more than just an absence of a male influence in her life: it is also the result of her estrangement from the sisterhood of black women. Guitar correctly identifies this handicap when he compares Hagar to his own sisters:

He thought of his two sisters, grown women now who could deal, and the litany of their growing up. Where's your daddy? Your mama know you out here in the street? Put something on your head. You gonna catch your death a cold. Ain't you hot? Ain't you cold? Ain't you scared you gonna get wet?...[Hagar] needed what most colored girls needed: a chorus of mamas, grandmamas, aunts, cousins, sisters, neighbors, Sunday school teachers, best girl friends, and what all to give her the strength life demanded of her—and the humor with which to live it. (310-11)

Similarly, it is this chorus of other women, this sisterhood, which Jadine is lacking. Erroneously assuming that the kind of woman Son wants her to be is inferior, passive, and ultimately spoiling, Jadine fails to realize that a connection with the "pie ladies" Son so admires could in fact be liberating. Through connections with such a community, Jadine could have learned what her aunt Ondine perceives as the fundamental lesson she has failed to teach Jadine: how to be a daughter. As Ondine tries to explain to her:

Jadine, a girl has got to be a daughter first. She have to learn that. And if she never learns how to be a daughter, she can't never learn how to be a woman. I mean a real woman: a woman good enough for a child, good enough for a man—good enough even for the respect of other women. (242)

As Cathleen Medwick notes, Morrison speaks "with high admiration" about such women," women who, when they called each other 'sister,' really meant something by it" (331). When such women say "daughter," Morrison explains," they mean someone who will carry it on. Carry on the race, carry on the culture, carry on the tribe" (Medwick 331). Deprived of the kind of sisterhood that would have given them knowledge of how to be a "real woman," Jadine and Hagar cannot carry on. Instead, Hagar dies and Jadine flees from the man who might have given her such a connection.

But if their status as only children prevents Hagar and Jadine from establishing sustaining, fulfilling bonds with other women, Morrison's character Denver in her fifth novel *Beloved* has no such handicap. The youngest of four children, Denver as a young girl enjoys a supportive, protective relationship with her two older brothers, brothers who were "polite to her during the quiet time and gave her the whole top of the bed," brothers with whom she finds pleasure in "sitting clustered on the white stairs—she between the knees of Howard or Buglar" (19). In addition, Denver also enjoys a connection with the ghost of her dead baby sister which haunts the house she and her mother Sethe share. The comfort Denver derives from this relationship is acknowledged when she compares her response to the ghost to that of her family:

None of them knew the downright pleasure of enchantment, of not suspecting but *knowing* the things behind things. Her brothers had known, but it scared them; Grandma Baby knew, but it saddened her. None could appreciate the safety of ghost company. (37)

When this ghost company is apparently driven away by Paul D at the beginning of the novel, the loneliness Denver already knew from her brothers' leaving sends her outside, alone, to "[s]lowly, methodically, miserably" eat a biscuit, her mother "upstairs with the man who had gotten rid of the only other company she had" (19).

This loneliness which is so vivid for the reader becomes apparent to Sethe and Paul D as well when the ghost returns to the house in the character of Beloved. Completely mesmerized by her, Denver is not only the first to immerse herself in caring for Beloved, but she is also the first to recognize her as her come-back-to-life dead sister. Jealously protective of her, Denver seeks in her sister the acceptance and companionship she so craves—and for a time Beloved provides it. In language strikingly similar to that used to describe Nel and Sula's relationship, Morrison writes that sometimes—at moments Denver could neither anticipate nor create—Beloved rested cheek on knuckles and looked at Denver with attention.

It was lovely. Not to be stared at, not seen, but being pulled into view by the interested, uncritical eyes of the other. Having her hair examined as part of her self, not as material or a style. Having her lips, nose, chin caressed as they might be if she were a moss rose a gardener paused to admire. (118)

Feeling herself alive with Beloved in a way she is with no other, Denver "will forgo the most violent of sunsets, stars as fat as dinner plates and all the blood of autumn and settle for the palest yellow if it comes from her Beloved" (121).

But though Denver believes she has found "the other" in Beloved, though she feels herself complete when looked at by Beloved's interested eyes, it becomes increasingly obvious that all is not as it seems. For Denver has lost her self in this relationship, has submerged herself so completely that when she suspects in the cold house that Beloved has disappeared for good, it

is worse than when Paul D came to 124 and she cried helplessly into the stove. This is worse. Then it was for herself. Now she is crying because she has no self. Death is a skipped meal compared to this. She can feel her thickness thinning, dissolving into nothing. She grabs the hair at her temples to get enough to uproot it and halt the melting for awhile. Teeth clamped shut, Denver brakes her sobs. She doesn't move to open the door because there is no world out there. She decides to stay in the cold house and let the dark swallow her like the minnows of light above. She won't put up with another leaving, another trick. Waking up to find one brother then another not at the bottom of the bed, his foot jabbing her spine. Sitting at the table eating turnips and saving the liquor for her grandmother to drink; her mother's hand on the keeping-room door and her voice saying, "Baby Suggs is gone, Denver." And when she got around to worrying about what would be the case if Sethe died or Paul D took her away, a dream-come-true comes true just to leave her on a pile of newspapers in the dark. (123)

Fortunately, Denver's story does not end here and neither does Beloved's influence on her or lesson for her. Having absorbed completely Denver's sense of self, Beloved unwittingly gives this self back to her near the book's end. Making it clear that she is concerned with nothing but Sethe's abandonment of her, Beloved seeks Sethe's life for that transgression, grows bigger as Sethe first diminishes, then literally starves. Beloved pushes Sethe to the edge and in so doing pushes Denver into a realization of the danger her mother is in. Recognizing, finally, that "the job she started out with, protecting Beloved from Sethe," has "changed to protecting her mother from Beloved," Denver is forced by Beloved's actions to "leave the yard, step off the edge of the world, leave the two behind and go ask somebody for help" (243). Having lost her self in loving Beloved, Denver finds her self in seeking protection for another, finds her self only when she begins to feel a "certain careful way" about her mother. Unlike Jadine, Denver has learned what it means to be a daughter. Unlike Hagar, who has available but does not use Pilate's example as an ancestor, Denver draws on the support of her own ancestor, Baby Suggs, to take the first steps out of 124 and into the community which stands ready to receive her:

Remembering those conversations and her grandmother's last and final words, Denver

stood on the porch in the sun and couldn't leave it. Her throat itched; her heart kicked—
and then Baby Suggs laughed, clear as anything. "You mean I never told you nothing
about Carolina? About your daddy? You don't remember nothing about how come I
walk the way I do and about your mother's feet, not to speak of her back? I never told
you all that? Is that why you can't walk down the steps? My Jesus my."
But you said there was no defense.
"There ain't."
Then what do I do?
"Know it, and go on out the yard. Go on." (244)

When Denver goes on "out the yard," she finds herself accepted by the
community of women who had once rejected her and her mother, a community
of sisters who, as Carolyn Denard notes, "are at the bidding of Sethe and
Denver and ready with patience, with songs, and with love strong enough to
exorcise a daughter-ghost destroying its mother" (323). In recognizing that she
does indeed have "a self to look out for and preserve," Denver is able to
approach Lady Jones, who responds to Denver's appeal for help with an "[o]h
baby." And as Morrison writes, Denver "did not know it then, but it was the
word 'baby,' said softly and with such kindness, that inaugurated her life in the
world as a woman" (248).

Initially abandoning herself to Beloved's overwhelming need for love and
to her own need for a sister to alleviate her loneliness, Denver in the end derives
from her sister a sense of self-sufficiency and independence, as well as a
concern about others. In this most complex of all Morrison's sibling
relationships, Denver finds a belief in herself which allows her to venture into
the world and into a larger relationship with the women of her community. And
it is her entry into this "sisterhood" which brings healing and redemption not
only to Denver, but to her mother Sethe as well.

In Morrison's first five novels, then, can be seen a provocative exploration
of the importance of sibling relationships to her wide-ranging cast of women
characters. In her novels, Morrison explores and indeed redefines the
boundaries of sibling relationships, making it clear that the word "sister" applies
not only to the supportive, sustaining biological bonds between Claudia and
Frieda MacTeer, but also to the emotional bonds between Sula and Nel, to the
unhampered-by-the-grave bond shared by Denver and Beloved, and, most
importantly, to the larger community of women with whom Morrison's female
characters must find a connection in order to find wholeness. Without such a
connection, without this identification with and membership in the sisterhood of
black women, characters like Pecola and Pauline, Jadine and Hagar, are doomed
to emotional and spiritual—if not physical—death.

But if Morrison's novels serve as a warning about the adverse effects of
estrangement from the sisterhood of black women, they at the same time reveal
a promise, they provide a portrait of what *could* be as regards sibling
relationships in their fullest sense. In her short essay "A Knowing So Deep,"
Morrison addresses this possibility when she links one's identification with the
sisterhood of black women to one's sense of wholeness and worth as an
individual. Here, in the form of a letter, she pays tribute to her black sisters who

have come before her, and invites the reader to see in her relationship to them an affirmation and celebration, a way to survive whole and to save the self:

> I think about us, women and girls, and I want to say something worth saying to a daughter, a friend, a mother, a sister—my self. And if I were to try, it might go like this:
> Dear Us:
> You were the rim of the world—its beginning. Primary. In the first shadow the new sun threw, you carried inside you all there was of startled and startling life. And you were there to do it when the things of the world needed words. Before you were named, you were already naming...
> You did all right, girl. Then, at the first naming, and now at the renaming. You did all right. You took the hands of the children and danced with them. You defended men who could not defend you. You turned grandparents over on their sides to freshen sheets and white pillows. You made meals from leavings, and leaving you was never a real separation because nobody needed your face to remember you by. And all along the way you had the best of company—others, we others, just like you. When you cried, I did too. When we fought, I was afraid you would break your fingernails or split a seam at the armhole of your jacket. And you made me laugh so hard the sound of it disappeared—returned, I guess, to its beginning when laughter and tears were sisters too.
> There is movement in the shadow of a sun that is old now. There, just there. Coming from the rim of the world. A disturbing disturbance that is not a hawk nor stormy weather, but a dark woman, of all things. My sister, my me—rustling, like life. (230)

Works Cited

Bakerman, Jane. "The Seams Can't Show: An Interview with Toni Morrison." *Black American Literature Forum* 12 (1978): 56-60.

Bonetti, Kay. "Toni Morrison Interview." *American Audio Prose Library*. Columbia, MO, May 1983, 78 minutes.

Christian, Barbara. *Black Women Novelists: The Development of a Tradition, 1892-1976*. Westport: Greenwood, 1980.

_____. "Community and Nature: The Novels of Toni Morrison." *The Journal of Ethnic Studies* 7 (1980): 65-78.

Denard, Carolyn C. "Toni Morrison." *Modern American Women Writers*. Ed. Elaine Showalter. New York: Macmillan, 1991: 317-38.

Medwick, Cathleen. "Toni Morrison." *Vogue* April 1981: 289, 330-32.

Morrison, Toni. "A Knowing So Deep." *Essence* May 1985: 230.

_____. *Beloved*. New York: Knopf, 1987.

_____. *Song of Solomon*. New York: Knopf, 1977.

_____. *Sula*. New York: Knopf, 1973.

_____. *Tar Baby*. New York: Knopf, 1981.

_____. *The Bluest Eye*. New York: Holt, Rinehart & Winston, 1970.

Parker, Bettye J. "Complexity: Toni Morrison's Women—An Interview Essay." *Sturdy Black Bridges: Visions of Black Women in Literature*. Ed. Roseann P. Bell, Bettye J. Parker and Beverly Guy. Garden City, NY: Anchor P, 1979: 215-58.

Russell, Sandi. "Conversation from Abroad." *Critical Essays on Toni Morrison*. Ed. Nellie McKay. Boston: G.K. Hall, 1988: 45-47.

Stepto, Robert B. " 'Intimate Things in Place': A Conversation with Toni Morrison." *Massachusetts Review* 18 (1977): 473-89.

"Fly, little sister, fly":
Sister Relationship and Identity in
Three Contemporary German Stories

Helga G. Braunbeck

"She was my vassal, my alter ego, my double: we could not do without each other....Thanks to my sister—my accomplice, my subject, my creature—I was asserting my independent self" (45,48). Translation H.B.

"For a woman the sister is the *other*" who is at the same time most like herself. "She is of the same gender and generation," has the same parents and "was exposed to the same values, assumptions," and "patterns of interaction" (Downing 11). Except for the case of the oldest child, siblings are, like parents, *primary* bonding figures. But even for the oldest child, younger siblings play a central role in the development of self, as Simone de Beauvoir's description illustrates.

Considering a sibling's strong influence on the process of subject formation, it is surprising that the sibling relationship has, thus far, captured only relatively little attention in psychoanalytic, psychological and literary research.[2] Vertical relationships are much more in the foreground, as for example relationships between father and son, father and daughter, and mother and son. Where the horizontal sibling relationship has been researched at all, gender specific experiences have been largely passed over and stereotypical gender roles have been accepted uncritically.

A glance at feminist research shows that here, too, a lot remains to be done. However, a few good beginnings have been made, for example, Christine Downing's study *Psyche's Sisters*, Elisabeth Fishel's research on *Sisters: Love and Rivalry Inside the Family and Beyond*, and from the Germanic world, Imme de Haen's book "*Aber die Jüngste war die Allerschönste.*"[3] Much more research has been devoted to the mother-daughter relationship.[4] By restricting their attention to vertical family relationships feminist scholars might have both consciously and unconsciously followed the pattern previously established by male-dominated psychoanalytic discourse. Moreover, feminist research might have been impeded by one of the most popular slogans of *political* feminism: "Sisterhood is powerful."[5] Traditionally positive concepts of sisterliness—trust, mutual care, solidarity—are here combined with a new element: women's power and strength. This one-sided metaphorical concept of sisterhood, which performs an idealizing function, has little in common with the reality of familial sister relationships. It contributes to women's denial and suppression of the difficult aspects of their sister relationships instead of making them work through these difficulties in a productive way. Competitiveness, rivalry and hostility between women have been chosen for investigation only in the most recent feminist research.

In fiction, the representation of vertical relationships and of the bonding of brothers predominates. One reason for this might be that many sister interactions take place outside of male experience. In fairy tales, brothers and brother-sister constellations grossly outnumber sister pairs. Tales like "Snow-White and Rose-Red" are exceptions to this pattern. Just like psychologists and literary critics, German women authors of the 70s and 80s focused attention on the working through of the mother-daughter relationship.[6] However, women's literature does explore a greater number of relationships between women in general and therefore also between sisters, as for example Waltraud Mitgutsch's novel *Die Züchtigung* or the two feature films by Germany's foremost woman director, Margarethe von Trotta, in which relationships between sisters are the central theme. These two films demonstrate in exemplary fashion two of the basic patterns which can shape the sister relationship: In *Schwestern oder Die Balance des Glücks*, von Trotta shows the dangers of a symbiotic relationship, in which one of the two sisters takes on the additional and dominant position of a parent figure. In *Die bleierne Zeit*, she identifies and develops the basic pattern of polarity between sisters. Polarity is caused not only by the need for differentiation from the other who is at the same time so much like the self, but also by the need to find one's own field of identity.

The formation and loss of identity and role of the sister in these processes are central themes in the three short stories by Marie Luise Kaschnitz, Botho Strauß and Angelika Jakob. We will be able to trace many similarities in the basic pattern of the sister relationships presented by these authors and even in the imagery associated with the sister figure. Yet the narratives also differ strikingly in the way they portray the sister relationship not merely as a sibling relationship, but also as one containing elements of other interpersonal relationships—these differences might be related to the author's gender. While the earliest story, by Kaschnitz, artfully describes a common pattern of sibling interaction, the two other later stories by Strauß and Jakob probe and explore the more extreme aspects of sisterhood, in the case of Strauß at the margins of the sibling relationship.

Marie Luise Kaschnitz' autobiographical short story of 1951, "Das dicke Kind," is narrated from the perspective of an adult recording her negative emotions when she meets a child who is repulsive to her, yet at the same time magically attracts her. This child, a girl at the onset of puberty and the process of self awareness, is immediately differentiated from the other neighborhood children who usually come to visit the narrator in order to borrow books from her: an obese intruder, she suddenly stands in the middle of the living room consuming her food like a caterpillar and hardly speaking any words at all. After a sluggish conversation the narrator feels an irresistible desire to follow this child, despite her revulsion. She speculates that she might be driven by the desire to see the child's sister, who was mentioned in the conversation, and whom the child will join for ice skating on a frozen lake. This sister is completely different from the child: she is "die Tänzerin, die Gewittersängerin, das Kind nach [ihrem—der Erzählerin] Herzen...dieses anmutige Wesen."[7] At the gloomy forest lake, the narrator watches as the fat child falls through the ice at the very spot where her sister had been dancing her pirouettes just moments before. From this shocking experience, the fat child suddenly develops "Willen und Leidenschaft"[8] for her own rescue—two characteristics she lacked previously and which mark a point of departure from her passivity and indifference. The narrator recognizes herself in this child. At the end we learn that the forest lake does not exist anymore, and as the narrator contemplates a snapshot of herself as a little girl, with the same white dress, "mit hellen, wäßrigen Augen und sehr dick"[9]—the descriptors used earlier for the child—the narrative retrospectively shifts the whole experience into the realm of the unreal, of the imagined, possibly of hallucination.

Thus far, critics have read this story primarily as "das Abenteuer der Selbstbegegnung,"[10] as an "Erzählfolge" which is built on the "Spannung zwischen *zwei* Individuen"[11]—the adult and the child—who in the last analysis merge into one person. What has largely been passed over is the role of the sister in the process of the girl's identity formation.[12] Yet the sister is the focus, climax and final point in the conversation between the narrator and the child. When talking about her sister, the girl eventually goes beyond monosyllabic answers and starts to narrate on her own. Simultaneously the child's "dumpfe[s] Gesicht" for the first time exhibits some emotion: "Schmerz und Trauer."[13]

The sister relationship in this narrative follows the basic pattern of polarity. In practically every way the child is the exact opposite of her sister: she is fat, her sister is slim; she lacks the curly black hair of her sister; she is a fearful person, her sister is courageous; she does not *do* anything while her sister writes poetry and sings, and not only does the sister sing, but she sings whatever she wants to sing, whereas the child does not even have a will of her own. The sister has many clearly defined roles: she is "the dancer" and "ballerina," "the poet," "the swimmer" and the "thunderstorm singer"—she is the agile one, the active one, the creative one. In comparison, the child's only concrete characteristic is her obesity; she is defined exclusively in terms of her external appearance and only through the gaze of others. She has internalized the label of "fatso" bestowed by others, and has accepted it as the sum total of herself. The sister is the unattainable ideal to which the child serves only as a negative contrast since she does not possess an identity of her own. Significantly, the child falls through the ice at the very moment when she tries to move into the place of the sister.

In this story, Kaschnitz describes the great influence which the sister exerts on the identity formation of the child and the difficulty of finding a place of one's own which is not merely defined by one's relationship to the other, a place which is defined neither by too much proximity, as in the imitation of the sister, nor by too much distance, as in the desire to be *completely different*. Imitation is the child's conscious goal when she practices ice skating;

characteristically she makes her attempt exactly in the area in which she is least likely to succeed. The other extreme, the extreme of distance, occurs unconsciously in the child's body which, through food addiction, acquires a shape *completely different* from her sister's. Also, from the range of her sister's activities—swimming, thunderstorm-singing, writing poetry and dancing on the ice—the fat child has chosen the one which is most clearly associated with the feminine. While her sister seems to be a positively androgynous figure, the fat girl is still confined to the sexually neutral role *of child* and—in German—the corresponding pronoun *it*.[14] This changes only when the fat child steps onto the ice, which, through the color white, is connected to her white dress as well as to the "cocoon"—the puberty stage of the caterpillar child—which it/she has to break in order to reach its/her (color)full and also gendered identity. Through her use of the imagery of the butterfly metamorphosis and the retrospective frame of the narrative the author points out that the strong identification with the sister during childhood and adolescence can be regarded as a developmental stage to be overcome.

Such a positive ending does not exist in Botho Strauß' short story "Marlenes Schwester," published in 1975. The story has as its central theme detachment from a sister which leads to a "Zerstreuung und Tilgung des Subjekts"[15] and, in the final analysis, to death. The sister relationship in this narrative is an extreme example of the emotional dependence of one sister on the other. Strauß depicts the slow process of death when one sister disintegrates following the unwanted and violent separation from the other. The mosaic of a sister relationship forms through the perspective of the dependent one who is unable, "sich aus der Verfallenheit an ihre jüngere, lebendigere Schwester zu lösen."[16] We see this happen by way of dream sequences, flashbacks, allegorical stories, and glimpses into the time after the separation.

As in Kaschnitz' tale here, too, the problem of not having an identity of one's own is closely tied to the sister relationship, yet the premise is reversed, since it is not life with the sister, but separation from the sister that reveals the failure to establish an independent self. The reader never learns the main character's proper name. When asked about herself in a dream, she responds: "Ich?...Ich bin Marlenes Schwester."[17] In order to compensate for the loss of this role which had, until then, provided her with a substitute for identity, her unconscious fills the empty space with something other:

"The ocean of voices in my head, the sum of the voices populating me—this is me, even though I no longer recognize myself in it. In the course of my dissolution, I, the singular being, am multiplying in boundless cell division. I am becoming a crowd, a society; I am becoming all others" (23-24).[18]

Separation from the sister has led to a loss of center, to a loss of the "Sinn alles Unverständlichen,"[19] which had been embodied in her sister. The inevitable outcome is the disintegration and dispersion of this self which does not possess itself anymore.

Little factual data is given about Marlene's sister: she is "[a]chtunddreißig Jahre alt, ehemals Deutschlehrerin, zuletzt wohnhaft in einer Landkommune in der Nähe von Aschaffenburg, vollkommen mittellos."[20] What is unusual and what shapes the unfolding relationship is that the sisters grew up separately. Because of an "inexplicable" blood disease, Marlene's sister spent her childhood and youth in California, where the necessary specialized clinics were available. For this reason Marlene meets her sister, who is nine years her senior, only after she has reached her thirteenth year.

That they did not grow up together in the same family means we are looking at an atypical sister relationship. The central shaping characteristic of a sister relationship is missing, which could be the reason why the relationship, when it finally occurs, is expressed in the form of a *love* relationship, with all the symptomatic manifestations: erotic attraction—"Sie lockt mich;" togetherness to a point of being trapped "in dieser schwirrenden Zwei-Personen-Wahn-Welt"; "Streit die ganze Nacht";[21] and finally permanent divorce.

The ultimately destructive course of precisely *this* relationship pattern is what Marlene's sister rebels against:

"One just doesn't lose a sister from one's life, like a husband, like a guy. A sister is an *innate* life companion" (19). Emphasis H.B.[22]

Through the use of blood imagery, Strauß gradually transforms the narrative, which began on a serious note into a satire on blood relations. Blood metaphors are present throughout the text: the "inexplicable" blood disease of Marlene's sister was the reason for their separation during childhood and adolescence; a few minutes before the sisters' second separation Marlene—almost sadistically—talks about her menstruation—"Mein Blut" (18)—which is two days early; Marlene's sister reminisces on the young boys' ritual of exchanging blood as a sign of their close bonding, and she states her desire for a similar yet more one-sided and vampiristic act with her sister: "Marlenes Blut trinken. Unsere Blutsverwandtschaft auffrischen."[23]

For family dependencies, especially the "Abhängigkeit...vom geliebten Anderen," Strauß employs "die denkbar stärkste Metapher: den Vampir."[24] The second half of the narrative is dominated by a story within the story about a vampiristic community, which can on one level be read as social criticism of the "Ausbeutung und Konsumption" which make up the "common wealth"[25] of our postmodern society. On another level this alternative family-like community demonstrates how dependencies among family members can be so all-consuming that the individuals are unable to live by themselves: they will lose their life substance–their blood, their name, their identity—and they will die.

The vampire story is told by Julien, a common friend of both sisters. While Marlene's sister, because of her "übergroße Zuneigung,"[26] slips into total dependence upon the beloved other—her sister—and ends up unable to distinguish fiction from reality, Julien, her male counterpart, navigates masterfully in both areas. He manages to have "eine ordentliche Doppel-

Existenz,"[27] an ability for which Marlene's sister envies him. He is able to love "nur mit dem Teil [seines] Innern, der unempfindlich und fühllos ist,"[28] as Botho Strauß asserts in the motto-like quotation by Maurice Blanchot placed at the beginning of the story.

In contrast, the love Marlene's sister has is absolute and unconditional; it exposes itself to injuries and leads from an obsession with the loss of the sister to a loss of self. By clandestinely exchanging their belongings—packed in suitcases—shortly before their final separation, Marlene's sister tries to retain part of her alter ego and later, by wearing her sister's clothes and assuming her role as a listener to Julien's stories, she tries to become her. But she only finds that the other's clothes refuse to grow together with her skin, as she would wish (14) and that Julien refuses her as his listener. Shortly before the end of the narrative and her own "Ende,"—death, Marlene's sister seems to realize that she is caught up in a vicious circle, unable to live with her sister and also unable to live separated from her. The futility of her situation is expressed in the regular repetition of one sentence throughout the narrative: "Sie versuchte es noch einmal."[29] In addition, the formal circular structure of the narrative—the closing sentence repeats the second sentence, and the two paragraphs before it are an exact copy of two paragraphs near the beginning—points to the impossibility of escape for Marlene's sister if all she does is repeat what obviously is not working for her.

Death is also of central concern in Angelika Jakob's short story "Flieg, Schwesterlein, flieg!," which appeared in 1984. A detailed description of the younger sister's funeral forms the skeleton of the narrative, which is then fleshed out with scenes from the sisters' common past, with the older one's contemplations and assumptions about the life and aspirations of the younger one, and with vivid imagery intended to make the dead sister come to life again. Before we join the funeral, the prelude-like first paragraphs of this dirge present us with an exchange between the sisters, which seems to have supplied the spark for the story: the younger sister Marianne, who knows that her older sister Christine writes stories and who is jealous of the "heroes" in these stories because Christine gives them "Leben...(und Liebe),"[30] wants Christine to write a story about *her*, "eine wahre Geschichte": "Mach mich so, wie ich bin."[31] When Christine starts to discuss problems of biography, for example how to transfer life into writing and where to find the "truth," which the sister naively requests, she has already "extinguished the fire in her little sister's head." Whereas Christine *writes* stories, Marianne *lives* them. Marianne's inability or unwillingness to separate reality from fantasy proves to be fatal later on. What follows in the opening scene is Marianne's suggestion that Christine describe her funeral, i.e. that she write her thanatography instead of her biography— Marianne then dramatically acts out the role of the corpse. By writing this story about her sister's life and death, Christine in a way executes her sister's last will, since this story was the only thing she ever refused her.[32]

At the same time, Christine writes the story for her own sake. It is told from her perspective and presents the view of the surviving older sister. As in

Kaschnitz' story, the relationship between her and the younger sister is characterized by extreme polarity. Christine works through this relationship by writing an account of her sister's life and death, and, by comparing their lives, she is not only able to recognize her own weaknesses, but can also reconfirm her own strength, a strength which manifests itself through the act of writing.

While Botho Strauß' sisters were entangled in the web of a life-draining love relationship, the relationship between Christine and Marianne is played out within the more finite parameters of a vertical mother-daughter relationship. Marianne is only three years old when the mother dies and Christine is pushed into the role of substitute mother. The duties, the responsibilities and the constant activities that accompany this role influence Christine's personality to such an extent that she continues performing them in her adult life. In contrast to Marianne, she has a profession and secure job as a German teacher, she is politically active on the city council; and she remains the "anchoring place" for the "little" sister, who is aimlessly fluttering about in the world.

Christine's identification with the role of the mother is so strong that it even predominates when her own love relationship is at stake: after Marianne has seduced Christine's boyfriend of seven years, on Christine's birthday nonetheless, and when she comes home the morning after, "naß wie eine junge Katze,"[33] Christine, instead of making a scene, makes a hot bath and milk with honey for the sister-daughter. At the end of her account of their relationship, Christine seems to realize that throughout her life she has waited for and waited on her sister. Shortly before Marianne's death she has even sent away her long time lover, so the house would be "purified" and ready for Marianne's eventual return to Christine.

While the traditionally adaptive Christine fulfills her familial and social tasks and has built a stable identity from these roles, Marianne has a constantly changing personality and cannot be pinned down. She resists any kind of familial control and seldom phones or corresponds. Instead she appears unannounced at their doorstep one day to visit and succeeds in seducing the whole family with her charisma and her stories, her "mündliche Prosa."[34] Marianne is often bodily present, yet what she tells has no presence: her stories only have a past and future, but they lack the present. As if to make up for that, she tells her stories partially with her body—she hates telephones, which convey voices without a body (88). Her constantly changing attire and appearance are more telling and truthful than her stories, yet Christine is the only one able to see the real person behind the iridescent plumage. Marianne is aimlessly on the move somewhere and questing for something indeterminate; she lives transitionally without reaching any destination. The narrator portrays this lifestyle with metaphors of flying: the title itself is an allusion to flight and to the well-known German nursery rhyme about the orphaned cock chafer.[35]

Marianne embodies everything Christine represses in herself: freedom, independence, femininity, sexual attractiveness and the ability to make herself popular despite her egocentricity. Marianne is "die ganz und gar Subjektive, die nur und ausschließlich ihre eigene Geschichte erlebte."[36] This role is that of the child who never grows up; Marianne dies with a "junge Seele" (129) though she is over 50 at the time. Christine becomes guilt-ridden when her sister's death coincides with Christine's refusal to play the mother role and her assertion for the first time, of her own life as a priority. She has pulled the mask from what appeared to be Marianne's independence and exposed it as false.

When Christine tries to remember her sister's face, her imagination produces a surreal montage of Marianne's face with a superimposed desert landscape and Marianne's miniature figure doubling as her own nose. Christine is the only one to realize Marianne's double existence, which eventually becomes fatal when Marianne can no longer integrate reality and fantasy. While investigating Marianne's life, Christine discovers the truth behind her beautifully seductive stories: her colorful years as a shepherdess and holy woman in a religious community in southern France turn out to have been the drudgery of factory work at a punching machine; the ascetic monk's hut in which she claims to have lived is, in reality, a camper without wheels and with an old sleeping bag inside.

In the act of writing her story about Marianne, Christine consistently dismantles her idealization of the sister and admits to herself her deep-rooted resentment, envy, jealousy, and even intense hatred of the dead sister. At the same time she discovers that the sister's death also endangers her own identity: "Nicht nur Mariannes Leben war Christine wie Sand durch die Finger gelaufen; ihr eigenes Leben war mitgezogen."[37] The story which she writes about Marianne's life is a last attempt to capture and pin down this elusive, incomprehensible sister. But the attempt fails and does not bring her sister back (128). "Christine weiß auch, daß es keinen Ort gibt, wo sie und die Schwester einander noch treffen können. Die Trennung gilt für immer."[38] Yet Christine finally allows her sister to enter into that area which she had always barred from her: her writing. The firm walls of Christine's identity have become penetrable; the sister has been recognized as an integral part of her own self, and will ultimately go on living, transformed into the female bird "Ariane" of Christine's next story.

In each of these three narratives one sister is perceived by the other as an ideal who becomes a polar opposite and at the same time constitutes an essential part of the self. All three authors portray the idealized sister as a free spirit who, in contrast to the "main" character of the narrative, has a positive relationship to her own body: she swims, dances or "flies" and is attractive to others. She also excels in being creative with words: she either writes poems (Kaschnitz) or invents funny and enticing new words (Strauß) or tells wonderful stories (Jakob). In the case of the stories by the two women writers (Kaschnitz and Jakob), this ability with words is transferred to the narrator later in her life.

But despite these similarities, the sister relationship is presented in a fundamentally different way in the man's and the women's stories. The male author, Botho Strauß, views the sister relationship as being determined by the fatal law of the love relationship, and he turns it into a model of vampiristic exploitation. His portrayal of the sister relationship is extreme: Strauß primarily exposes the darker aspects of symbiosis between two women. He responds to these threatening aspects by destroying the symbiosis and transforming it into a deadly psychosis. Kaschnitz and Jakob, on the other hand, depict a more female-centered view which privileges the problems of mutual differentiation and polarity in the sister relationship. Their figures ultimately work through their feelings of envy, jealousy and hatred by taking up writing. In Strauß' narrative, the sisters are denied such a solution and remain confined to the role of the listeners, while the story of their relationship rests firmly in the hands of the males, Julien and Strauß, who control fact and fiction (Julien is also the director of the Paris doll and puppet museum!). In Kaschnitz' story, the narrative frame, which stages the sister relationship retrospectively as a hallucination, but also as a developmental stage in identity formation, functions like a mirror: it may reflect the reader's own experience while it distances it at the same time.

The subtle complexities and ambiguities of the sister relationship, in particular the ever-present feeling of being unable to live up to the demands of this relationship, are more thoroughly explored and more effectively expressed in Angelika Jakob's story. In this story, little Marianne, while sitting on the swing, says to Christine: "Schwesterlein, stößt du mich ab?—Ja, flieg du nur...."[39] While Marianne is asking to be pushed away so she can fly, she nevertheless needs to be anchored in her sister. Christine, although she is constantly trying to tie her sister down, needs her to fly. Jakob's image of the swing brilliantly encapsulates the constitutive dynamic in all of these fictional relationships: the constant back and forth, the moving away from each other and towards each other, the repulsion and attraction between sisters.

Notes

[1]Elle était mon homme lige, mon second, mon double: nous ne pouvions pas nous passer l'une de l'autre....Grâce à ma soeur—ma complice, ma sujette, ma créature—j'affirmais mon autonomie. Simone de Beauvoir.

[2]Cf. Elisabeth Fishel: "Freud, Deutsch, Adler, Horney, Jung: an occasional reference to sibling rivalry, but usually in a neurotic patient and, if then, likely to be male. More recently, Erikson, Eric Borne, Robert White: an intermittent reference to sibling patterns along the life cycle, but no real frame-work or overview..." (20). Judy Dunn and Carol Kendrick also found that despite the importance of the sibling relationship in child development, "psychologists have paid scant attention to it" and that there exists "pitifully little...systematic research" (1). However, two additional studies appeared in the same year: Bank/Kahn and Lamb/Sutton-Smith.

[3]Fishels and de Haens books are based primarily on authentic interviews. This method insures that, first of all, sisterly experience is described and represented. Short biographies of well-known sister-pairs in the English-speaking literary world are presented by Toni A.H. McNaron.

[4]The most influential socio-psychological study is by Nancy Chodorow; more recent research on the mother-daughter theme was done by Marianne Hirsch; for additional literature in the German-speaking world see Maria-Regina Knecht.

[5]The slogan used for one of the most widely-known collections of feminist texts, edited by Robin Morgan.

[6]Examples are Karin Struck and Elfriede Jelinek. For additional literature see Maria-Regina Knecht.

[7]"The dancer, the thunderstorm-singer, the child after [her—the narrator's] heart,...this graceful creature" (63).

[8]"Will and passion" (65).

[9]"With light, watery eyes and very fat" (66).

[10]"The adventure of an encounter with the self" (Zimmermann 67).

[11]"Narrative sequence,"..."tension between *two* individuals" (Baus 263). Emphasis H.B.

[12]In addition to Zimmermann and Baus, Schweikert and Pulver ignore the sister.

[13]"Dull face"..."pain and sadness" (60,61).

[14]Unfortunately this is lost in the English translation of the story which uses "girl."

[15]"Diffusion and effacement of the subject," vom Hofe 114.

[16]"To detach herself from the emotional enslavement she experiences in the relationship with her younger, livelier sister." Text on the cover of the third edition by Deutscher Taschenbuch Verlag (1980).

[17]"Me?...I am Marlene's sister" (16).

[18]Das Stimmenmeer im Kopf, die Summe der mich bevölkernden fremden Stimmen—das bin ich, obwohl ich mich nicht mehr darin erkenne. Ich, das Einzelwesen, vermehre mich, im Verlaufe meiner Auflösung, in grenzenloser Zellteilung. Ich werde eine Menschenansammlung, eine Gesellschaft, ich werde alle anderen.

[19]"Meaning of everything incomprehensible" (22).

[20]"Thirty-eight years old, formerly a teacher of German, a recent resident in a county commune near Aschaffenburg, completely destitute" (10).

[21]"She is alluring me" (12,13),..."buzzing insanity of a two-people-world" (17), "arguments all through the night" (16).

[22]Eine Schwester verliert man doch nicht, wie einen Mann, wie einen Kerl, aus dem Leben. Eine Schwester ist eine *angeborene* Lebensgefährtin.

[23]"To drink Marlene's blood. To refresh our consanguinity" (19).

[24]"Dependence on the beloved other,"..."the strongest metaphor imaginable: the vampire" (vom Hofe 114).

[25]"Exploitation and consumption"; "common wealth" is English in the original (vom Hofe 114).

[26]"Overly great affection" (41).

[27]"An orderly double existence" (29).

[28]"Only with that part of his inner self which is detached and without feeling" (8).

[29]"She tried it once more" (9,16,24,42).

[30]"Life...(and love)" (114-115).

[31]"A true story": "Make me the way I am" (81).

[32]Except for one more request, which Christine had not fulfilled and which might have contributed to Marianne's death and certainly caused a lot of guilt feelings in Christine.

[33]"Wet like a young cat" (121).

[34]"Oral prose" (96).

[35]"Maikäfer, flieg!/Dein Vater ist im Krieg!/Die Mutter ist in Pommerland,/Pommerland ist abgebrannt./Maikäfer, flieg!" (Cock chafer, fly/your father is in the war/your mother is in Pommerland/Pommerland has burnt down/cock chafer, fly!) (Heidenreich 133).

[36]"The one who is completely subjective, who experiences nothing except for her own story" (84).

[37]"Not only Marianne's life had run through Christine's fingers like sand; her own

life had gone along with it" (128).

³⁸"Christine also knows that there exists no place where she and the sister could still meet. The separation is valid forever" (129).

³⁹"Dear sister, will you give me a push? Yes, go ahead and fly..." (93).

Works Cited

Bank, Stephen P. and Michael D. Kahn. *The Sibling Bond.* New York: Basic, 1982.

Baus, Anita. *Standortbestimmung als Prozeß: Eine Untersuchung zur Prosa von Marie Luise Kaschnitz.* Bonn: Bouvier, 1974.

Beauvoir, Simone de. *Mémoires d'une jeune fille rangée.* Paris: Gallimard, 1958.

Downing, Christine. *Psyche's Sisters: ReImagining the Meaning of Sisterhood.* San Francisco: Harper, 1988.

Dunn, Judy and Carol Kendrick. *Siblings: Love, Envy & Understanding.* Cambridge: Harvard UP, 1982.

Fishel, Elisabeth. *Sisters: Love and Rivalry inside the Family and Beyond.* New York: William Morrow, 1979.

Haen, Imme de. *"Aber die Jüngste war die Allerschönste": Schwesternerfahrungen und weibliche Rolle.* Frankfurt/M. Fischer, 1983.

Heidenreich, Gert. *Das Kinder-Lieder-Buch: Texte und Noten mit Begleit-Akkorden.* Frankfurt am Main: Fischer, 1981.

Hirsch, Marianne. *The Mother/Daughter Plot: Narrative, Psychoanalysis, Feminism.* Bloomington: Indiana UP, 1989.

Hofe, Gerhard vom. *Das Elend des Polyphem: zum Thema der Subjektivität bei Thomas Bernhard, Peter Handke, Wolfgang Koeppen und Botho Strauß.* Königstein/Ts.: Athenäum, 1980.

Jakob, Angelika. *Flieg, Schwesterlein, flieg!: Erzählungen.* Siegen: Machwerk Verlag, 1984. 81-129.

Jelinek, Elfriede. *Die Klavierspielerin.* Reinbek bei Hamburg: Rowohlt, 1983.

Kaschnitz, Marie Luise. "Das Dicke Kind." *Gesammelte Werke* IV. Ed. Christian Büttrich and Norbert Müller. Frankfurt am Main: Insel, 1983: 58-66.

_____. "The Fat Girl." *Circe's Mountain: Stories by Marie Luise Kaschnitz.* Trans. Lisel Mueller. Minneapolis: Milkweed, 1990.

Knecht, Maria-Regina. " 'In the Name of Obedience, Reason, and Fear': Mother-Daughter Relations in W.A. Mitgutsch and E. Jelinek." *The German Quarterly* 62/3 (Summer 1989): 357-72.

Lamb, Michael E. and Brian Sutton-Smith. *Sibling Relationships: Their Nature and Significance Across the Lifespan.* Hillsdale: Lawrence Erlbaum, 1982.

McNaron, Toni A.H. *The Sister Bond: A Feminist View of a Timeless Connection.* New York: Pergamon, 1985.

Morgan, Robin, ed. *Sisterhood is Powerful: an anthology of writings from the women's liberation movement.* New York: Vintage, 1970.

Mitgutsch, Waltraud. *Die Züchtigung.* Düsseldorf: Claassen, 1985. English translation by Lisel Mueller. *Three Daughters.* San Diego: Harcourt, 1987.

Pulver, Elsbeth. *Marie Luise Kaschnitz.* Autorenbücher 40. München: Beck, 1984.

Schweikert, Use. "Das eingekreiste Ich." *Marie Luise Kaschnitz.* Ed. Uwe Schweikert. Frankfurt am Main: Suhrkamp, 1984: 58-77.

Strauß, Botho. "Marlenes Schwester." *Marlenes Schwester: Zwei Erzählungen.* München: Hanser, 1975.

Struck, Karin. *Die Mutter.* Frankfurt: Suhrkamp, 1975.

Trotta, Margarethe von, dir. *Schwestern—oder die Balance des Glücks (Sisters, or the Balance of Happiness)*. Bioskop: WDR, 1979.

_____. *Die Bleierne Zeit (The German Sisters/Marianne and Juliane)*. Bioskop, 1981.

Zimmermann, Werner. "Marie Luise Kaschnitz: Das dicke Kind (1952)." *Deutsche Prosadichtungen unseres Jahrhunderts: Interpretationen für Lehrende und Lernende* II. Düsseldorf: Schwann, 1969: 67-73.

List of Primary Works Discussed

*work is discussed at some length

The Living is Easy by Dorothy West
    Rueschmann*
Manservant and Maidservant by Ivy
    Compton-Burnett
    Colt
Mansfield Park by Jane Austen
    Cohen
    Gruner*
"Marlenes Schwester" by Botho Strauß
    Braunbeck*
Marriage by Susan Ferrier
    Cohen*
Mary Barton by Elizabeth Gaskell
    Cohen
Middlemarch by George Eliot
    Cohen
    Colt
The Mill on the Floss by George Eliot
    Colt
    Waddell*
The Mists of Avalon by Marion Zimmer
    Bradley
    Benko*
Morte d'Arthur by Sir Thomas Malory
    Benko*
The New Magdalen by Wilkie Collins
    Cohen
Northanger Abbey by Jane Austen
    Gruner
The Old Curiosity Shop by Charles Dickens
    Colt*
Oliver Twist by Charles Dickens
    Colt
Pendennis by Sir Walter Scott
    Gruner
Plum Bun by Jessie Redmon Fauset
    Rueschmann*
Pride and Prejudice by Jane Austen
    Cohen
Puddn-head Wilson by Mark Twain
    Mangum
Rhoda Fleming by George Meredith
    Cohen
Romola by George Eliot
    Waddell
A Room of One's Own by Virginia Woolf
    Benko
Saint Maybe by Anne Tyler
    Madden*
Scenes of Clerical Life by George Eliot
    Waddell

Searching for Caleb by Anne Tyler
    Madden*
Sense and Sensibility by Jane Austen
    Cohen
A Serious Proposal to the Ladies by Mary
    Astell
    Cohen
Sir Gawain and the Green Knight
    Benko
Song of Solomon by Toni Morrison
    Schomburg*
Sophia by Charlotte Lennox
    Cohen*
Sula by Toni Morrison
    Schomburg*
Tar Baby by Toni Morrison
    Schomburg*
The Tin Can Tree by Anne Tyler
    Madden*
The Vicar of Wakefield by Oliver Goldsmith
    Cohen
To the Lighthouse by Virginia Woolf
    Colt
A Vindication of the Rights of Woman by
    Mary Wollstonecraft
    Cohen*
The Violent Bear It Away by Flannery
    O'Connor
    Colt
The Wanderer by Frances (Fanny) Burney
    Gruner
We Have Always Lived in the Castle by
    Shirley Jackson
    Hall*
What Maisie Knew by Henry James
    Colt*
Wives and Daughters by Elizabeth Gaskell
    Cohen
The Woman in White by Wilkie Collins
    Cohen
Wuthering Heights by Emily Brontë
    Colt
    Gruner*
    Mangum

Contributors

Debra A. Benko is a doctoral student in English at Bowling Green State University. Her study, "Transformations of Morgan le Fay in Arthurian Literature: From Healer to Witch to Priestess," completed when she was a 1987 National Endowment for the Humanities Younger Scholar research grant recipient, formed the foundation for her recent research on Morgan le Fay and King Arthur as siblings.

Helga G. Braunbeck is an assistant professor of German at North Carolina State University. She has presented papers on sisterhood and feminism in Christa Wolf's *Cassandra*, the intersection of the visual and the textual in Kleist and Günderrode, forms of displacement in Moníková, the medium of film in Dürrenmatt's recent works, and computer assisted foreign language instruction. She has published on the female paradigm of writing double biography in Bettina von Arnim and Christa Wolf and is the author of *Autorschaft und Subjektgenese: Christa Wolfs* Kein Ort. Nirgends (Vienna: Passagen, 1992).

Michael Cohen is the author of *Hamlet in My Mind's Eye* (Georgia, 1989), which won the South Atlantic Modern Language Association Studies Award, and *Engaging English Art: Entering the Work in Two Centuries of English Painting and Poetry* (Alabama, 1987). Co-author, with Robert E. Bourdette, of *The Poem in Question* (Harcourt, 1983), Cohen is a professor of English at Murray State University and lives on Kentucky Lake.

Rosemary M. Colt is Assistant Editor at *Novel* and an instructor in the Brown University Learning Community. She has presented papers and published articles on modern British fiction. She is co-editor of *Writers of the Old School: British Novelists of the 1930s* (Macmillan, 1992) and is currently working on a collection of essays on modern British women writers.

Elisabeth Rose Gruner is a lecturer in Victorian literature at the University of California, Los Angeles. She has presented papers and published articles on eighteenth- and nineteenth-century fiction, focusing especially on the fictional construction of female identity within the family. The essay published here is derived from her dissertation, which treats sister-brother relationships in fiction by women from the eighteenth and nineteenth centuries.

Karen J. Hall is a graduate student at The Ohio State University in the Department of English. She is currently involved in work in the fields of gay and lesbian studies.

Deanna Madden has been a Visiting Assistant Professor at the University of Hawaii at Manoa and other colleges. Her short stories have appeared in literary journals, and she has published articles on women writers and gender issues. She is interested in British and American novels of the nineteenth and twentieth centuries and contemporary novels.

Teresa Mangum is an assistant professor of English at the University of Iowa. Her essay "George Eliot and the Journalists: The Making of a Moral Mistress" is forthcoming in *Victorian Scandals*, ed. by Kristine Garrigan (Ohio UP). She has presented and published work on literary uses of eugenics, on turn-of-the-century lace co-operatives, and on Robert Louis Stevenson's pirates. At present, she is completing a book on Sarah Grand.

Leila S. May teaches in the English department at the University of California at Berkeley, where she is currently completing her doctorate. Her presentations and research have been primarily on Victorian literature. Her dissertation is entitled "Relatively Speaking: Representations of Siblings in Nineteenth-Century British Literature."

JoAnna Stephens Mink is an assistant professor of English at Mankato State University. She has presented papers and published articles on nineteenth- and twentieth-century fiction and authors, as well as on strategies for integrating writing and literature. She is co-editor of *Joinings and Disjoinings: The Significance of Marital Status in Literature* (BGSU Popular Press, 1991) and is currently working on two anthologies, one focusing on the relationship between communication and women's friendships in literature and the other, on feminist collaboration.

Allison Pingree is a lecturer on History and Literature at Harvard University, specializing in nineteenth- and twentieth-century American fiction and culture. Her research interests include: cultural constructions of personal identity, and their inversion in figures of replication; kinship and literature in the American South; and ethnicity and American writers of color. She is also a Teaching Consultant at the Derek Bok Center for Teaching and Learning at Harvard.

Eva Rueschmann received her B.A. from the University of Heidelberg and is currently a doctoral candidate in Comparative Literature at the University of Massachusetts, Amherst, where she also works as the Assistant to the Director of the Interdepartmental Program in Film Studies. Her article "Desire and Loss in Alan Rudolph's *The Moderns*" is forthcoming in *Literature/Film Quarterly*, and "Female Self-Definition and the African Community in Mariama Bâ's *So Long a Letter*" will be published in a collection on international women's writing. She is currently completing her dissertation, a psychoanalytic study of sister relationships in twentieth-century literature and film.

Connie R. Schomburg is an assistant professor of English at Midland Lutheran College in Fremont, Nebraska. Her book, "*Safe Harbor and Ship*": *The Evolution of*

174 The Significance of Sibling Relationships

Self in the Novels of Toni Morrison, is forthcoming in the Peter Lang Series Studies in African and African-American Culture.

Julia Waddell is completing her dissertation at The Ohio State University on the language theory of Gerard Manley Hopkins and its significance for closure in his poetry. She has presented papers on the religious impulse in the bird poems of Coleridge, Shelley, and Hopkins; on Maggie Tulliver's struggle for autonomy in *The Mill on the Floss*; and on Swift's ironic mask in *Gulliver's Travels*.

Janet Doubler Ward teaches at Illinois Central College in East Peoria, Illinois. She has presented papers on women in literature and on composition studies at several conferences. She is co-editor of *Joinings and Disjoinings: The Significance of Marital Status in Literature* (BGSU Popular Press, 1991) and is currently working on an anthology focusing on the relationship between communication and women's friendships in literature.

CPSIA information can be obtained
at www.ICGtesting.com
Printed in the USA
LVOW10s0835260217

525454LV00001B/121/P